The Impact of Medical Cost Offset on Practice and Research: Making It Work for You

The Impact of Medical Cost Offset on Practice and Research: Making It Work for You

A Report of the First Reno Conference On Medical Cost Offset

Editors:
Nicholas A. Cummings, Ph.D., Sc.D.
William T. O'Donohue, Ph.D.
Kyle E. Ferguson, M.S.

Foundation for Behavioral Health:
Healthcare Utilization and Cost Series,
Volume 5
2002

Context Press
Reno, Nevada

The Impact of Medical Cost Offset on Practice and Research:
Making It Work for You

Hardback 218 pp.

Library of Congress Cataloging-in-Publication Data

Reno Conference On Medical Cost Offset (1st : 2001 : University of Nevada,
Reno)
   The impact of medical cost offset on practice and research : making it work
for you : a report of the First Reno Conference On Medical Cost Offset ;
editors, Nicholas A. Cummings, William T. O'Donohue, Kyle E. Ferguson.
       p. cm. – (Healthcare utilization and cost series ; v. 5)
   ISBN 1-878978-41-1
  1. Mental health services–Cost effectiveness–Congresses. 2. Medical care–
Utilization–Congresses. I. Cummings, Nicholas A. II. O'Donohue, William T.
III. Ferguson, Kyle E. IV. Title. V. Series.
   RA790.A2 R46 2001
   338.4'33622–dc21

                                                              2002012939

© 2002 CONTEXT PRESS
933 Gear Street, Reno, NV   89503-2729

Printed in the United States of America

The Healthcare Utilization and Cost Series of the Foundation for Behavioral Health

Volume 1 (1991):
> *Medical Cost Offset: A Reprinting of the Seminal Research Conducted at Kaiser Permanente, 1963-1981*
> Nicholas A. Cummings, Ph.D. and William T. Follette, M.D.

Volume 2 (1993):
> *Medicaid, Managed Behavioral Health and Implications for Public Policy: A report of the HCFA-Hawaii Medicaid Project and Other Readings.*
> Nicholas A. Cummings, Ph.D., Herbert Dorken, Ph.D., Michael S. Pallak, Ph.D. and Curtis Henke, Ph.D.

Volume 3 (1994):
> *The Financing and Organization of Universal Healthcare: A proposal to the National Academies of Practice.*
> Herbert Dorken, Ph.D. (Forward by Nicholas Cummings, Ph.D.).

Volume 4 (1995):
> *The Impact of the Biodyne Model on Medical Cost Offset: A sampling of Research Projects.*
> Nicholas A. Cummings, Ph.D., Sc.D., Editor.

The Reno Conferences

The First Reno Conference on Medical Cost Offset was convened at the University of Nevada, Reno on January 19 and 20, 2001 and is reported in this volume. It was co-sponsored by the University of Nevada, Reno and The Nicholas & Dorothy Cummings Foundation.

The Second Reno Conference on Medical Cost Offset was Convened at the University of Nevada, Reno on May 17 and 18, 2002 and will be reported in a subsequent volume. It was co-sponsored by the University of Nevada, Reno and The Nicholas & Dorothy Cummings Foundation.

Preface

This book contains expanded papers presented at a conference held at the University of Nevada, Reno on January 19-20, 2001. This conference was generously supported by grants from The Nicholas and Dorothy Cummings Foundation and the University of Nevada, Reno.

The purpose of this conference was to explore the phenomenon often called "medical cost offset." There are conflicting reports concerning this—some report success; some report failure. The questions arise: What is going on? Are the positive reports doing something different than the negative reports? If so, what? Are the reports different methodologically (i.e., better controlled, costs better measured, etc.)? What are the implications of all this for future research and practice?

The context of this conference was and still is the healthcare crisis facing the United States as well as many other nations. Costs are escalating and yet few seem very satisfied with the current state of healthcare delivery. What can be done to contain costs? If restricting the supply of medical services is not an acceptable answer, then what is? Can demand be legitimately reduced? If so, how? How can we have more quality in our healthcare system?

Nicholas Cummings and his colleagues discovered the medical cost offset phenomenon in 1961 at the Kaiser Permanente Health Plan, and conducted the subsequent seminal research. In a series of studies discussed in this book they found that future medical utilization can be significantly reduced by providing a certain type of psychotherapy to particular types of patients. Some studies did not find this. One can come to the conclusion that this phenomenon like so many, requires special attention to key details. The reader will see some of what the experts see as these keys.

This book owes a special thanks to Stephanie Dmytriw who provided such excellent assistance in organizing the conference. It also owes a special debt of gratitude to Janet Cummings, Psy.D., President of the Nicholas and Dorothy Cummings Foundation. Without her decision to support the conference it would not have happened. Steven Hayes, Chair of the Department of Psychology, deserves thanks also as he ably served as the key conference moderator. To our copy editor, Emily Neilan, we are indebted for many useful suggestions as to how the text could be improved, and we are grateful for the great care and attention she brought to her immense task. Finally, we owe a special debt of gratitude to all the conference presenters and chapter authors. They are the experts whose contributions hold the keys to addressing these critical problems.

Forward

With the publication of this volume, the Foundation for Behavioral Health is pleased to resume publication, in association with Context Press, of its popular *Healthcare Utilization and Cost Series*. In so doing, FBH is also pleased to continue the tradition of distributing complimentary copies to the directors of American Psychological Association approved doctoral programs, to selected leaders in psychology, and to key persons in the field of behavioral healthcare. It is also available upon request as long as supplies last.

It is hoped you will find this series useful in your work. The Foundation for Behavioral Health requests that after you have finished reading it, you donate it to the library of the institution with which you are afiliated.

Additional copies for individuals may be obtained by sending $4.00 to cover postage and handling to the following address:

> Janet L. Cummings, Psy.D.
> Foundation for Behavioral Health
> 561 Keystone Avenue, #212
> Reno, NV 89503

Library copies may be ordered from Context Press for a charge of $29.95 plus shipping and handling.

Table of Contents

Introduction: Reflections on the Medical Cost Offset Effect

William T. O'Donohue
University of Nevada, Reno
Kyle E. Ferguson
University of Nevada, Reno
Nicholas A. Cummings
University of Nevada, Reno and
The Nicholas and Dorothy Cummings Foundation

While several industrialized countries are comparatively healthier, Americans spend more on healthcare than any other nation (Wessel, 2001). In 2000 healthcare expenses in the United States were expected to reach $1.3 trillion, which represents approximately 14% of the Gross Domestic Product (Phelps, 1997). Said differently, one in every seven dollars exchanging hands in 2000 was involved in purchases or payment for healthcare. In spite of a slight drop in 1996, spending continues to rise at multiples of the general rate of inflation, with little or no indication that things will change anytime soon (Chambliss, 2000).

A basic concept in economics is "opportunity cost." Opportunity costs are defined as the price of forgone alternatives. If a person chooses to watch a basketball game Tuesday night, this costs her the opportunity to talk with her partner. Therefore watching the basketball game "costs" her the forgone opportunity to talk with her significant other. Medical expenditures involve opportunity costs: the more we pay for these the less money we have left over for other goods and services. Thus, it is reasonable to want to spend healthcare dollars in a prudent, cost-effective manner.

A second basic concept in economics that is relevant to our present discussion is free market competition. In the latter half of the 20th century with the emergence of Japan and Europe from their post-war declines, economic markets have become increasingly international. Many nations of the world now compete internationally to sell their electronic goods, cars, steel, and other raw materials or products. For the United States to remain competitive in this new world market, American companies have to better manage their expenses on domestic soil. Above all, managing healthcare expenses is critical for corporate competitiveness.

Employers in the United States pay for a very large percentage of healthcare. For example, in 1997 large employers spent an average of $4,400 per employee on healthcare (England, 1999). The U.S. tax code makes this coverage tax exempt and thus when healthcare coverage is offered by employers workers pay less for coverage. However, it is a real expense for employers and this expense must be passed on to consumers in the price of goods and services they buy from this employer.

Accordingly, as healthcare costs continue to rise, U.S. companies are becoming less competitive internationally due to inflated prices. Here again there are pressures to find ways to spend healthcare dollars in prudent, cost effective ways.

Healthcare economists point out two unusual aspects of medical expenditures. One, consumers are partially or sometimes entirely shielded from the cost of their "purchases". Bills are simply sent to third party payers and little or nothing comes out of the consumer's pocketbook. Hence, consumers are generally unaware what healthcare actually costs. Two, there are vast asymmetries of knowledge. Medical professionals making or influencing purchasing decisions have much more knowledge about key matters than consumers or payers. This point is best reflected in two axioms that shaped healthcare delivery from the Second World War until about a decade ago: "The doctor knows best" and "We must spend whatever is needed" (Chambliss, 2000). This imbalance can obviously influence the amount or kind of purchases made and the extent to which patients are appropriately matched with effective treatment.

For these and other reasons, many have asserted that our nation has been and is in a "healthcare crisis." Healthcare expenditures had for many years increased yearly at 2, 3, and 4 times the rate of general inflation (Phelps, 1997). Managed care was created to attempt to contain these spiraling costs. And it was temporarily successful. Healthcare spending during the last decade no longer increased at some multiple of the rate of general inflation.

Managed care lost a complex public relations battle, and now is being dismantled (Cummings, 2000). Once again, prices are rising dramatically. Healthcare premiums in 2001 increased an average of 14% (about 4 times the general rate of inflation) (Institute of Medicine's Committee on the Quality of Health Care in America, 2001). Note that a 14% rate compounded over 5 years essentially doubles the price in that period.

Finally, an important issue that we can only briefly mention is that many suggest that the United States is having a healthcare crisis because there are approximately 41 million uninsured individuals (American Medical Association, 1995). Unlike the insured who access healthcare more appropriately with a focus on prevention and early detection (e.g., annual check ups), the uninsured usually don't access the healthcare system until numerous complications arise. What otherwise might have been inexpensively treated in a physician's office becomes extremely expensive when left untreated for months or even years (e.g., necessitating emergency care). Accordingly, a large population of the uninsured drives the cost of healthcare up, and as costs are driven up, so too are the number of uninsured individuals who can't afford increasingly expensive health insurance.

In summary, healthcare expenditures are large, they have wide implications, they have interesting and unusual causes, and they are very much seen as a critical problem to be solved. Having set this macro-economic context, we also need to keep focused on the fundamental issue: people are in need of some kind of care. We all worry about healthcare and its affordability because we know not having a quality system in place can mean the difference between life and death or between pain and disability for loved ones and ourselves. Generally good willed people want everyone to get needed, appropriate, and effective care. However, as the old saw goes this is much more easily said then done.

Medical Cost Offset

"Medical cost offset" is a phrase coined by Nicholas Cummings et al. (1962). In its most general meaning, cost offset, denotes the savings produced by some intervention which itself has some cost. Inoculations which cost $5 can prevent and thereby offset hundreds of thousands of dollars of medical expenditures if the person were not inoculated and actually needed to be treated because he or she contracted the disease. More specifically it can mean: to what extent are the costs of providing treatment X now compensated by reduced medical expenditures in the future?

Clearly there are many uncontroversial cases of this. In fact much of medicine is implicitly based on this premise: e.g., the cost of successfully treating an infected wound through antibiotics and clean dressings is offset by avoiding the costs of amputation, hospital costs, and prosthetic devices, etc., if the untreated infected wound were to become more severe.

Our concern in the present chapter is narrower and it is based on that fact that traditionally the healthcare community has placed far greater emphasis on medical aspects of patient visits relative to psychological and social factors (Chamblis, 2000; Cummings, Cummings, & Johnson, 1997). Namely, medical screening attempts to ascertain organic causes underlying physical dysfunction. This should come as no surprise given that primary care physicians whom patients see early on are trained to identify organic etiology and treatments, rather than problems due to psychiatric/psychosocial disturbances. This almost sole emphasis on the "biological/physical" side of healthcare phenomena is called the "biomedical model".

Screening only for organic etiology, however, often leads to a dead end. Namely, in spite of a barrage of (often expensive) clinical and laboratory tests, the etiology driving the patient to seek help remains unknown. For example, upon reviewing over 1,000 patients' records in an internal medicine clinic Kroenke and Mangelsdorff (1989) found that less than 16% of somatic complaints (e.g., chest pain, fatigue, dizziness, headache, back pain, numbness, cough, constipation) had an identifiable organic cause.

More recently, in a sample of 25,000 at Kaiser, Strosahl (1998) estimated that 70% of all primary care visits were driven by psychological factors. Analyzed further, 35% of visits were initiated by panic, Generalized Anxiety, Major Depression and somatization (i.e., physical symptoms manifesting from psychological illness or distress). Thirty-five percent were driven by stress and adjustment difficulties. The remaining 30% were identifiable medical difficulties. Interestingly at follow-up, even after 10 years, no organic conditions were found to explain the somatized complaints.

The specific question that interests us in this book is: *Can the cost of detecting and treating patients' psychosocial problems (from subclinical problems such as stress, to mental disorders such as depression, to adjunctive problems such as treatment adherence, or finally, lifestyle issues such as poor exercise habits) be offset by decreased medical utilization in the future?* Implicit in this question are two key components: (a) The patient is being treated more appropriately. All their problems (medical and psychological) are being more effectively detected and treated. (b) The initial costs of this approach are higher. Patients receive more treatment initially. This is in contradistinction to concerns raised about managed care that they sought to restrict access to care in order to save money. This question assumes a return on investment model.

Achieving Demand Relation

How might this be achieved? Friedman et al. (1995) suggest that managed care has traditionally focused on "supply side" strategies such as restricting access to healthcare, decreasing practice variation and by improving the efficiency of services. The "demand side" strategies of examining behavioral and psychosocial variances influencing medical help seeking behavior have been ignored. Friedman et al. suggest that there are six major pathways (demand side) whereby psychosocial factors influence medical help seeking behavior:

1. *Information and Decision-Support Pathway.* Teaching patients appropriate self-care, medical utilization, and providing them with appropriate information about their problems and treatment options can result in healthier and less costly clinical outcomes. Example:

   Forty-nine controlled experiments that used psychoeducational preparation before surgery reported an average of 1.31 fewer days in the hospital relative to those who received treatment as usual (Devine & Cook, 1983).

2. *Psychophysiological Pathway.* Stress management programs can be effective in helping patients handle the stress of everyday life, chronic disease, medical procedures, and other life problems. Example:

   In a review of asthma self-management studies Klingelhofer & Gershwin (1988) concluded that for every dollar spent on these programs, resulted in a cost savings between $3 and $10 in medical services.

3. *Behavior Change Pathway.* How a person eats, drinks, smokes, uses prescribed or illicit drugs and exercises has a significant impact on health. Lifestyle change groups, bibliotherapy, smoking cessation psychotherapy, and substance abuse treatment are ways of capturing this pathway. Example:

   Failure to treat alcohol and substance abuse can result in a marked increase in medical costs. Based on the Hawaii Medicaid data (addressed later in this chapter), patients diagnosed as chemically dependent who did not go into treatment increased their medical costs by 91% during the study period (Cummings, 1990a). By contrast, certain types of interventions produced net decreases of medical costs by about $514 per person in the 12 months following treatment.

4. *Social Support Pathway.* Some patients enter the healthcare system to obtain social support. Even patients who have high levels of social support under ordinary circumstances may develop feelings of isolation when experiencing chronic illness. Increasing social support through peer-led groups and activation of natural support networks have been shown to improve health and reduce future medical-surgical utilization. Example:

It is well known that after a year or two following the death of a spouse, there is a precipitous rise in healthcare utilization seen in surviving widows. Based on the notion that increased utilization was related to bereavement and severe sadness, using an outreach program Cummings (1997) contacted survivors shortly after the spouse's death and referred them to one of two groups if he or she wasn't coping well with the loss. For those who screened positively for signs of depression, they were triaged into psychotherapy for depression. For those who were mourning with severe sadness, they were triaged into a bereavement program. The program consisted of 5 to 8 mourners that among other things used the "buddy system." 323 were in this experimental condition and 278 widowed older adults who resided in a nearby center served as the control group. The savings in medical utilization shown in the experimental group versus the control group was $1,400 per patient for 2 years following participation in the program.

5. *Undiagnosed Psychological Problem Pathway.* In many cases patients present with medical complaints but actually have an undiagnosed psychological problem such as depression and anxiety. Training in making the accurate diagnoses such as these as well as the use of less expensive but highly effective psychological treatments results in significantly less medial utilization. Example:

Katon et al. (1990) examined the characteristics of "high utilizers" of general medical services and found high rates of depressive illness. In their sample of two large primary care clinics, for those deemed as "high utilizers" (i.e., highest 10% of patient visits) they found prevalence rates of 25% for current depression and 68% for lifetime depression.

6. *Somatization Pathway.* Some patients who very frequently present with multiple somatic complaints may have increased emotional reactivity to bodily changes. These individuals tend to be high utilizers of medical services. Psychological consultation reduces medical costs

significantly with somatizing patients. Example:

Smith (1994) targeted patients diagnosed with somatization disorder (n=19 in both the somatization group and control group). Treatment involved assessment and recommendations for participants' primary care physicians as to how to manage these cases. The intervention was related to a subsequent decrease of 53% in quarterly healthcare costs relative to the control group.

How these Pathways Converge into Disease Management

Value Health Sciences reviewed medical claims and determined the following. Many of these pathways converge into disease management. A few examples of these include:

1. *Diabetes*: While only slightly more than 3% of the population is diagnosed with diabetes, it represents 14% of all healthcare costs. *Forty percent of diabetes treatment cost is estimated to be inpatient costs associated with difficulties in lifestyle management.* (Also note that the American Diabetes Association estimates there is one person with undiagnosed diabetes for every one diagnosed; American Diabetes Association, 2001).
2. *Chronic Obstructive Pulmonary Disorder (COPD)*: Asthma and emphysema impact 5% of the population and represent 10% of all health costs. Pediatric asthma difficulties represent 40% of all pediatric inpatient admissions. Episodic costs of COPD care are among the highest of all disorders and, significantly, *the need for inpatient care is related to unstable lifestyle.*
3. *Pain*: Pain related issues significantly impact the functioning (absentee-ism, disability) of 12% of the population. Arthritis alone accounts for 12% of all office visits by the elderly.
4. *Hypertension*: Fifteen percent of the population is diagnosed with hypertension. This is the single most frequent diagnosis, which represented over 27 million people in 1996. Over 50% of people diagnosed are without medical care for twelve months. Of those in care, *less than 50% are following the prescribed medical plan.*

With that as background, let us turn to a brief discussion of the history of medical cost offset research.

Brief History of Medical Cost Offset

As mentioned, Cummings coined the term "medical cost offset." He was also the first to systematically investigate the medical cost offset phenomenon. In the first of a series of experiments, Cummings and colleagues tabulated the incidence by occurrence of all health services (physician visits, days in the hospital, x-rays, laboratory tests, etc.) for the full year before the patient's first psychotherapy session, and then made a similar tabulation of all occurrences for the years following the first psychotherapy visit (Cummings, Kahn, & Sparkman, 1962). Eventually there were

18 years of follow-up evaluations before the experiments were terminated. The results of this research revealed that although their patients were high utilizers of all medical facilities, three or fewer psychotherapy sessions reduced their utilization by 65% the first year following the initial psychotherapy visit, and brief therapy (i.e., an average of 6.2 sessions) reduced their utilization by 75%. Both of these reductions took into account the added psychotherapy visits in computing total health utilization. Patients receiving long term therapy (i.e., an average of 17.5 sessions) added psychotherapy to their utilization so that total utilization was not reduced for outpatient care, but their hospitalization rate decreased by two-thirds, resulting in an even more significant cost savings. Over the years Cummings' research has yielded approximately 60 interventions targeted for specific psychological conditions in primary and collaborative care settings. High specificity eliminates the time and labor intensity of traditional therapy and makes treatment even more therapeutically effective.

In the 1980's Dr. Cummings was awarded an $8 million federal grant to conduct a 7-year project to study the entire Medicaid population of the Island of Oahu (Cummings, Dorken, Pallak, & Henke, 1993). All Medicaid eligibles (N= 36,000) and Federal employees (N=90,000) were randomly assigned to an experimental or control group. Dr. Cummings trained psychotherapists, had them spend 15% of their time in quality assurance, used empirically derived treatment protocols, and an aggressive outreach program, and targeted 15% of the highest utilizers of health services. He found that medical-surgical savings recovered the cost of creating the behavioral health care system within 18 months, and the significant reduction in medical utilization continued thereafter with no additional behavioral healthcare required to maintain the cost savings. These were estimated to be $8 million per year in constant dollars. In contrast, the control group revealed a 17% increase in medical–surgical utilization, while there was a 27% increase in control patients who received no psychotherapy services whatsoever.

In a more recent example of the medical cost offset effect, Pallak and Cummings (1992) examined the effects of inpatient or outpatient treatment for psychiatric disorders on posttreatment hospital days in a large Midwestern HMO. The main purpose of their study was to determine the extent to which patients referred to intensive outpatient services rather than inpatient treatment were subsequently hospitalized under psychiatric or medical-surgical diagnoses.

The researchers examined all patients from the HMO population of 67,000 who presented for inpatient psychiatric hospitalization during a 6-month period in 1989. Their healthcare utilization (hospital days for psychiatric and medical-surgical diagnoses) was tracked for 12 months following their initial admission in 1989.

Approximately 20% of patients referred themselves for admission, while the remaining 80% were admitted through hospital emergency and admitting rooms. Postdischarge outpatient treatment was integrated into participants' treatment plans (for both inpatient and outpatient conditions). The intense outpatient treatment increased available treatment options and was provided without co-payment, without any cap on the number of visits, and without deductible requirements. Intensive outpatient treatment, among other things, consisted of brief, intermittent therapy throughout the life cycle (Cummings, 1990b).

1,259 participants were given outpatient or inpatient mental health treatment during the initial 6-month period; 106 of whom presented for inpatient psychiatric admission (48 men, 58 women, with a mean age of 33). Of the 106 participants based on an on-site evaluation (mental status examination), 16 were admitted to inpatient treatment and the remaining 90 were referred to intensive outpatient treatment.

The results were as follows. Patients who were admitted to inpatient psychiatric treatment had an average of 9 inpatient treatment days and an average of 8.5 follow-up outpatient visits. In the year following treatment these patients, while not requiring further inpatient or outpatient psychiatric services, had a total of 14 hospital days under medical-surgical diagnoses. Patients referred to intensive outpatient treatment were not admitted for inpatient psychiatric treatment and averaged about 16 outpatient visits during the treatment episode. In the subsequent year, these patients had a total of 12 days under medical-surgical diagnoses and required no further outpatient psychiatric treatment. This difference between the inpatient group and the outpatient group with respect to medical-surgical utilization was statistically significant ($t=3.59$, $p<.01$). Accordingly, the results of this study suggest that with immediate identification of problems and referral to clinically appropriate levels of treatment might reduce the number of medical-surgical days and decrease unnecessary inpatient treatment without leading to the "revolving door" phenomenon (i.e., repeat psychiatric admissions).

The Medical Cost Offset Literature

Since Cummings and his colleagues' seminal work, there have been scores of medical cost offset studies published in the literature. Due to the sheer volume of published studies, an exhaustive review is beyond the scope of the present chapter. Moreover, there have already been several recent reviews of the cost offset literature (Gabbard, Lazar, Hornberger, & Spiegel, 1997; Groth-Marnat & Edkins, 1996; Katon, 1995) and two meta-analyses, making a review somewhat redundant for our present purposes (Chiles, Lambert, & Hatch, 1999; Mumford, Schlesinger, Glass, Patrick, & Cuerdon, 1984). Accordingly, in what follows we are going to highlight main findings from the two meta-analyses and critique the literature more generally.

Mumford et al. (1984) published the first meta-analysis of the medical cost offset literature. In their review they examined data from 58 articles published before 1984 that dealt with the effects of mental health treatment on medical utilization and costs. They also conducted a second meta-analytic review of health insurance claims files (for the Blue Cross and Blue Shield Federal Employees Plan for 1974-1978). Their analyses revealed two major findings. One, "the clearest cost-offset effect appears largely in the reduction of inpatient rather than outpatient costs" (p.

1156). Two, "older patients (over age 55) show larger cost-offset effects than younger ones" (p. 1156).

While these data clearly point to ways in which cost offsets might be achieved (develop outpatient programs in lieu of inpatient programs and target the elderly), the Mumford et al. review had several limitations that mitigate against these findings: (a) some of which concerned data analytic strategies; (b) and several had to do with the studies themselves, included in the review.

Regarding (a), these authors neglected to break down the literature according to the kinds and quality of interventions that were employed, they were vague in detailing study characteristics, and it wasn't clear, the participants' severity of illness (Chiles et al., 1999). Hence, the numbers that were factored into analyses, although treated as if they were homogenous, actually weren't. With these confounds in mind, it can't be determined from their review what treatments are optimal for what populations, when the benefits of treatments can be realized (i.e., immediate gains versus longer-term outcomes), and in what settings certain treatments work best (e.g., rehabilitation settings versus acute facilities). Indeed, as will be taken up shortly, medical cost offset research must address these questions with respect to specific populations otherwise they are of limited use, providing little or no guidance as far as policy implications are concerned. And this is the level of analysis that concerns us most (i.e., how we treat patient populations that cluster around distinct problems).

Regarding (b), in consideration of the studies themselves that went into the analyses, three additional methodological criticisms can be raised (Katon, 1995). One, the subjects in the treatment conditions and no treatment conditions were often poorly matched. Poorly matching subjects between conditions poses a severe threat to internal validity. Namely, to what extent did certain subject characteristics differentially interact with the interventions in question? Moreover, to what extent were cost offset effects due to statistical regression (see Fraser, 1996)? As is the case with most populations, statistical outliers or extreme cases tend to "regress" to the mean over time. Even those clients with severe problems are expected to eventually experience some alleviation of symptoms independently, in the absence of treatment. For the sake of argument, if those participants in the treatment condition were comprised of severe cases (i.e., statistical outliers) one would expect noticeable improvements across target areas in spite of any intervention employed. Statistically speaking this would manifest as regression to the mean. If the comparison group wasn't comprised of similar cases this threat to internal validity can't safely be ruled out.

A second methodological criticism concerns the measures used in these investigations. While the studies considered for review reported healthcare utilization other measures of import were not mentioned (e.g., clinical outcome measures). Indeed, a major criticism of the cost offset literature is that interventions target managing costs instead of managing care (Cummings et al., 1997). For example, restricting access to treatment also produces cost savings (though, arguably only in the short-term) all the while clients' problems become progressively worse. Simply monitoring utilization wouldn't necessarily capture this and other areas of related interest (e.g., employee absenteeism rates due to illness).

A third methodological criticism concerns the underlying factors which purportedly produce cost offsets. Namely, the studies reviewed didn't examine the mechanisms that might have produced these outcomes. These studies can't answer the most important question about an intervention's effects: to what extent was a given cost offset related to the intervention in question (e.g., treating a previously undiagnosed psychological problem), as opposed to being due to some other unspecified factor or factors?

Due to methodological shortcomings as seen in Mumford et al.'s original review and because over a decade later their findings had become somewhat outdated (e.g., reimbursement for services had drastically changed since then), Chiles and his colleagues conducted another meta-analysis; one that cast a wider net so as to include more contemporary examples of the medical cost offset. For their review they included original studies reviewed by Mumford et al., and added more recent studies, covering a span of 30 years (1967-1997). This yielded 91 studies in all.

Improving on the original meta-analyses Chiles et al. examined components involved in producing cost offset effects, as well as length of stay, the number of healthcare visits, and financial data. Specifically, they addressed the following questions:

1. Is there a measurable medical cost offset found in the literature?
2. Are there particular psychological interventions or settings related to cost offset effects?
3. Is there a difference between inpatient offset studies and outpatient offset studies?
4. What patient characteristics are more amenable to psychological interventions?
5. If, in fact, the cost offset phenomenon is indeed present, what are the likely mechanisms responsible for producing this effect?

Because the Chiles et al. methodology will be discussed in detail elsewhere in the present volume (see Chapter 3), it won't be taken up here. Rather, let us now proceed to the results of their analysis.

Of the studies considered for review, 90% reported a decrease in medical utilization following the psychological intervention. More specific findings were as follows:

1. an average of 15.7% reduction in utilization shown in the treatment conditions versus a 12.27% average increase found in the control conditions
2. the articles reported a cost savings of 20-30%

3. about 1/3 of the articles demonstrated marked cost savings even after the cost of employing the psychological intervention was subtracted from the savings

4. the type of professional (psychologist, social worker, psychiatrist) delivering the intervention was not a significant factor in producing the medical cost offset effect

5. behavioral medicine interventions tended to fare better relative to psychotherapeutic approaches, in spite of the setting

6. with respect to psychoeducational methods, their analysis revealed that the more specific interventions tended to produce better outcomes

7. a comparison of child relative to adult relative to elderly samples suggested that mean effect sizes were marginally larger for child (.35) and elderly (.34) studies versus adult (.12) studies

8. as with gender, larger effect sizes were associated with all female subjects (.82; especially females undergoing surgical procedures) versus all male subjects (.26)

9. those participants with severe medical difficulties tended to respond better to treatment than those with severe psychological problems

10. regarding medical cases, those undergoing surgical procedures tended to respond better to treatment (e.g., fewer hospital days) when compared to mixed-medical patients.

Regarding probable factors responsible for medical cost offset phenomena, while the Chiles et al. (1999) review provides greater detail and is more current relative to Mumford et al.'s original review, similar methodological problems remain in the literature that limit our confidence in their findings. Chiles et al. note that: (a) it was common to find researchers still failing to control for severity of illness; (b) treatments were often only loosely described, thus making it difficult to replicate findings; (c) threats to internal validity remain as many studies failed to randomize subjects to conditions; (d) many studies didn't control for experimenter biases (e.g., because experimenters weren't "blind" to conditions perhaps they discharged patients prematurely in accord with expected outcomes); (e) studies often didn't report whether therapists adhered to the operationally defined treatment protocols (e.g., patients were potentially receiving different treatments unbeknownst to the experimenters due to clinicians failing to adhere to the treatment proper).

Other criticisms of the Chiles et al. (1999) review reflect problems in the contemporary literature more generally. Since the Mumford et al. (1984) review healthcare delivery has markedly changed. Unlike today, the Mumford et al. review reflected a system where mental health benefits weren't covered by third party payers or if they were, strict limitations were placed on the number of sessions allotted to mental health treatment. This, of course, changed with the Mental Health Parity Act of 1996. This act mandated that health insurance plans that provide mental health services to beneficiaries may not differentially impose annual dollar caps on those services relative to other surgical-medical services (Budman, 1999). Moreover, at about this time membership in managed behavioral health organizations ("carve outs") had proliferated from 78 to over 150 million in just five years, from 1992 to 1997 (Oss et al., 1997, as cited in Sturm, 1999). Hence, unlike the "parachuting" in of treatment protocols into traditional medical settings as was commonly seen spanning the period of Mumford et al.'s review, the contemporary healthcare system has become more inclusionary, more collaborative. One must then ask upon examining Chiles et al.'s review: (a) To what extent were mental health treatments delivered in organized settings versus traditional locations? (b) What was the specificity of the interventions employed (i.e., did they target health-related variables or were they more nebulous)? (c) To what extent did mental health services providers collaborate with primary care providers? All of these questions, unanswered by the Chiles et al. review and by the literature at large, are critical to a better understanding of what works for whom and where (Cummings, 1999).

In summary, in consideration of the medical cost offset literature taken as a whole, the contemporary literature is in need of vast methodological improvement. Moreover, because the three issues mentioned above are only sporadically addressed by researchers, the medical cost offset literature is of limited practical use, providing little in the way of how organized healthcare delivery systems ought to employ effective behavioral health treatments in contemporary primary care and integrated care settings.

However, criticisms aside, there have been powerful demonstrations of the medical cost offset phenomenon in the literature for more than a quarter of a century. And as found in the scientific literature more generally, we find some "strong" experiments (i.e., rigorous) mixed in with a lot of "weaker" ones. The medical cost offset literature is no exception to this rule. Nevertheless, by virtue of the fact that medical cost offsets have been produced under well controlled conditions and under a variety of different healthcare delivery systems, we have good reason to remain hopeful that our understanding of this phenomenon will continue to develop as new treatments and delivery systems are examined. We are confident that, after reading the chapters in the present volume, the reader will also come away with a similar sense of optimism.

Conclusion

While healthcare premiums continue to rise at some multiple of the rates of general inflation several decades of medical cost offset research suggest that, given the right combination of behavioral health and primary care treatment, these spiraling costs can potentially be better managed through a more appropriate healthcare delivery system. Most importantly, healthcare costs are reduced through effective treatment not by restricting access to care as was the case decades ago. Although specific algorithms presently escape us with respect to what will work for whom and in what settings, there are a handful of "diamonds in the rough" (researchers) who are pointing us in the right direction. It is in this spirit that we publish this collection of papers. The authors who have contributed to this volume represent those "diamonds in the rough".

References

American Diabetes Association. (2001). American Diabetes Association: Cinical practice recommendations 2001. *Diabetes Care, 24*. Retrieved February 19, 2002, from http://journal.diabetes.org/CareSup1Jan01.htm.

American Medical Association. (1995). *American Medical News 1994 Data Survey summary*. Chicago: Author.

Budman, S. H. (1999). Whither medical cost offset? Comments on Chiles et al. *Clinical Psychology: Science and Practice, 6*, 228-231.

Chambliss, C. H. (2000). *Psychotherapy and managed care: Reconciling research and reality*. Boston: Allyn and Bacon.

Chiles, J. A., Lambert, M. J., & Hatch, A. L. (1999). The impact of psychological interventions on medical cost offset: A meta-analytic review. *Clinical Psychology, 6*, 204-220.

Cummings, N. A. (1990). *Psychologists: An essential component to cost-effective, innovative care*. Paper presented to the American College of Healthcare Executives, February, 1990.

Cummings, N. A. (1990). The Biodyne model of brief intermittent therapy throughout the life cycle. In N. A. Cummings, H. Dorken, M. S. Pallack, & C. J. Henke (Eds.), *The impact of psychological intervention on healthcare utilization and costs* (Tech. Rep. No. 11-C-9834419, Appendix II, pp. 152-177). San Francisco: Foundation for Behavioral Health.

Cummings, N. A. (1997). Behavioral health in primary care: Dollars and sense. In N. A. Cummings, J. L. Cummings, J. N. Johnson (Eds.), *Behavioral health in primary care: A guide for clinical integration* (pp. 3-21). Madison, WI: Psychosocial Press.

Cummings, N. A. (1999). Medical cost offset, meta-analysis, and implications for future research and practice. *Clinical Psychology: Science and Practice, 6*, 221-224.

Cummings, N. A. (2000). The first decade of managed behavior care: What went right and what went wrong? In R. D. Weitz (Ed.), *Managed care in mental health in the new millennium* (pp. 19-37). New York: The Haworth Press.

Cummings, N. A., Cummings, J. L., Johnson, J. N. (1997). (Eds.). *Behavioral health in primary care: A guide for clinical integration*. Madison, WI: Psychosocial Press.

Cummings, N. A., Dorken, H., Pallak, M. S., & Henke, C. J. (1991). The impact of psychological intervention on health care costs and utilization. The Hawaii Medicaid Project. HCFA *Contract Report #11-C-983344/9*.

Cummings, N. A., Dorken, H., Pallack, M. S., & Henke, C. J. (1993). Managed mental health care, Medicaid, and cost-offset: The impact of psychological services in the Hawaii-HCFA-Medicaid project. In N. A. Cummings, H. Dorken, M. S. Pallack, & C. J. Henke (Eds.), *Medicaid, managed behavioral health and implications for public policy: Volume 2. Healthcare and utilization cost series* (pp. 3-23). San Francisco: Foundation for Behavioral Health.

Cummings, N. A., Kahn, B. I., & Sparkman, B. (1962). *Psychotherapy and medical utilization: A pilot study.* Oakland, CA: Annual Reports of Kaiser Permanente Research projects.

Devine, F. L., & Cook, T. D. (1983). A meta-analytic analysis of effects of psycho-educational intervention on length of post-surgical hospital stay. *Nursing Research, 32,* 267-274.

England, M. J. (1999). Capturing mental health cost offsets. *Health Affairs, 18,* 91-93.

Fraser, J. S. (1996). All that glitters is not always gold: Medical cost offset effects and managed behavioral health care. *Professional Psychology: Research and Practice, 27,* 335-344.

Friedman, R., Sobel, D., Myers, P., Caudill, M., & Benson, H. (1995). Behavioral Medicine, Clinical Health Psychology, and Cost Offset. *Health Psychology, 14* (6), 509-518.

Gabbard, G. O., Lazar, S. G., Hornberger, J., & Spiegel, D. (1997). The economic impact of psychotherapy: A review. *American Journal of Psychiatry, 154,* 147-155.

Groth-Marnat, G., & Edkins, G. (1996). Professional psychologists in general health care settings: A review of the financial efficacy of direct treatment interventions. *Professional Psychology: Research and Practice, 27,* 161-174.

Institute of Medicine's Committee on the Quality of Health Care in America (2001). Crossing the Quality Chasm. *Qual. Lett. Healthc. Lead., 13,* 14-5.

Katon, W., Von Korff, M., Lin, E., Lipscomb, P., Russo, J., Wagner, E., & Polk, E. (1990). Distressed high utilizers of medical care: DSM-III-R diagnoses and treatment needs. *General Hospital Psychiatry, 12,* 355-362.

Katon, W. (1995). Collaborative care: Patient satisfaction, outcomes, and medical cost offset. *Family Systems Medicine, 13,* 351-365.

Klingelhofer, E. L., & Gershwin, M. E. (1988). Asthma self-management programs: Premises, not promises. *Journal of Asthma, 25,* 89-101.

Kroenke, K., & Mangelsdorff, D. (1989). Common symptoms in ambulatory care: Incidence, evaluation, therapy, and outcome. *The American Journal of Medicine, 86,* 262-266.

Mumford, E., Schlesinger, H. J., Glass, G. V., Patrick, C., & Cuerdon, T. (1984). A new look at evidence about reduced cost of medical utilization following mental health treatment. *American Journal of Psychiatry, 141,* 1145-1158.

Pallak, M. S., & Cummings, N. A. (1992). In patient and outpatient psychiatric treatment: The effect of matching patients to appropriate level of treatment on psychiatric and medical-surgical hospital days. *Applied and Preventive Psychology: Current Scientific Perspectives, 1,* 83-87.

Phelps, C. E. (1997). *Health economics* (2nd ed.). Reading, Massachusetts: Addison-Wesley.

Smith, G. R. (1994). The course of somatization and its effects on utilization of health care resources. *Psychosomatics, 35,* 263-267.

Strosahl, K. (1998). *A model for integrating behavioral health and primary care medicine.* Paper presented at the annual meeting of the American Psychological Association, San Francisco, USA.

Strum, R. (1999). Cost and quality trends under managed care: Is there a learning curve in behavioral health carve-out plans? *Journal of Health Economics, 18,* 593-604.

Wessel, D. (2001). Rising medical costs can be a good thing. *Wall Street Journal, July 26.*

Medical Cost Offset as a Roadmap to Behavioral Entrepreneurship: Lessons from the Hawaii Project

Nicholas A. Cummings
University of Nevada, Reno
and The Nicholas and Dorothy Cummings Foundation

The things that need to be learned before we do them are often the things that we must first do in order to learn them.
- Aristotle

If the knowledge of organizational behavior were a true guide to entrepreneurship, the Silicon Valley would be populated by college professors. That this is not so is neither surprising, nor does it diminish the importance of behavioral analysis. But it does indicate that other crucial and over-riding factors are present. It is the purpose of this paper to identify some of those factors, using the case history of the first and only successful, clinically-driven, national psychology-run behavioral care system. It was created and administered by psychologists at its headquarters on the edge of the Silicon Valley during the early 1980s, the hey-day of e-commerce and the new economy. Intensive research went hand-in-hand with extensive field demonstrations, interrelated and timed so that each led to the identification of the next step in the other.

Although there are no immutable reasons that academia and entrepreneurship should not mutually proceed, certain intrinsic characteristics of each result in an unfortunate chasm between the two. The first and perhaps the most defining of these characteristics is *risk aversion*. Academia prefers the security of tenure to the uncertainties of the sweat equity model of a start-up, while the entrepreneur flourishes on the concept of risk and ultimate reward for this risk. Further, academia leans heavily toward order and planning, and hence favors a planned economy, the very antithesis of entrepreneurial endeavor, while the entrepreneur insists there has never been a planned economy that was able to out-produce free-market capitalism. It is not surprising, therefore, that the universities are populated by one, and the Silicon Valleys of the nation are populated by the other.

There are a number of striking exceptions in which renown academics have founded and run successful start-ups, and although these are few, the author is not aware of a single example of the reverse, where a highly successful entrepreneur later became a scientist of stature. An obvious example of the former is Ed Fredkin of the Massachusetts Institute of Technology (MIT) faculty who achieved such wealth from the company he founded that he bought his own Caribbean island where he hosted for many years top level scientific conferences by special invitation.

An even more unlikely example is that of Stephen Wolfram whose academic credentials are dazzling and his entrepreneurial success most impressive. He attended Oxford on a scholarship and by age 14 he had written his own book on particle physics. At the age of 17 he published a scientific paper in the journal *Nuclear Physics,* and shortly thereafter he went to work in the High Energy Physics Groups at the Argonne National Laboratory. While there, and at the age of 18, he wrote a scientific paper on heavy quark production that soon became a classic in the field. At 19 he received an invitation from the legendary scientist Murray Gell-Mann to attend the California Institute of Technology (CalTech) where he earned his Ph.D. the first year. The following year he joined the CalTech faculty, and at the age of 21 he was awarded a MacArthur "Genius" Fellowship. In his late twenties he founded a highly successful software firm whose *Mathematica* is the most used computer program in mathematics, physics, chemistry and biology. Now in his early forties, he spends from 10:00 o'clock every night, and until 5:00 in the morning, in his home laboratory working on his new conceptualizations of cellular automata. He awakens at noon and spends every afternoon as CEO of his company. His highly remarkable conceptualizations challenge much of the fundamentals of mathematics, as well as the basic notion of natural selection in biology. His latest book, *A New Kind of Science,* was published in 2002 and it enjoyed the largest advance sales of any scientific book in history. Wolfram is a celebrated and dedicated scientist, as well as a consummate entrepreneur, and demonstrates that these seemingly disparate qualities are not necessarily so.

Characteristics of the New Economy

The Beginnings

Forty years before the IT revolution, two young Stanford engineering graduates named Dave Packard and Bill Hewlitt defined the sequence under which struggling "techies" would one day be creating their start-ups in the Santa Clara Valley, later to be dubbed the Silicon Valley. Unable to afford either an office or a laboratory, they rented a garage with a leaky roof in the home of a widow who did not drive. They never dreamed that if their pioneering work could survive the frequent rain damage, Hewlitt-Packard would one day be one of the Fortune 500 companies. Their start-up was in the midst of the Great Depression of the 1930s, and although the economy was strong during the growth of the Silicon Valley in the 1980s, the garage, attic, bedroom and basement were the beginning locations of what are now the giants of the new economy. Capital was difficult to come by, necessitating use of meager savings and asking relatives and friends to invest. This was the ambiance in which the author founded his own company, sharing hard times with such legendary figures as Steve Jobs and Michael Dell, and learning much from Dave Packard, himself. Most Americans are not aware that Oracle, second in size only to MicroSoft in the IT world, was capitalized with only half a million dollars, the exact sum that launched American Biodyne in the early 1980s.

The Irrational Exuberance

All of this changed in the mid-1990s. The success of the IT revolution found investors, a predictable type of herd animal, almost throwing money at start-ups as long as their corporate name was followed by dot-com. The average start-up capitalization jumped from a few hundred thousand dollars to thirty million dollars. Every young MBA with any modicum of an idea rushed to take advantage of the opportunities, and investors rewarded them with money. The garage was replaced by the posh office, and fast-talking marginal business types, several of whom had been convicted of fraud in the past, moved in to take command of the fledgling companies and their naive founders. Much of the millions in capitalization were spent on slick advertising, a lot of it incomprehensible, which nevertheless gave the illusion the dot-com was doing well. Investors took the bait and kept bidding the tech stocks up in the absence of any earnings until the bubble burst in 2000. Again in predictable herd animal fashion, investors abandoned the dot-coms as rapidly as they had espoused them. The new economy had its first shake-out.

During the period described by Alan Greenspan of the Federal Reserve Board as irrational exuberance (1997-1999), the author had occasion to advise a venture capital firm on a number of the start-ups seeking funding. The ideas were at best questionable, with little indication they could ever be profitable. There was a preponderance of young, patently opportunistic MBAs and an absence of technologists. One company, which would create a data bank of customers who would list the significant dates of friends, family and associates, and to whom the company would dispatch a gift, sought a $5 million initial capitalization. For this the founders were willing to give-up only 10% of the company in spite of their being at the stage where they had not even begun to develop the software. The principles were four MBAs just out of school, and anyone with IT ability was glaringly absent. On advice the venture capital firm refused them, but they easily got their money from others. The company was launched and it went bankrupt two years later. The author's favorite, however, was DogDoo.com that sent canine excrement neatly packaged to whomever the customer selected, obviously as a prank. The company actually got liberally capitalized, but it never established much of a customer base and it quickly vanished when the start-up money was spent.

Characteristics of the Start-up Winners, 1997-2000

Over 130 dot-coms launched during this period met their financial demise in the year 2000. *Inc Magazine* (Mangelsdorf, 2000) gathered data on these companies and found them to resemble those described above: high initial capitalization, mediocre business ideas, little likelihood of profitability, founders who were oriented toward a quick cash-in, and an absence of founders with the requisite IT. In contrast, the 500 companies that were founded in 1997 and that achieved a revenue stream of 100 million or more within three years reflected characteristics of the companies that started-up in the mid-1980s rather than those of the mid-1990s.

As Tables 1 and 2 reveal, 42% of these successful start-ups had an initial capitalization of under $10,000, an amazing 79% had an initial capitalization of under $100,000, while only 21% had such a capitalization of over $100,000. These funds were derived from personal assets (92%), cofounders personal assets (36%), and assets of family and friends (33%). Obviously many of these companies had a combination of all three. The startling statistic is that only 4% of these 500 successful start-ups received initial funding from venture capitalists (VCs). This latter fact rendered them free of the pressures that VCs, who usually are business-oriented and lack technological knowledge, frequently impose on a company, often to its detriment. And the final figure is the most crucial of all: fully 100% of these founding CEOs of successful start-ups were intimately acquainted with the technology involved in their company. In other words, they were techies who had the vision for their company, and who knew how to tap the necessary business/financial expertise.

Less than $1,000	16%
$1,000 to $10,000	26%
$10,001 to $20,000	16%
$20,001 to $50,000	10%
$50,001 to $100,000	11%
More than $100,000	21%

Table 1. Amount of initial start-up capital available to the 2000 Inc. 500 companies. The criterion for inclusion was $100 million or more in annual revenue within three years. All were 1997 start-ups. (Source: Mangelsdorf, 2000).

Used personal assets	92%
Used cofounders personal assets	36%
Tapped assets of family or friends	33%
Received venture capital	4%

Table 2. Method of raising initial start-up Capital for the 2000 Inc. 500 companies. The Criterion for inclusion was $100 million or more in annual revenue within three years. All were 1997 start-ups. (Source: Mangelsdorf, 2000).

With these facts and background in mind, it is time to consider how a successful entrepreneurial behavioral care company was established. The similarities with successful IT companies will be apparent. The difference, however, was the way the requisite technology was derived: field-testing of various models in a cohesive at-risk delivery system, using medical cost offset as the criterion for adoption of the protocols.

Elicitation and Application of Behavioral Care Technology

In the late 1970s the author became convinced that the industrialization of healthcare was inevitable. Not only was it the last major sector of our economy that was not industrialized, it was predicted to account for 12% of the gross national product (GNP). All other major sectors of the economy had industrialized:

Manufacturing in the 1900s, mining in the 1930s, transportation in the 1950s, and retailing in the 1970s. In addition, he was convinced that the government would seek private sector solutions inasmuch as the thrust toward government sponsored universal care had gone nowhere. This was loudly signaled by the Congress when in 1974 it passed the HMO enabling Act, rendering moot many of the state laws that prevented what had been defined as "the corporate practice of medicine." However, attempts by the author and a number of others in the late 1970s to interest the private sector in an organized system of psychological healthcare failed. At that time psychological services were such a small part of the overall health expenditures that it hardly seemed worth the effort. The only large healthcare provider that foresaw how behavioral interventions could save medical/surgical costs was Kaiser Permanente.

This all changed in the early 1980s when the Congress created a system of Diagnosis Related Groups (DRGs), for these inadvertently ushered in the era of managed care. However, the impossibility of writing DRGs for psychiatry threatened the existence of mental health and chemical dependency (MH/CD) as a covered healthcare benefit. The cost of MH/CD skyrocketed at a time when medicine and surgery costs were beginning to be tethered, and insurers were dropping the benefit. As an alternative to psychiatric DRGs, the government opened the way for the private sector to contain MH/CD costs, and the author responded rapidly with a plan to create a national behavioral healthcare company.

The Mission

As there were no effective precedents in existence, a mission statement for the new company was enunciated with the following requirements:

1. Since health plans wanted to be rid of the responsibility for the MH/CD benefit because they neither understood it nor knew how to deliver it without unacceptable costs, the new company would have to be independent and freestanding (later to be termed a carve-out).
2. It would have to be able to go at risk, relieving the contracting (client) health plan of any downside or liability while guaranteeing to provide the promised services.
3. In assuming such responsibility, it would have to be able to accept capitation (or other prospective reimbursement) rather than fee-for-service. The latter would leave the client health plan still at risk.
4. The cost to the client health plan would have to be competitive, reducing and capping its run-away MH/CD costs while expanding the benefit.
5. Cost-efficiencies would be achieved by therapeutic effectiveness, not by limiting services or access. Procedures that at the time were rapidly becoming popular in an attempt to reduce untoward MH/CD costs would not be used. These included therapy session limits, utilization review, pre-certification, case management, and therapist profiling.
6. The use of the best in behavioral care technology (protocols, guidelines, quality assurances) would be the basis of an MH/CD system that made

use of these in a cohesive, reliable delivery system that was consistent on a nationwide basis, but flexible enough to accommodate regional demands.

Scouting

The entrepreneurial activity of scouting involves the determination of market needs and the technology available to meet these demands. The difference between the technology available and that required to produce the product and accomplish its application and delivery constitutes the research and development that must be immediately tackled by the start-up. The striking features of behavioral health was first the surprising amount of behavioral care technology that existed in 1981, and second the remarkable degree to which it was being ignored by the mental health professions.

There existed at the time brief, behaviorally oriented therapies that were being developed by a number of practitioner researchers, but these were essentially open ended. Whereas they demonstrated therapeutic effectiveness to a greater or lesser degree, none had been subjected to the criterion of cost effectiveness in an at-risk delivery system. The researchers were largely in university and other non-profit environments where the concern was therapeutic effectiveness, not cost. Therefore, nothing decidedly useful to an at-risk, capitated delivery system existed beyond the extensive, but incomplete work on group and individual protocols under development by the author and his colleagues the 25 years he was at Kaiser Permanente in San Francisco. As important as these were, they were tested within the world's largest HMO and its attendant limiting bureaucracy, leaving the question of how well these would or would not operate in a carve-out.

It was apparent from the beginning, therefore, that most of the technology would have to be redeveloped and re-tested, a daunting task, indeed. In the words of Dave Biegelson, longtime scientist at Xerox Parc in the Silicon Valley, "The best way to change the future is to invent it" (personal communication, 1983). This is what in effect the Biodyne Institute, a non-profit research organization and predecessor to American Biodyne, a for-profit outgrowth and start-up, set out to do.

The Funding, the Setting and the Population

Whereas the private sector generally showed little interest in a study of this kind, the exception was Albert Yuen, the president of the Hawaii Medical Services Association (HMSA, the Blue Cross/Blue Shield affiliate in Hawaii), who was keenly concerned with runaway health care costs. In addition, several United States Senators, and particularly Daniel K. Inouye (D-HI), saw the importance of an empirically-derived delivery system that had the potential of saving significant dollars in Medicaid and Medicare. It was not long before the Health Care Financing Administration (HCFA) put together a four-way contract for a several year demonstration project among the State of Hawaii, HMSA, the Biodyne Institute, and HCFA. The combined state/federal funding exceeded $8 million, and the Hawaii Project, as it came to be called, originally scheduled for five years actually went seven (1981-1988) with such efficiency that no additional funding was necessary. In fact, the Biodyne Institute actually returned several hundred thousand dollars to the federal government at the conclusion of the project.

The Hawaii Project has been extensively reported (Cummings, Dorken, Pallak, Henke, 1991 & 1993; Pallak, Cummings, Dorken, & Henke, 1994 & 1995), and only a few salient features will be discussed here. The setting was the Island of Oahu (Honolulu) and the population included both the 36,000 Medicaid recipients and 90,000 federal employees participating in a prospective study. These 126,000 subjects were randomly assigned two-thirds to the experimental group and one-third to the control, accomplished in a manner that kept nuclear families intact. The control group received the extant Medicaid benefit of 52 sessions of psychotherapy a year, renewable each January 1st, with any licensed psychiatrist or psychologist of the patient's choice. This was perhaps the most liberal psychotherapy Medicaid MH/CD benefit in the United States, and one that was extensively utilized since by Hawaii state law a patient on "emotional or mental disability" had to be in continuous therapy. The study, therefore, did not compare MH/CD services with no such services. Rather, it compared fee-for-service psychotherapy in the private community with capitated MH/CD services offered in a highly organized setting.

The experimental group would receive its MH/CD benefit through a new delivery system that was created from the ground-up. Well-placed Biodyne Centers were established, a staff of psychologists was hired and intensely trained, and communication with potential patients through newsletters, bulletins and phone calls became routine. In addition, an outreach program directed toward the 15% highest utilizers of medicine was instrumental in bringing the somatizers in for therapy, and in addition six medical conditions were targeted: asthma, emphysema and other chronic airways diseases, diabetes, hypertension, ischemic heart disease, and rheumatoid arthritis. These conditions account for 40% of medical expenditures in the ages 20 to 55.

For ease in acquiring a large number of practitioners in a short time, all psychotherapists were hired half-time and were encouraged to maintain their private practices the other half-time. Since all of them did, a number of comparisons that otherwise would not be possible were made. HMSA was the state's fiscal intermediary, so data on what practitioners did in their independent offices versus their performance at the Biodyne Centers were readily available. Table 3 portrays the number of comparisons possible among patients in this study: control group patients seen privately by Biodyne and non-Biodyne therapists; experimental group patients seen by Biodyne; all patients seen in these settings according to experimental versus control, and as to diagnosis of the six chronic medical diseases; and finally all patients seen in all of these settings with a diagnosis of substance abuse.

Data Analysis

The psychotherapists received extensive training during the initial period of six months in which infrastructure of the Biodyne Centers was being created. The author, who was the principal investigator for the Hawaii Project, flew to Honolulu

Experimental Group patients:
    (a) seen by Biodyne therapists at the Biodyne Centers.
    (b) seen by Biodyne therapists in their private practices.
    (c) seen by non-Biodyne therapists in their private practices.
    (d) not seen by any therepist.

Control Group patients:
    (e) seen by non-Biodyne therapists in their private practices.
    (f) seen by Biodyne therepists in their private practice.
    (g) not seen by any therapist.

Table 3. The four possibilities for treatment for the Experimental Group and the three possibilities for treatment for the Control Group as found in the Hawaii HCFA Project. The critical feature is that in addition to comparison of the Biodyne therapists with private practitioners in the community, it also allows a comparison of the way Biodyne therapists operated in their private offices versus how they conducted therapy in the Biodyne Centers. By definition Control Group patients could not be seen in the Biodyne Centers.

every other week to conduct the hands-on training, which included the direct delivery of services by the trainees. The intervening weeks the trainees conducted their own practices in their private offices. Thus, the trainees received 480 hours of hands-on training (12 weeks times 40 hours per week) during which they were on salary. At the conclusion of training they became salaried half-time staff members, and 15% of their time was devoted to quality assurance in the forms of supervision and clinical case conferencing.

The trainees (all doctoral level psychologists or board certified psychiatrists) were specifically trained in Focused, Intermittent Psychotherapy Throughout the Life Cycle which is designed to raise the motivational level of the patient by making her or him a partner in the therapeutic process. This therapeutic approach was developed over 25 years at Kaiser Permanente (1957-1982) and has been extensively described (Cummings and Sayama, 1995). The trainees were also trained in 68 individual and group protocols that were developed over the same quarter century at Kaiser Permanente.

The psychotherapists' performance by protocol was measured in terms of both its therapeutic effectiveness and its cost efficiency. Thus, the results with each patient was measured on a cost-therapeutic efficiency-effectiveness ratio. The criterion for therapeutic effectiveness was medical cost offset; i.e., reduction in the patient's medical and surgical utilization following the beginning of therapy as compared to the full year's utilization in the year prior to the beginning of therapy. The criterion for efficiency was a combination of number of sessions and the weight of each session. For example, an individual session would count as one hour of a therapist's time, while a group session lasting two hours with one therapist and eight patients is weighed one-fourth of an hour per patient. This weighting would depend on whether there are more or fewer patients per group, as well as whether the group session is one, one-and-a-half, or two hours. Finally, the individual session would also be weighted as to whether it was one hour, half an hour, or one-quarter hour, or a seldom used two-hours. (For a full description of this method, see Cummings, 1994).

The Cost/Effectiveness Ratio is the average number of medical services tabulated for a group of patients for the year before psychotherapy began (1B), divided by the average tabulation of medical utilization the year after (1A) plus the average number of weighted psychotherapy sessions for that group of patients. Additionally, this can be tabulated for two (2A), three (3A) or more years after. It is written as follows:

$$r = \frac{\text{medical utilization 1B}}{\text{medical utilization 1A + number therapy sessions}}$$

For example, if a group of patients averaged 1B utilization of 128, while their average 1A utilization was 62, but it required an average of 46 sessions to accomplish this, the ratio would be:

$$r = \frac{128}{62 + 46} = 1.02$$

This ratio is low, indicating that the intervention was therapeutically effective (average medical utilization was cut to less than half), but the gain was obviated by the large average number of therapy sessions to accomplish it. In such an event, the protocol would be accepted as therapeutically effective and it would be continued, but additional research would be conducted toward refinement of the protocol to make it more efficient. No protocol was accepted as efficient but not therapeutically effective, as this would constitute an oxymoron. For a protocol or an intervention to be accepted as part of the clinical delivery system, it must consistently result in a ratio of 9.0 or above. In time the median score for all Biodyne Model interventions was 15.2. A troublesome exception is the protocol for borderline personality disorder. No matter what was done, this never exceeded a ratio of 7.8, mostly because of the large number of individual and group therapy sessions required for a medical cost offset sufficient to relieve the physicians of constant barrages of non-medical issues from this kind of patient.

It would be useful to trace this procedure through the development of this difficult protocol (Cummings, 1994). A group of 83 borderline disordered patients was placed in individual focused psychotherapy as described by Cummings and Sayama (1995). The result was that medical utilization declined slightly, but at an enormous expenditure of both individual sessions and emergency room visits:

$$r = \frac{163}{141 + 68} = .8$$

The ratio is low, indicating that interventions were neither therapeutically effective (reduction in medical utilization) nor cost efficient (number of mental health units). The staff over time created a focused set of interventions more appropriate to this kind of patient, but again in individual psychotherapy. In a group of 73 patients there was some improvement in cost efficiency, but little impact on therapeutic effectiveness:

$$r = \frac{167}{148 + 51} = .7$$

The overall effectiveness/efficiency ratio actually declined. With another population of 76 patients suffering from borderline personality disorder, a great deal of care and effort was expended in designing a 20-session group therapy, augmented with 10 sessions of individual therapy, then with monthly follow-up sessions. Emergency room visits were virtually eliminated, and the ratio rose dramatically:

$$r = \frac{166}{27+31} = 2.8$$

Learning a great deal from this group of patients, the therapy was sharpened to 15 group sessions, followed by 10 psychoeducational sessions, and with subsequent monthly follow-up sessions. Critical was the feature that paired-off patients with the requirement that they call each other for help between sessions, not the therapist. This resulted in a dramatic diminution of acting out behavior, yielding a markedly improved ratio:

$$r = \frac{171}{11+12} = 7.8$$

The research team continued to experiment with honing the program even further. However, the work with borderline personality disorder, a category of resistant and highly acting out patients, never achieved the ideal of 9.0 or higher, which became the standard, and remained less than half the median ratio of 15.2 found in most of the 68 protocols. This protocol was adopted, nonetheless, because of consistent reports of satisfaction from both physicians and patients. As this illustrates, medical cost offset does not always yield the degree of therapeutic cost efficiency sought, but it helps define the primary component: the most effective, not the cheapest treatment.

A Caveat

In order to conduct medical cost offset research, the system must have in place a sophisticated electronic system in which computerized medical records can be compared with the computerized psychological records. Often these requirements are not in place. In other instances, the sophisticated automated records of the medical system do not interface with the equally sophisticated records of the behavioral carve-out. And in still others, the management information systems (MIS) of either or both the medical and behavioral delivery systems are inadequate.

In the case of the Hawaii Project, the MIS of HMSA was state of the art. Furthermore, HMSA was the physical intermediary for both Medicaid and the Federal Employees Benefits Program (FEBP). In addition, HMSA was the payor for the independently practicing psychiatrists and psychologists in Hawaii, making possible the extension of medical cost offset research into the fee-for-service sector.

Results and Conclusions

Levels of Comparison

The design and implementation of the Hawaii Project made possible the comparison of several groups on the medical cost offset dimension.

1. Experimental group patients receiving treatment from Biodyne.
2. Experimental group patients receiving no behavioral health treatment.
3. Control group patients receiving fee-for-service psychotherapy from private practitioners in the community.
4. Control group patients receiving fee-for-service psychotherapy from private practitioners in the community who practiced half-time at Biodyne.
5. Control group patients who received no behavioral health care.

Within these five conditions, the patients were further delineated as having one of the following characteristics:

1. Psychological problems with no diagnosed chronic medical condition.
2. Psychological problems plus one of six diagnosed chronic medical conditions.
3. Psychological problems plus diagnosed addiction or chemical abuse.

Results

It is important to point out that the data were collected, tabulated and stored by both HMSA in Honolulu and HCFA in Washington. The final report of the Hawaii Project (HCFA No. 11-C-98344/9) was distributed by the Health Care Financing Administration. It included a number of results that will be only summarized here, and are displayed graphically in Figures 1, 2 and 3.

The State of Hawaii funded the creation of the Biodyne carve-out on the Island of Oahu (Honolulu and environs), as well as the training of the practitioners in the Biodyne Model. It recovered its investment through medical cost offset within 18 months, and the savings continued to accrue throughout the three years of the clinical demonstration. This was the result of outreach and subsequent interventions with the experimental group patients seen, with several hundred dollars of medical cost offset in the non-chronic medical condition group and twice that in the chronic medical condition group. The medical cost offset demonstrated by the substance abuse group was the largest of all three groups, resulting in substantial savings in the high-risk Hawaii Medicaid population.

A substantial group of patients responded to none of the various outreach methods that were successful in bringing in most other patients. Attempts to send

Non-Chronic Group

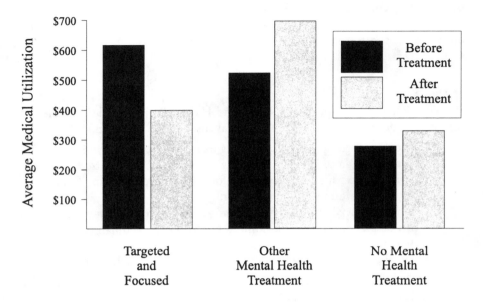

Figure 1. Nonchronic Group. Average medical utilization in constant dollars for the Hawaii Project Nonchronic group for the year before (darker shaded columns) for those receiving targeted and focused treatment, or other mental health treatment in the private practice community, and no mental health treatment, and for the year after (lighter shaded columns) for each condition treatment (Cummings, Dorken, Pallak, & Henke, 1993).

psychologists to the home failed, but substituting nurses dressed in full regalia resulted in 100% admittance into the home. It was found that these patients were not only resistant to seeking medical care, they also manifested a wide range of serious and neglected medical conditions. The task was to get these patients into the medical system as soon as possible, thus raising substantially their medical utilization. Getting these patients to a physician was often critical, and was both the appropriate medical and ethical response. Even with the increase of medical utilization among these needy patients, the impressive overall medical cost offset prevailed. The Hawaii Project was committed to the appropriateness of care, whether this be medical, behavioral or both.

The private fee-for-service sector significantly raised medical costs among all patients seen, but particularly among those suffering from chronic medical conditions. Subsequent interviews with the independently practicing psychiatrists and psychologists revealed that these psychotherapists, rather than addressing somatization issues or the lack of compliance with medical regimen, concentrated

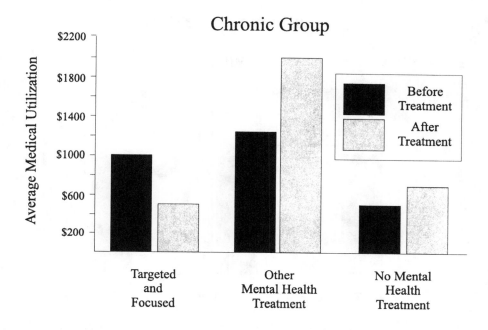

Figure 2. Chronically ill Group. Average medical utilization in constant dollars for the Hawaii Project chronically ill group for the year before (darker shaded columns) for those receiving targeted and focused treatment, other mental health treatment in the private practice community, and no mental health treatment, and for the year after (lighter shaded columns) for each condition of treatment (Cummings, Dorken, Pallak, & Henke, 1993).

on assertiveness issues. Patients were admonished and encouraged to go back to their physicians and demand more laboratory tests and/or a different treatment. This had the effect of increasing medical costs without resolving the patient's somatizing or non-compliance.

The private fee-for-service sector increased the already high medical utilization of the chemical abusers. Patient abstinence was the successful goal with the experimental patients, while "social" drinking or drug use was the theme of the independent practitioners. Consequently, there was a significant drop in the medical utilization among the addiction/chemical dependency patients.

The Biodyne therapists, who were instrumental in bringing about medical cost savings while practicing at the Biodyne Centers, actually raised medical utilization in the patients they treated in their private offices. Although the increases in medical costs were not as dramatic as those resulting from non-Biodyne private practitioners, it demonstrated that once out of the Biodyne environment psychotherapists reverted to the treatment approaches they used before their intensive re-training.

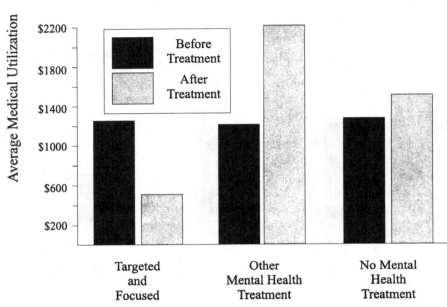

Figure 3. Substance abuse Group. Average medical utilization in constant dollars for the Hawaii Project substance abuse group for the year before (darker shaded columns) for those receiving targeted and focused treatment, other mental health treatment in the private practice community, and no mental health treatment, and for the year after (lighter shaded columns) for each treatment condition (Cummings, Dorken, Pallak, & Henke, 1993).

Implications for Entrepreneurship

After only three years of research and experience with the Hawaii Project, there followed in 1985 the launching of American Biodyne, a clinically driven organized behavioral healthcare carve-out. This was permitted by newly enacted federal legislation that encouraged the translation into the private sector of findings resulting from government funded research. The new delivery system was launched into uncharted waters and at considerable risk were it not for the knowledge gained through the use of medical cost offset research in the preceding Hawaii Project. Overcoming risk aversion, therefore, does not involve behavior that resembles closing one's eyes in the face of fear and diving into what turns out to be the shallow end of the swimming pool. It is the deliberate movement forward from data and experience that enables the formation of a start-up based on knowledge, albeit the type of comprehensive knowledge that cannot emerge from the laboratory alone. Consequently, risk is still extant, but it is mitigated by research, as well as its applications beyond the laboratory.

One is reminded in this regard of the development of new drugs and their certification by the federal Food and Drug Administration (FDA). The laboratory can only provide a standard of safety, substantial as it is. Eventually the FDA must take the risk and certify the drug for use. It is now that heretofore undiscovered side-effects, some of which may prove disfiguring or fatal, are discovered. Drugs, such as the benzodiazapines and others that revealed no addictive properties on clinical trials are found by experience to be highly addictive or subject to abuse. Others have resulted over time to cause such severe physical harm that they have been withdrawn after a period of use by the medical community with its patients. All of these untoward effects were not foreseen during the clinical trials. Similarly, when one moves from the laboratory to entrepreneurship, the risk can never be zero. Consequences must be weighed with the degree of assurance, but many excellent researchers are not able to successfully bridge the gap because they are reluctant to take the next step and move out of the laboratory. For those that do, the risk must be tempered by data and experience.

Well-conducted medical cost offset research, embodying both laboratory research and field demonstration in an optimal timing and mix, is one key to behavioral healthcare entrepreneurship. In the experience of this author it gives the practitioner the basis and courage to use newly discovered, effective interventions, it satisfies the investor who must finance the endeavor, and it emboldens the health payor system that must ultimately share the risk.

In addition to these general considerations, there are lessons learned from the new economy. The organized delivery of behavioral healthcare involves technology, and the ultimate decisions are best vested in those who fully understand the technology, not in those trained only in business. All decision-makers at American Biodyne were clinicians who were further trained in business procedures and management. No matter how high up the ladder these clinicians were promoted, each had to spend at least one full day a week in hands-on clinical work with patients. Their involvement was also required in the ongoing research, both medical cost offset as well as other empirical studies, which were characteristically built into the delivery system.

Critical Considerations in Organizing a Behavioral Care Delivery System

Expanding and Redefining the Technology

Treatment protocols empirically derived in the laboratory are invaluable, but not sufficient. The academic researcher is interested in normative data, along with effectiveness. In the field the therapist is concerned with the individual case, and how much protocol noncompliance is necessary to respond to exigencies. Furthermore, in the search for effectiveness, laboratory-derived treatments are open-ended. A delivery system is a closed-system, having to be efficient (cost effective) as well as therapeutically effective. Scouting reveals the extant technology; entrepreneurs must expand and redefine this technology to make it applicable and appropriate in the real world. The success of this extrapolation will depend on the reliability and validity of the field demonstrations where the pristine controls of the laboratory are absent, but the loose variables extant in a delivery system are paramount. The author and his colleagues found medical cost offset measures reliable and rewarding. Thus they were able to create from scratch a system with 14.5 million eligible lives nationally, and one that in the seven years the author was founding CEO there was not a single malpractice suit or a complaint that had to be adjudicated. The business-driven systems of behavioral care are plagued with malpractice suits, and the lack of technology is forcing most to abandon delivery while becoming essentially third-party intermediaries.

Infusing the Technology

It is critical, but not sufficient that the leadership be steeped in the technology that will drive the delivery system. It is also important that this technology be infused throughout the delivery system, and especially to those who will be doing the hands-on treatment. If the technology is not present at the point of treatment application, no amount of administrative business monitoring, such as pre-certification, utilization review, case management, and therapist profiling, will render effective/efficient results. This is another reason why the present industry is failing as a delivery system of care.

Training in the Technology

Since the organized behavioral system has defined the technology, it does not yet exist in its potential practitioners. Training of the practitioners hired, therefore, is essential. But Biodyne found that merely exposing hires to the technology is far from enough. Practitioners tend to not heed the retraining, to keep doing what they were taught in graduate school, and to remain loyal to the particular system, or psycho-religion, in which they were trained. In order to assure the infusion of the technology, there was developed an intensive training system that came to be known as the "Biodyne bootcamp." This involved intensive, hands-on participatory training for 12 hours a day and for 14 straight days with no time off. This was necessary to break through the resistance, and it was akin to a cowboy breaking a horse. But it worked. The practitioners moved through the 14 days from resistance, to hostility, to rejection, to taking a second look, and to finally appreciation. After the bootcamp they embarked with trepidation on applying the technology in their treatment rooms, and they were accorded the support and supervision to enable them to make the transition from the old to the new. Within six months the therapists not only became facile in the new technology, but they also became enthusiastic because it accorded them new, effective skills.

Continuous Quality Assurance

Even with the retraining, most therapists who are left to their own devices will drift back to their original approaches. Therefore, to maintain quality and prevent drift, fully 15% of every therapist's time was spent in quality assurance. This included three hours of clinical case conferencing every Friday morning, as well as weekly individual and group supervision. As costly as it is spending 15% of the therapist's time in this way, the system more than recovered these expenditures in effective outcomes, patient satisfaction, and the total absence of malpractice suits.

A unique feature of the ideal Biodyne Center as it eventually evolved was the placing of all the therapist's offices in a circle or a hollow square, with the director's office in the center. That office would have one-way mirrored screens into every therapists office (the usual Biodyne Center was five psychotherapists and the supervisor) along with a sound system. At any moment the center director could observe and hear whatever was going on in any therapy session. This direct observation greatly energized the supervisory sessions, and in extreme cases in which the therapist was off on a tangent with the patient, the center director could ask that the therapist step out for a two minute consultation with the supervisor.

This degree of scrutiny worked because a deliberately non-punitive atmosphere was created and meticulously maintained. The psychotherapist was never chastised or demeaned. This atmosphere of acceptance and help was so pervasive that the therapists would save their worst failures to present to the CEO on his frequent visits to the centers throughout the country.

Patient Participation

Every patient who presented at Biodyne for treatment was asked to sign a form acknowledging that in the interest of assuring that the patient received the best possible care, his or her case could be monitored at any time, either directly or indirectly. For the exception of a handful of paranoids who refused, and whose refusal was honored, the patients agreed to, and expected monitoring. In scores of difficult and baffling cases, the therapist, patient and CEO conducted a session while the entire center staff observed through a one-way screen. These procedures were implemented with fanatic dedication to quality patient care, an attitude that did not escape the patient, who responded with appreciation. Interestingly, there was never an instance where the therapist lost favor or stature in the patient's eye because the CEO or other supervisor had come to recoup a stalled therapy.

Self-Selection

One of the things that often insures success in entrepreneurial ventures is an incentive system known as "sweat equity." The participants accept low salaries in exchange for an ownership of the new company. If the company succeeds, the rewards are extensive. If the company fails, then the participants worked several years at "minimum wages." The author often refers to this as the Bunsen-burner at the behinds of the participants, propelling them to put in as much sweat as may be necessary to succeed. This is one of the secret weapons of the Silicon Valley success, for the participants have self-selected, with those who may be risk-aversive, or unwilling to work back-breaking hours, opting out. Biodyne also learned that practitioners will also self-select. There are those who are appalled when they first hear what is expected of them, while others (about 10%) will quit in the middle of the training.

Opportunity to advance was a significant feature of Biodyne employment. The company was growing 200% a year, and met this by promoting and relocating successful, but willing therapists to staff the new centers. It was not unusual for a skillful therapist to advance in one year from staff psychotherapist to center director to state director. But in all cases of advancement, which often involved relocation, the clinician agreed. Those who did not desire such advancement could work toward achieving the status of master clinician that had a different set of rewards: supervisor, researcher and higher pay with no administrative duties. This was an extension of the original system of self-selection.

Outcomes Research

Research was an ever-present feature, with the research built into the delivery system so as to cause the least amount of interference or disruption. Outcomes research was ongoing, as was the refinement of the protocols and the delivery system. Of importance were the kinds of studies that elicited regional differences necessitating adaptations in the procedures and protocols. These studies underscored what has come to be a given in the industry: healthcare is a local and regional matter.

Organized Systems of Care

Medical cost offset can only be demonstrated in large, appropriately organized systems of care. Solo practitioners or small group practices can never have the critical mass necessary to provide the wide range of services addressing each of the many conditions that must be appropriately treated. Purchasers of behavioral healthcare prefer one-stop shopping where all the services are offered. Even if a solo practitioner or small group practice were to succeed in carving a niche market, such as anorexia for example, the impact on the total medical system would be too small to measure. But even more importantly, the ability to track the patient's psychotherapy vis-à-vis the same patient's medical care through a sophisticated electronic system would be absent. Medical cost offset would be difficult to assess or prove.

Addendum

The managed behavioral care organizations (MBCOs) have not been successful in delivering quality care that is both within their financial constraints and is satisfactory to the consumer. Consequently, they are rapidly getting out of the delivery of care, leaving it open to providers to form at-risk delivery systems while the MBCOs fall back to being intermediaries in the healthcare industry. This is underway as of this writing, and will be largely completed by 2002, leaving tremendous opportunities for providers to create at risk delivery systems.

The psychologists who will be able to seize the opportunity are those who not only have the clinical technology, but are also those who can expand this technology to meet the exigencies of a healthcare system in flux and jeopardy. The difficulties and failures of managed behavioral care today are the kinds of problems that foster risk-aversion. In addition, most psychologists when it comes to entrepreneurship seem to have a hefty amount of their own free-floating risk-aversion. Medical cost offset research, properly conducted, can reduce risk by serving as a roadmap to the creation of an effective, efficient delivery system, and to the continued success and growth of such a system by keeping it grounded in data.

Finally, this paper would be remiss in not mentioning the potential savings in medicine, and the lack of potential savings in behavioral care. All of the fat has beenremoved from behavioral care, leaving it under-funded. Yet there are enormous potential savings in a medical system that is over-burdened by patients manifesting stress, depression, non-compliance to their medical regimens while suffering from chronic diseases, and faulty life styles. A 10% to 15% reduction in medical utilization as a result organized behavioral interventions is conservative in most medical cost offset research. Yet it would result in a savings to the health system of $120 billion to $180 billion dollars a year.

References

Cummings, N.A. (1994). The successful application of medical offset in program planning and clinical delivery. *Managed Care Quarterly*, 2(2), 1-6.

Cummings, N.A., Dorken, H., Pallak, M.S., & Henke, C.J. (1991). The impact of psychological intervention on health care costs and utilization. The Hawaii Medicaid Project. *HCFA Contract report #11-C-983344/9*.

Cummings, N.A., Dorken, H., Pallak, M.S., & Henke, C.J. (1993). The impact of psychological intervention on health care costs and utilization: The Hawaii Medicaid Project. In N.A. Cummings & M.S. Pallak (Eds.), *Medicaid, managed behavioral health and implications for public policy, Vol. 2: Healthcare and utilization cost series (pp.* 3-23). South San Francisco, CA: Foundation for Behavioral Health.

Cummings, N. & Sayama, M. (1995). *Focused psychotherapy: A casebook of brief, Intermittent psychotherapy throughout the life cycle.* New York, NY: Brunner/Mazel.

Mangelsdorf, M.L. (2000). The 2000 Inc. 500. *Inc. Magazine*, (November 27), 57-69.

Pallak, M.S., Cummings, N.A., Dorken, H., & Henke, C.J. (1994). Medical costs, Medicaid, an d managed mental health treatment: The Hawaii Study. *Managed Care Quarterly*, 2(2), 64-70.

Pallak, M.S., Cummings, N.A., Dorken, H., & Henke, C.J. (1995). Effects of mental health treatment on medical costs. *Mind/Body Medicine, 1,* 7-12.

Medical Cost Offset:
A Review of the Impact of
Psychological Interventions on Medical
Utilization Over the Past Three Decades

Jeremy A. Chiles
Davis Behavioral Health, Bountiful, Utah
Michael J. Lambert
Brigham Young University
Arlin L. Hatch
Brigham Young University

The rising cost of health care has become a major concern. In 1965 Americans spent $41.7 billion dollars on health care needs, compared to $250.1 billion in 1980, $540 billion in 1988, and $751.8 billion in 1991. Further, 9.6% of the Gross National Domestic Product was spent on health care in 1981 but reached over 15.0% in 1994 (Cockerham, 1995). At this rate, it was anticipated that $5,551 would be spent per person annually on health in the year 2000 (Cockerham, 1995). It is not surprising that a variety of measures have been taken by the insurance industry and government to contain costs. Incidental to these efforts is the discovery that psychological interventions may reduce general medical costs. In recent years, this has been referred to as the "medical cost-offset effect."

Based on a variety of research studies, there is reason to believe that an offset effect may exist. First, there is a growing body of literature that suggests people with mental health problems go to medical doctors and medical clinics for treatment of physical disorders rather than emotional disorders. For example, Shapiro (1971) reported nationally based estimates indicating that 50-80% of medical visits are by persons without any identifiable physical problem. Second, unwarranted physician visits and over-utilization of medical care also occurs in patients who experience co-occurring medical and psychological complaints. The psychiatric disorders that are common in patients who excessively seek medical services are mood disorders, anxiety disorders, substance abuse disorders, psychotic disorders, and adjustment disorders (Fulop & Strain, 1991; Goldberg, 1995; & Jencks, 1985).

Because medical patients' mental health can impact the treatment and recovery process, medical hospitals and clinics are likely to see greater length of stay for patients who also have psychological problems (Cohen, Shapiro, Manson, & Kondi, 1985; Levenson, Hamer, & Rossiter, 1990; & Saravay & Lavin, 1994). From a medical administrator's viewpoint, increased length of stay translates into higher patient costs, and a higher overall cost of providing medical services. This, in turn, translates into decreased hospital and clinic resources available to other patients, as well as increased costs that must be passed on to the patient, other taxpayers, and the insured public.

With the American health care system's gravitation toward managed health care, the focus has been on increasing the efficiency and cost-effectiveness of service and delivery (Budman, Simeone, Reilly, & Demby, 1994; Klein, Brabender, & Fallon, 1994). Considering this trend, higher utilization of medical services by those with psychological disturbance becomes especially important. It is a likely deduction that mental health problems are related to the use of primary medical care services, and it seems reasonable to suggest that the implementation of psychological interventions in primary care medical facilities could decrease mental health problems resulting in overall decreases in medical care costs and a *medical cost offset*.

The present meta-analytic review attempts to address a number of cost-offset questions. First, is there a measurable cost-offset effect in the extant literature? Second, are there particular psychological interventions or specific treatment settings (i.e., behavioral medicine in hospital settings) that have an increased offset effect? Third, is there a demonstrated difference in the offset effect between inpatient hospital offset studies where medical utilization is the focus and outpatient mental health offset studies where medical utilization is only a piece in a much larger psychological puzzle? Fourth, are psychological interventions cost-effective in terms of "offset" savings exceeding the cost of the interventions? Fifth, if an offset effect exists in the literature, to what mechanism of change (e.g., mental health intervention or medical system response) can this reduction in medical costs, inpatient length of stay, or outpatient medical visits be attributed?

Method

Literature Search

Articles pertinent to the study of offset effects were identified through several approaches. A computer search was conducted for the period January 1967 through July 1997, using the old and new Psychlit and Medline databases. Search terms related to cost offset were crossed with treatment terms and psychological and medical diagnostic terms to identify additional articles. After potential articles were identified for the study, articles were either included or excluded based on criteria including size of the study, whether or not a psychological intervention was measured, specific outcome measures reported, and scientific rigor of the study. A pool of 91 studies with 128 different treatment groups was chosen based on the inclusion/exclusion criteria. The studies were published between 1967 and 1997.

Coding of the Studies

Studies were coded for patient demographics (e.g., mean age, age range, gender, prior therapy experience), treatment settings (e.g., outpatient mental health clinics or inpatient medical hospitals), provider training (e.g., psychologist, psychiatrist, social worker, substance abuse counselor), types of intervention, outcome measures (e.g., length of hospital stay (LOS), number of doctor visits, lab/X-ray visits, actual treatment costs, intensive care days), cost of psychological intervention, and experimenter bias. Effect-size and percentage calculations were carried out independently of coding to avoid contamination. An undergraduate research team, trained to code empirical articles, used a coding sheet and coding format to independently code 25% of the selected studies. Mean interrater agreement (k) across pairs of coders reached 90% agreement (k = .90) for all coded categories.

Effect Size or "D"

Effect-size values were calculated from the outcome statistics reported in each study (e.g., significance levels, means and standard deviations, t-tests, F-tests) according to the within-study meta-analysis formula $d = (M1 - M2)/Sp$, where d is the estimated effect size, M1 and M2 (typically the control group) are the posttest means of the groups being compared, and Sp is the pooled within-group standard deviation of the posttest (Cohen, 1977). Thus, an effect size of 1.00 would indicate that the M1 group achieved an effect one standard deviation above that obtained by the M2 group. It could then be stated that the average person in the M1 group achieved an outcome that was better than 84% of the people in the M2 group. Likewise, an effect size of –1.00 would indicate that the average person in the M1 group fared worse than 84% of the subjects in the M2 group.

A *small effect size* ($d = 0.2$) would be interpreted to mean that the likelihood of the treatment being responsible for the outcome is minimal. A *medium effect size* ($d = 0.5$) is conceived as an effect size large enough to be visible to the naked eye. Finally, a *large effect size* ($d = 0.7$) is interpreted to mean that 14% of the variance is attributed to the difference between the treatment and the comparison group.

Results

Analysis of Percentage Change and Difference Among Groups

Of the 91 studies analyzed, 90% reported a decrease in medical utilization following some form of psychological intervention. Table 1 summarizes average improvement rates. Percentages are reported for studies that included a contrast between treated patients and control patients. Percentage data reported in the "treatment-comparison" condition in Table 1 indicate that the average treatment group exhibited a reduction in utilization across all dependent variables within a study by 15.7%, while the control group utilization rate increased an average of 12.27% (4).

Table 1. Average percentage, differences, average LOS in hospital following treatment, average per person savings, for treatment-control only, and studies combined.

	Percentage Difference				
	Treatment Group	Control Group	Total	Average Hospital LOS in days	Estimated savings[a] per person
Treatment-comparison	-15.70[b]	12.27[b]	-25.08[b]	-2.52	$2,205.00
Pre-post experimental only	-33.79[b]		-34.72[b]	-3.32	$2,905.00
Studies combined	-23.57[b]	12.27[b]	-28.06[b]	-2.01	$1,758.75

[a]Based on an estimated cost of $875 per day (Cockerham, 1998).
[b]Represents the sum of each study's combined percentage difference, totaled across the 91 studies and averaged.

Table 1. Dollar savings for one of the dependent measures-length of hospital stay (LOS)-were estimated based on an average reduction of 2.52 hospital days per person (5). The savings per person was then estimated to be $2,205.00 (projected savings data are based on an average one day hospital cost of $875 in 1993; Cockerham, 1998). The dollar estimate reported above is a projected dollar amount. This same process could be conducted with doctor visits, prescriptions, or other outcome measures. Length of stay in hospitals was chosen because it is a common outcome measure in the medical offset literature. Savings of 20-30% were reported across cost-offset articles. Furthermore, of the 28 articles that report dollar savings, 31% reported savings after the cost of mental health treatment was subtracted from the original savings figure. Two out of the 28 articles reporting dollar savings indicated that costs of mental health treatment exceeded savings resulting from the intervention.

Preliminary Analysis of Effect-Size Values

A possible confound in analyzing effect-size values across multiple studies is that studies reporting larger effect-size values tend to have less weight in the meta-analysis because they usually involve smaller sample sizes and larger variances than do smaller effect-size values (Weisz, Weiss, Han, Granger, & Morton, 1995). As a result, overall effect-size values are reported for weighted and unweighted analyses for 40 treatment-comparison group articles (weighted = .34, unweighted = .34; both significantly different from 0, $p < .001$), and 17 experimental pretest/posttest only articles (weighed = .16, unweighted = .24; both significantly different from 0, $p < .001$, weighted vs. unweighted comparison, t-test = 2.33, $p < .025$; see Table 2.) The weighted versus unweighted effect-size values for the treatment-comparison group are not statistically significant, which indicates that large and small N studies did not exhibit differences large enough to be impacted by weighting procedures. The weighted versus unweighted effect-size values for the experimental pre-post test only group did follow the trend commonly found following weighting procedures; that is, studies with a smaller N had slightly larger effect sizes.

Table 2. Effectiveness of psychological interventions by comparison group: unweighted and weighted.

Treatment Group x Design Type	N of Studies	Effect Size			
		M	SE	95% Confidence Interval	p[a]
Unweighted					
Treatment-comparison group	40	.34	.17	.25-.43	.001
Pre-post experimental only group	17	.24[b]	.12	.18-.30	.001
Weighted					
Treatment-comparison group	40	.34	.17	.25-.43	.001
Pre-post experimental only group	17	.16[b]	.08	.15-.17	.001

[a]Significance levels are based on a t-test examining whether the effect sizes differ significantly from zero.
[b]The t-value for testing significance of difference between the effect-size values of the unweighted and weighted group means is $5 - 2.33$, $p < .025$, df = 32.

Table 2. Characteristic Groupings are reflected here. Based on the literature review, it was anticipated that various study characteristics within this meta-analysis would be differentially related to the overall mean effect size. Analyzing characteristics contributing to the overall effect-size estimate is essential to identify components of the offset literature where an offset is most pronounced.

Treatment Settings

Analysis of treatment setting effects revealed marginally significant ($p < .10$) results, with a marginally larger mean effect size for inpatient (.53) than outpatient (.23) settings (see Table 3). This suggests that patients undergoing medical procedures that require inpatient care (e.g., surgery patients, cancer patients, heart conditions patients) may account for a larger offset effect than patients who seek outpatient medical care (e.g., doctor visits for illness, accidents, skin conditions, gynecological checkups, or infections), although more studies are needed in the analysis before the differences would reach statistical significance.

Types of Treatment

Treatment characteristics were grouped according to psychotherapy or equivalent and instruction or psychoeducation. The psychotherapy condition consisted of psychiatric consultation, crisis intervention, short-term psychotherapy, relaxation training, and group therapy. Psychoeducation included behavioral medicine, biofeedback, vocational training, and specific instructions on how to improve and what sensations to expect following surgery. When comparing psychoeducational techniques that included behavioral medicine studies with psychotherapy, there was a significant effect ($p < .05$), with significantly larger effects for psychoeducation (.52) than for psychotherapy (.20; see Table 3). This result suggests that the more specific psychoeducational interventions were more effective regardless of the settings in which they occurred. It should be noted that of the psychoeducational techniques utilized, behavioral medicine with surgery patients was the most effective.

Table 3. Effect-sizes for key variable groups, analyzed with meta-analytic procedures.

Studies with treatment-control groups inclusive	N of Studies	Effect Size		95% Confidence Interval	p[a]
		M	SE		
Treatment setting conditions					
Outpatient settings	16[b]	.23	.11	.06 to .71	.01
Inpatient settings	18[b]	.53	.26	.25 to .81	.001
Type of treatment conditions					
Psychotherapy	21[c]	.20	.10	.01 to .39	.03
Psychoeducation (e.g. behavioral medicine)	15[c]	.52	.25	.27 to .76	.001
Subject medical conditions					
Presurgery	11[d]	.69	.33	.35 to 1.02	.001
Mixed-medical	18[d]	.26	.13	.07 to .45	.003
Provider training conditions					
Psychologist	11[e]	.27	.13	.04 to .49	.002
Psychiatrist	10[e]	.18	.09	.00 to .36	.04

[a]Significance levels are based on a t-test examining whether the effect sizes differ significantly from zero.
[b]The t-value for testing the significance of the difference between effect-size values of these two group means is t = 2.00, p < .10, df = 32.
[c]Psychotherapy and psychoeducation mean effect-size values were contrasted via a t-test with a resulting t value of 2.35, p < .05, df = 34.
[d]The t-value for the mean effect-size values in this comparison is 2.49, p < .02, df = 27.
[e]The t-value for significance of difference between the effect-size values of these group means is .69, p < .20, df = 19.

Table 3. This compares outcomes across treatment settings, types of treatment, types of medical conditions, and provider training, including N of studies, effect-size values, confidence intervals, significance levels from zero, and significance levels between comparisons in each characteristic category. Additional variables were analyzed in the original meta-analysis by this author. Please refer to the original meta-analysis for a more comprehensive list of variables analyzed.

Subject Medical Condition

Subject medical variables consisted of two conditions: patients hospitalized for surgical procedures (mean effect size = .69), and subjects seeking treatment at inpatient and outpatient medical settings for various medical difficulties (mean effect size = .26; see Table 3). The results suggest that patients hospitalized for surgical procedures and other hospitalized patients are affected by mental health interventions, but interventions have a greater impact on the recovery of surgery patients than on mixed-medical patients (p < .02).

Comparison of Psychologists and Psychiatrists

Differences between medical offset outcomes across provider types were confounded by differences in types of intervention employed (see Table 3 for effect-size data). Typically, psychiatrists' roles included providing psychiatric consultation for medical patients in hospital settings. Consultation consisted of talking with patients about how they were feeling and what physical and emotional problems they were experiencing while in the hospital. In the studies analyzed, psychiatric consultation was considered more of an evaluation than actual therapy. Psychologists and social workers typically were responsible for providing individual, family, and group psychotherapy to patients. In contrast to psychiatrists who worked in medical settings with hospital patients, psychologists and social workers worked in outpatient mental health centers with individuals seeking treatment for psychological problems yet prone to overutilization of medical services.

Whether a psychologist, social worker, or psychiatrist is performing the mental health intervention was not a significant factor in medical cost offset. Each of these disciplines appears to utilize treatment techniques that tend to reduce patients' recovery time, resulting in decreased medical care utilization and cost savings but no differential treatment effect.

Discussion

Analyses of effect size and percentage change across studies included herein yielded positive findings pertaining to the cost offset of psychological interventions used among a wide variety of patients. The most dramatic treatment effects involved the use of behavioral medicine to treat surgical inpatients. Such interventions lead to a significant decrease in length of stay and an increase in psychological well being, as is the goal of behavioral medicine. In essence, health psychology and behavioral medicine techniques in the context of surgery offer consistent support for the cost-offset effect.

The effects of behavioral medicine are not exclusive to a specific surgical procedure or patient with a certain psychiatric complication. Improved recovery rates were observed among hip fracture, hysterectomy, cholecystectomy, and cardiac surgery patients with various comorbid psychiatric difficulties. The cost benefit to health care providers and improved mental status among patients make behavioral medicine practices a worthwhile investment for all parties involved, including patients' families.

An incidental finding in the present review is the observation that, in addition to representing cost savings attributed to reduced medical utilization (cost offset), mental health interventions also appear to pay for themselves (are cost-effective) in studies that reported the cost of psychological services. Of the 28 studies that reported the costs of providing psychological interventions, only two indicated that the cost of treatment either exceeded or was equal to the savings that resulted from reduced patient medical utilization. Because approximately one third of the studies reported estimates of psychological treatment costs, this observation is anecdotal and needs more systematic study.

Several limitations to this study were presented in the original paper published in 1999 in Clinical Psychology: Science and Practice. Please refer to that publication for specific details on limitations to the meta-analysis itself, as well as confounds in the cost-offset literature.

Despite the difficulties involved in meta-analyses and in the cost-offset literature, psychological interventions including brief psychotherapy, psychiatric consultation, psychosocial interventions, psychoeducation, and behavioral medicine appear to result in economic savings to some degree. The effectiveness of the various mental health interventions from a statistical viewpoint, with the exception of behavioral medicine, remains inconsistent despite the many studies reporting economic dividends. Although it is common across the medical offset literature to talk of cost reduction and economic savings, less attention is paid in this literature to the main objective of medical and psychological providers, which is to improve a patient's quality of life. Although many psychological interventions lead to reduced costs while also improving patient's physical and psychological well-being, some mental health treatments may increase costs. As seen with cancer patients, support groups may extend life while actually increasing overall medical expenditures (Friedman, Sobel, Myers, Caudill, & Benson, 1995). In an age of booming health care costs and the watchful eye of managed care organizations, mental health and medical care providers must do their part to balance the patient's quality of life with economic realities (Yates, 1997). To date, it is a relatively consistent finding across the medical cost-offset literature that behavioral medicine is an effective intervention for reducing unnecessary medical usage and costs. As for the future of the medical cost-offset literature, scientific and clinical efforts still require improvement in screening, in identifying patients receptive to behavioral medicine and other psychological treatments, and in further understanding the role of mental health interventions in physical health. More research with improved rigor is necessary to answer the remaining medical cost-offset questions. More medical effectiveness studies are particularly needed with patients suffering from severe psychological disorders (e.g., borderline personality disorder) and with patients who have disorders that are especially prone to overutilization of services (e.g., panic disorder, somatization disorders). The present review considers studies that were undertaken across a wide variety of payer systems. Nevertheless, questions about the impact of psychological interventions on health care costs and recovery from physical disease, as well as the advantages of recognizing and treating psychological disorders in medical patients should be a high priority for future research.

Future Trends

Several responses were written to the original meta-analysis published in 1999. Although each author offered insightful responses to the meta-analysis along with progressive ideas about the future of cost offset literature, three authors in particular presented cutting-edge ideas. Nicholas Cummings (1999) delineated criteria for efficiency/effectiveness in savings as proposed by the Bethesda Conference. These are (a) organized settings in contrast to traditional ones, (b) specificity in terms of focused and targeted interventions, and (c) collaboration with primary care. A primary point he communicated in his commentary of the meta-analysis is that medical cost offset research must clearly delineate treatment interventions that are effective through hands-on training for therapists providing treatment interventions, supervised therapy instruction to ensure that the treatment protocol is being followed, and conducted in a collaborative setting especially created for research.

Simon Budman (1999) in his commentary to the above meta-analysis discussed the importance of future studies and meta-analyses in this area to attempt to look at offset systematically (i.e., within the context of the delivery system), focus on offset that occurs as a function of behavioral medicine interventions, and examine the mechanisms underlying the offset effect. By approaching the cost offset research in this manner, Budman hypothesizes the following may occur in patients that overutilize health care services: (a) patients may develop insight into psychological problems that may lead them to recognize that medical utilization is not the solution to their physical/psychological problems, (b) patients may develop insight into illness behavior and resulting secondary gain, leading to reduced medical utilization, and (c) patients may potentially recognize a relationship between stress and resulting medical problems.

In Dennis Russo and Heidi Howard's (1999) commentary, they describe four types of patients: the worried well, the worried unwell, the chronically disabled, and the chronically ill. They suggested the importance of having specific behavioral medicine interventions for each of these types of patients, and that research should drive practice techniques. Further, they posit a multifactor model of treatment that involves gathering an understanding of behavioral, cognitive, biochemical, medical, personality, and environmental factors. The combination of these factors is used to provide an overall picture of each patient's clinical characteristics leading to the appropriate treatment and positive clinical outcomes.

The benefits of behavioral medicine and other psychological interventions in improving patient well-being and reducing medical utilization are apparent. Despite the cost offset research that exists, refinement is needed in delineating the most useful psychological interventions for the treatment of patients with varying psychological sequelae in divergent treatment settings.

References

Budman, S. H. (1999). Whither medical cost offset? Comments on Chiles et al. *Clinical Psychology: Science and Practice, 6* (2), 228-231.

Budman, S. H., Simeone, P. G., Reilly, R., & Demby, A. (1994). Progress in short-term and time-limited group psychotherapy: Evidence and implications. In A. Fuhriman & G. M. Burlingame (Eds.) *Handbook of group psychotherapy* (pp. 370-415). New York: Wiley.

Cockerham, W. C. (1998). *Medical sociology* (7ᵗʰ ed.). Englewood Cliffs, NJ: Prentice Hall.

Cohen, J. (1977). *Statistical power analysis for the behavioral sciences* (rev. ed.). New York: Academic Press.

Cohen, L. M., Shapiro, E., Manson, J. E., & Kondi, E. S. (1985). The high cost of treating a psychiatric disorder as a medical/surgical illness. *Psychosomatics, 26,* 453-455.Cockerham, W. C. (1995). *Medical sociology* (6ᵗʰ ed.). Englewood Cliffs, NJ: Prentice Hall.

Cummings, N. A. (1999). Medical cost offset, meta-analysis, and implications for future research and practice. *Clinical Psychology: Science and Practice, 6*(2), 221-224.

Friedman, R., Sobel, D., Myers, P., Caudill, M., & Benson, H. (1995). Behavioral medicine, clinical health psychology, and cost offset. *Health Psychology, 14,* 509-518.

Fulop, G., Strain, J. J. (1991). Diagnosis and treatment of psychiatric disorder in medically ill patients. *Hospital and Community Psychiatry, 42,* 389-394.

Goldberg, R. J. (1995). Psychiatry and the practice of medicine: The need to integrate psychiatry into comprehensive medical care. *Southern Medical Journal, 88,* 260-267.

Jencks, S. F. (1985). Recognition of mental health distress and diagnosis of mental disorder in primary care. *Journal of the American Medical Association, 253,* 1903-1907.

Klein, R. H., Brabender, V., & Fallon, A. (1994). Inpatient group therapy. In A. Fuhriman & G. M. Burlingame (Eds.), *Handbook of group psychotherapy* (pp, 370-415). New York: Wiley.

Levenson, J. L., Hamer, R. M., & Rossiter, L. F. (1990). Relation of psychopathology in general medical inpatients use and cost of services. *American Journal of Psychiatry, 147,* 1498-1503.

Russo, D. C., & Howard, H. A. 1999). The evolving role of clinical psychology in health care systems. *Clinical Psychology: Science and Practice, 6* (2), 232-238.

Saravay, S. M., & Lavin, M. (1994). Psychiatric co-morbidity and length of stay in the general hospital: A critical review of studies, *Psychosomatics, 35,* 233-252.

Shapiro, A. K. (1971). Placebo effects in medicine, psychotherapy and psycho-analysis. In Garfield, S. L., & Bergin, A. E. (Eds.), *Handbook of psychotherapy and behavior change: An empirical analysis* (pp. 439-473). New York: John Wiley.

Weisz, J. R., Weiss, B., Han, S. S., Granger, D. A., & Morton, T. (1995). Effects of psychotherapy with children and adolescents revisited: A meta-analysis of treatment outcome studies. *Psychological Bulletin, 117,* 450-468.

Yates, B. T. (1997). From psychotherapy research to cost-outcome research: What resources are necessary to implement which therapy procedures that change what processes to yield which outcomes. *Psychotherapy Research, 7,* 345-364.

Identifying and Capitalizing on the Economic Benefits of Primary Behavioral Health Care

Kirk Strosahl
Mountainview Consulting Group
Moxee, Washington

The evolution of health care reform in general, and managed care in particular, has profoundly affected the health and behavioral health delivery systems of the United States. While Generation 1 of managed care was characterized by an excessive emphasis on supply side cost containment strategies (i.e., "managed cost"), Generation 2 is aimed at achieving a better balance between cost and quality (i.e., managed care). This is due to the fact that the "floor" of cost containment achievable through cost cutting alone has been reached. Unfortunately, the early emphasis on cost containment resulted in a general neglect of much more basic flaws in the American healthcare system. These institutionalized defects have not been corrected by managed care practices. In a recent report, the Institute of Medicine describes the American healthcare system as "broken" (Richardson, 2001). Among other problems, this report cites the excessive fragmentation of healthcare, poor to non-existent coordination of care, basic inadequacies in the health care financing system and a singular lack of emphasis on quality in most health care systems. Indeed, the report implies that it is a minor miracle when a patient with relatively complicated healthcare issues is able to successfully navigate this tangled system of care. Note that this sad state of affairs is occurring in the most expensive healthcare system in the history of mankind. The United States spends a greater percentage of its Gross National Product on healthcare than any other country in the civilized world (approximately 1.2 trillion dollars in 2000). Yet, as the Institute of Medicine report suggests, inadequacies in this system of care are resulting in the premature deaths of thousands of patients each year (Richardson, 2001). In the last three years, we have witnessed yet another disconcerting theme: the resumption of health care inflation. It is now estimated that health care inflation in the year 2001 will approach 14%. This inflation rate is nearing the yearly rate that triggered the managed cost movement in the first place.

Looking at the dilemmas confronting contemporary healthcare, it is obvious that a basic re-engineering of goals, systems, processes and financing models will be required. For example, the cumbersome and overlapping systems that provide health and behavioral health services will be pressured to consolidate, as the marketplace seeks ways to reduce administrative redundancy and increase delivery system efficiencies. There is already a great deal of interest nationwide in the integration of primary care and behavioral health services (cf., Strosahl, 1998, 1997, 1996a, 1996b, 1994; Cummings, 1995). Healthcare systems as diverse as the HRSA Bureau of Primary Healthcare, United States Air Force, Veteran's Administration and Kaiser Permanente Northern California are already engaged in significant primary care behavioral health integration initiatives. As will become obvious, the segregation of behavioral health and primary medicine has not only had a destructive impact upon the health of the general population, but may also be one of the primary reasons the health care cost crisis continues to persist (Strosahl & Sobel, 1996).

This chapter will attempt to explain the economic pressures facing contemporary healthcare systems as well as the potential economic benefits of integrating primary care and behavioral health services. In order to achieve this objective, it will be useful to review trends in the financing of general health care, as well as the impact which behavioral health factors exert on the delivery system. It will then be possible to more closely examine three basic economic arguments for the integration of primary care and behavioral health services. Behavioral health, as used in the chapter, is a broader concept than "mental health and substance abuse". The latter are undoubtedly factors in medical service use; however there are many other behavioral factors that lead to health care seeking behavior. Collectively, this chapter will examine these behavioral health "pathways" and suggest programmatic strategies for controlling their associated medical service costs. Finally, this chapter will examine the practicalities involved in designing and implementing programs that generate medical cost savings.

The New Economics of Health Care

The economic forces pushing the integration of behavioral health and primary care are closely tied to basic changes in the healthcare financing environment. The methods used to achieve cost containment in managed care can generally be described as "risk shifting" and supply side constriction. Risk shifting has involved putting healthcare providers and systems at risk for not being paid or being underpaid if they provide care that is deemed excessive or unnecessary. Tactics such as capitation, case rates, pre-certification, utilization review are all designed to shift the risk from the payer to the provider. This is in stark contrast to the pre-managed care era, where the payer accepted virtually all of the risk. In that era, systems of healthcare that were inefficient and wasteful actually became rich, because virtually any service would be compensated. The concept of supply side constriction basically involves making it harder for patients to access all healthcare services. Strategies such as benefit exclusions, benefit limits, co-insurance and "gatekeeper" models all have the effect of deflecting consumers away from unrestricted service use.

Contemporary trends in healthcare financing indicate that risk shifting is evolving toward a greater reliance on capitation-based strategies. Capitation essentially involves paying the health care vendor "up front" based upon an agreed upon formula for determining the likely cost of caring for a particular population. Normally, capitation rates are computed on a "per member per month" (PMPM) basis. This is the amount of money it should theoretically take to provide healthcare for one person in a month. For example, the Medicaid Prospective Payment System scheduled to take effect in January 2002, is essentially a risk adjusted captitation model. The significance of this shift should not be lost on the reader, for this is the largest insurance plan in the world. Precedents established in the Medicaid payment system usually effect the strategies that are used by commercial insurance companies in their employer sponsored health plans. Indeed, some managed health care organizations (e.g., United Healthcare) are moving away from expensive secondary review systems (i.e., pre-certification and utilization review) in favor of "pay for performance" contracting methods. In this type of arrangement, payment is based upon the health care provider achieving contractually agreed to health care outcomes (i.e., percentage of eligible patients seen annually, percentage of eligible patients with PAP smears or breast cancer screens annually). The gist of these changes is that health care systems are going to be given more flexibility in how they deploy financial resources, but these same systems are going to have to identify, manage and/or eliminate controllable "cost centers." A controllable cost center is a source of unnecessary financial waste, due to factors such as clinically ineffective care, poor system design, ineffective population health management or administrative waste.

Health care administrators are understandably anxious about the movement to such at risk financing models. Implicit in this change is a requirement that systems of care be relentless about addressing waste and inefficiency. They understand that patients never leave the health care system, so when service needs are not addressed; the patient's general health status deteriorates, leading to increased medical costs in the future. Further, the burden in capitated health care is to do more with less. A system that cannot deliver a very high volume of effective medical services will not "come in under the cap". Inefficient delivery systems that shackle the capacity of medical providers will simply not be able to compete in the public or commercial health care marketplace. At the same time, as productivity standards have increased (i.e., some general physicians now are responsible for as many as 3,200 patients), the feedback from medical providers is that their productivity is severely hampered by the ongoing problem of having to address behavioral health needs when their basic training is in general medicine. Medical visits that are scheduled to last 15 minutes (the basic unit of service in general medicine) can take 30-45 minutes with little improvement in clinical results. This limits the number of patient visits a general medical provider can generate in a typical practice day, which in turn limits the amount of revenue that physician can generate. Furthermore, the ongoing mismatch between patient need and the service delivered is demoralizing to medical providers, increases the risk of burnout and creates difficulties in recruiting and retaining medical providers. Interestingly, most of the major primary care behavioral health integration initiatives are originating out of primary medicine, not in the mental health system. This reflects a growing consensus among health care leaders that behavioral health is a major controllable cost center in general medicine.

Behavioral Factors Underpinning Medical Service Utilization: A Controllable Cost Center

One of the basic flaws in medicine is that there is a mismatch between the reasons a person seeks medical care and the ensuing service response. The result is many missed opportunities to identify and manage the demand for health services. Consequently, wasted resources, poor quality, unsatisfied patients, and frustrated providers characterize contemporary primary care medicine. Understanding the basic processes which influence health care seeking as well as the delivery system factors that drive the provision of medical care is essential if one is to design programs to increase medical cost savings.

Primary Care: The United States De Facto Mental Health System

The Epidemiological Catchment Area project, a large multi-site study of over 18,000 households in the United States, provides a sobering picture of the delivery of behavioral health services in the United States. The approximate one-year incidence of diagnosable mental disorders, including substance addiction, is approximately 17% (Regier, et al., 1993). Of such patients, only half seek any form of mental health care. Of the half that do seek mental health care, 50% receive it solely from their general physician. This means that general medical providers deliver half of all the formal mental health care (Narrow, Regier, Rae, Manderscheid & Locke, 1993). A very similar service utilization picture emerged in the more recent National Co-Morbidity Study (Kessler, et al., 1994). The Substance Abuse and Mental Health Services Administration (SAMHSA) report on mental health expenditures between 1987 and 1997 suggests that the claims submitted out of general medical settings were essentially equal to the claims submitted by the formal mental health system (Coffey, et al., 2000). These data do not address the service use characteristics of the bewildering number of patients with life stress, losses, conflicts and illnesses requiring lifestyle adjustment that are routinely seen in primary care. For example, waiting room studies have consistently suggested that 50% of primary care patients have clinically elevated depression or anxiety levels (VonKorff, et al., 1987). The extent of behavioral health services provided in general health care is best illustrated in prescribing practices. General physicians (Beardsley, et al., 1988) prescribe 70% of all psychotropic medications, including 80% of all anti-depressants.

Health Care Seeking Is A Multi-Dimensional Phenomenon

Whether or not people are physically ill, and even how ill they are, is *not* the primary determinant of whether they decide to seek medical care. Studies have suggested that only a quarter of the decision to seek health care is explained by disability or morbidity alone (Berkanovic, Telesky & Reeder, 1981). As Lynch (1993) suggests that the demand for health care may be triggered by a genuine health concern (the patient is vomiting blood), the patient's need for reassurance (the patient has a bad cold and just wants it "checked out"), the patient's preference for a specific service (the patient wants a woman's health specialist to evaluate a physical health concern) and psychosocial motives (the health care context is the most comfortable place to discuss a sensitive sexual issue).

Psychosocial Stress Drives Medical Utilization

A variety of studies, using different methodologies, have generally concluded that 70% of all health care visits have primarily a psychosocial basis (Fries, Koop & Beadle, 1993; Shapiro, et al., 1984). A recent study of the 14 most common complaints seen in primary care revealed that less than 10% were due to an organic etiology (Kroenke & Mangelsdorff, 1989). The most frequent psychosocial drivers of medical utilization are mental disorders, alcoholism/drug addiction, deficient social support, lack of coping skills, and a stressful home/work environment (cf. Friedman, Sobel, Myers, Caudill & Benson, 1995). To make matters worse, these factors frequently occur in combination among the highest utilizers of medical services (Katon, et al., 1992). For example, the top 10% of medical utilizers consume approximately 33% of ambulatory medical services and nearly 50% of hospital services. A significant percentage of these patients have medical profiles that do not explain their medical service use. Not surprisingly, disproportionate percentages have diagnosable mental disorders, drug/alcohol addiction and highly stressful living environments. (Katon, et al., 1992). Finally, several recent studies have found distressed primary care patients use approximately 2 times the amount of health care services as their non-depressed counterparts (Simon, 1992; Simon, VonKorff & Barlow, 1995; VonKorff & Simon, 1996).

Psychosocial Stress Influences General Health Status

There are several studies showing that psychosocial factors are positively related to poor general health status, functional disability and long-term health morbidity and mortality (Frasure-Smith, 1991; Fawzy, Fawzy & Hyun, 1993). These studies suggest that when behavioral factors are systematically addressed, there will be a corresponding reduction in negative health outcomes. Not surprisingly, each of these health outcomes is a strong predictor of elevated medical costs. Self-perceptions of health status are related not only to the decision to seek health care, but also predict eventual objective health status (Sobel, 1995). Many patients respond to psychosocial stresses by developing vaguely defined, distressing physical symptoms that have no organic basis. These stress-related health concerns create a motivation to seek out a health care provider (Smith, Rost & Kashner, 1995). Further, basic process factors can be compromised by psychosocial stresses. For example, adherence to medical treatment and disease management regimes can be negatively effected by depression, anxiety, alcohol & drug abuse, family conflicts or patient beliefs and expectancies (cf. Robinson, Wischman & Del Vento, 1996).

Functional impairment is a major determinant of health-related quality of life and well being. Functional impairment involves the loss of adaptive physical, social or occupational role functioning in response to a physical or mental illness. The negative impact of psychosocial distress on functional impairment can be greater than most common chronic medical conditions. For example, the Medical Outcomes Study revealed that depression results in more functional impairment than chronic diseases such as diabetes, arthritis and angina (Wells, et al., 1989). Functional disabilities not only are related to increased medical expense, but also are a primary concern for employers because of work absenteeism and reduced job productivity.

Service Availability Drives Medical Decision Making

Primary care is the final resting place for patients who have not had their psychosocial needs addressed in other social service delivery systems. With the virtual collapse of the community mental health system over the last decade, a huge population of patients with complicated health and behavioral health needs have converged on the primary care setting. Faced with this daily onslaught, primary care providers are forced to adapt their practice styles to cope with this new type of service demand. Simply ignoring the psychosocial needs of the patient often invites uncontrolled escalation in medical visits, hospitalizations and/or consumer dissatisfaction. Yet, the provider must address these in the "15 minute" hour model of general medical practice. Ordinarily, the medical provider will lack access to on-site, integrated behavioral health programs that can address the psychosocial needs of the patient. If the primary care provider cannot address the patient's psychosocial issues in the context of the medical visit, what options are open? Unfortunately, the all too common answer is to reach for the prescription pad. In the time-pressured world of the primary care provider, the pill is a major practice management tool. It is an action that is universally interpreted to mean that the provider has listened to the problem and is now going to do something to help. The pill also has the effect of ending a medical visit that has exceeded the scheduled amount of time, a factor that is not lost on most medical providers. Referring the patient to an offsite behavioral health provider is usually the only other alternative, but most patients are not willing to accept such a referral. Discussions about the need for counseling are often viewed as stigmatizing ("It's all in your head") and tend to further segregate health and behavioral health care.

The result is a one size fits all service response that can be very costly. For example, most health care systems are struggling to contain pharmacy costs related to anti-depressant medications and other psychoactive medicines. Recent studies suggest that only 50% of depressed primary care patients who are prescribed anti-depressants meet diagnostic criteria to establish suitability for anti-depressant therapy (Katon, et al., 1996). Another costly effect is that patients that do not have their psychosocial needs addressed often end up using acute and emergency care services. In a study of emergency room patients with chest pain, nearly 41% met criteria for either an anxiety or depressive disorder as a primary medical diagnosis (Yingling, et al., 1993). Patients with psychosocial needs will continue to "travel" in both primary and specialty medicine as long as there are no behavioral health services available at the point of contact.

Three Economic Benefits of
Primary Care Behavioral Health Integration

In the previous section, the behavioral factors that have led to an uncontrolled escalation in medical costs have been explored in detail. The basic picture that emerges is simple. The majority of patients with behavioral health issues prefer to seek services in general medicine, but the structure of general health care precludes responding in a meaningful way. This results in ineffective services being delivered by the general medical provider, often with considerable negative impact on the efficiency of the medical provider. In effect, costly, time consuming services are being delivered with little clinical impact. A revolving door is created that leads to increasing levels of functional and health impairment in the patient and a corresponding increase in the provision of expensive medical services on the part of the delivery system. This analysis suggests that there are three major economic opportunities available to systems that integrate services: to increase the cost effectiveness of behavioral health interventions in medicine, to "leverage" medical provider time by shifting patients with complicated behavioral factors to a lower priced, appropriately trained, behavioral clinician and to target the provision of behavioral health services with the aim of reducing medical service utilization and its associated cost. Although these three concepts will be examined separately, in truth, they are often highly interdependent.

Cost Effectiveness: The Value of Doing the Job Right the First Time

Health care is an industry that has only continued to grow in cost over the years. Although health care administrators will suggest otherwise, the truth of the matter is that health care budgets always grow; they never shrink. As this growth occurs, the question of relevance is how decisions are made to add new tests and procedures. After all, this always involves adding cost to a system. One common method is to evaluate the incremental cost effectiveness of a new test or procedure. Essentially, incremental cost effectiveness is a measure of how much "value" is added by adding a test or a procedure with a certain fixed cost. Value is often viewed as an increase in diagnostic precision or treatment efficacy, relative to existing medical practices. When the cost of adding a new test or procedure is significantly outweighed by its documented ability to improve care, it is deemed to have incremental cost effectiveness.

From a cost effectiveness perspective, the services currently offered to patient's with behavioral health needs lack any real value. Medical costs are being incurred, but patients are not getting better. For example, the outcomes for depressed primary care patients in primary care barely exceed the spontaneous remission rate for depression (Katon, et al., 1996; Hunkeler, et al., 2000). What is often lost in the discussion of whether integrated behavioral care is "worth it" is that fact that there is no such thing as "not treating" a primary care patient. Studies conducted at Group Health Cooperative indicated that "untreated" depressed patients on average rang up approximately $1000 annually in ambulatory medical services (Katon, et al., 1996), yet less than 42% were evaluated as clinically improved. Adding integrated behavioral health services increased the annual cost of medical services by approximately $250, but improved clinical response rates to nearly 71%. In incremental cost effectiveness terms, adding the $250 of additional medical cost returned a "value" of approximately $500 per case of depression treated. Unlike other medical tests or procedures, where the incremental cost effectiveness may be measured in single or double digits, health care administrators can expect to see very large incremental gains with integrated behavioral services. Rather than confining these benefits to a small percentage of the patient population, integrated behavioral services can be delivered to a large segment of the population. For example, if one multiplied the $500 incremental cost effectiveness figure for providing services to depressed primary care patients by the number of depressed patients in a primary care setting (between 6-20%), the resulting cost benefit to the system would be astronomical.

Leveraging Productive Capacity

Simply put, leveraging is a strategy designed to improve the productive capacity of a medical provider by shifting patients with behavioral health needs to a lower priced behavioral clinician. It will be of value to examine how this works in practice so as to appreciate the significant revenue generation capacity of this strategy. In a previous section, we described a common healthcare scenario: a patient with complicated behavioral health issues comes in for a 15-minute medical appointment. The medical provider may have 6-12 patients scheduled consecutively in 15 minute blocks. However, the patient with behavioral health problems breaks down during the medical visit and is inconsolable. The medical provider offers medication, but the patient just wants someone to talk to and refuses drugs. Suddenly, the scheduled 15-minute visit has increased to a 45-minute visit. Two or three patients in the waiting room have to be rescheduled because the provider's schedule is tied up. The financial impact of this common situation is relatively easy to calculate. The schedule overrun means that two billable visits have been lost. Assuming the patient is insured by Medicaid, the amount billable for a 15 minute medical visit is approximately $120, while the billable amount for the 45 minute visit has not increased appreciably over the base rate of a 15 minute visit ($140). If the medical provider had seen three unique patients as scheduled, the revenue generated would be $360. Instead, it is $140, or a 150% drop in productivity. Further, in some payment systems, billing is based in part upon the Relative Value Unit (RVU) of the medical encounter. In other words, as the degree of medical complexity (as opposed to behavioral health complexity) increases, the amount that can be billed increases. Consequently, the magnitude of productivity loss would increase to the extent that our hypothetical patient did not have significant medical morbidity. This scenario is not the exception in health care. It is an every day occurrence. In economic terms, the mismatch between what the patient needs and what the provider has to offer results in diminished system productivity. There is a direct link between the productivity of a system and the revenue it can generate. When "high priced" medical providers are constantly forced to provide behavioral care to medically uncomplicated patients, the revenue producing capacity of the system is shackled. The magnitude of shackling is impossible to calculate exactly, but it is probably in the vicinity of 25%. Many health care systems have launched workload and productivity initiatives precisely because there is a general perception that medical providers are not generating a sufficiently high visit load. It should be noted that similar leveraging strategies on the medical side have become a popular component of many redesign initiatives in general medicine. For example, the use of "mid-level" medical practitioners (PAC, ARNP) and flexible contact strategies (nursing driven phone follow-up, group care clinics, open access scheduling) are classic examples of the leveraging concept at work.

One potential solution to this problem is to leverage medical provider time by making behavioral health services available in the context of routine health care. Leveraging involves shifting the patient with behavioral health problems from the medical provider to the behavioral health provider. If this transfer is made in "real time," then the medical provider is in a position to return to the practice schedule without losing billable visits. Taking the earlier example, if the patient was immediately transferred to a team based behavioral clinician, the medical provider's revenue generation capacity for that hour would approach the $360 target. This would be offset by the unit cost of staffing a behavioral clinician; however, a significant portion of this cost would be recouped through billing for the behavioral clinician's services. Further, the patient is now placed with a provider that is equipped to address behavioral health issues in a clinically effective way. This could lead to significant incremental cost effectiveness in addition to increasing visit related revenues. Given the magnitude of the leveraging effect, it is entirely conceivable that implementing integrated behavioral health services within the health care team milieu would drive up productive capacity to the point that the additional revenues would more than cover the costs of adding behavioral health providers.

Medical Cost Offset

Cummings and VandenBos (1981) first examined the medical cost offset effect. Specifically, they proposed that since there is a strong relationship between psychological distress and medical service utilization, the provision of appropriately targeted behavioral health services should reverse the effect. In essence, medical cost offsets are the savings generated when medical service use is reduced as result of providing the patient with effective behavioral care. Therefore, the more appropriate term to use is medical cost savings, which is the amount of money returned to the health care system net of the cost of providing behavioral health services. While medical cost savings can be generated by providing targeted services to the index patient, research suggests that reductions in medical utilization can also occur in the family members of the identified patient. (McDonnell-Douglas, 1989). One classic economic argument for integrated care is that sizable medical cost savings can be obtained through the integration of medical and behavioral health services (Chiles, Lambert & Hatch, 1999; Friedman, et al., 1995; Mumford, et al., 1984; Sobel, 1995; Strosahl & Sobel, 1996). It will be useful to examine some basic assumptions that drive the medical cost savings strategy.

The cost offset literature contains many studies that suggest it may be a major medical cost containment strategy. Cost savings in the vicinity of 20-40% are not uncommon for well-designed programs. A recent meta-analysis of 57 controlled cost offset studies revealed an average 27% cost return (Chiles, Lambert & Hatch, 1999). For example, an intervention program focused on elderly patients hospitalized with hip fracture cost $40,000 in psychological and psychiatric consultative services, but reduced in-patient lengths of stay and associated medical expenses by $270,000. The associated medical cost savings was approximately $1300 per patient (Strain, et al., 1991). A targeted psychosocial intervention with "high utilizing" Medicaid outpatients found that medical costs declined by 21% at 18-months compared to a rise of 22% in those not receiving any mental health treatment (Pallak, et al., 1995).

As noted previously, integrated behavioral interventions can improve cost effectiveness while simultaneously reducing overall medical costs. This type of cost return is often substantial. A recent study showed that a consultative intervention for somaticizing patients reduced annual medical charges by $289 (33%) and simultaneously improved general functioning (Smith, Rost & Kashner, 1995). In the current 2.2 trillion dollar climate of healthcare, a set of strategies with the capacity to reduce health care expenditures by even 20% would generate nearly 500 billion dollars in real dollar returns!

Cost offsets have been observed in a number of health populations: parents with sick children, patients with chronic illness, arthritis, asthma, coronary artery disease, poor health habits (i.e., smoking, obesity, sedentary lifestyle), mental disorders (i.e., depression, anxiety/panic, somatization) and chronic pain syndrome. An equally diverse set of intervention strategies have been employed: individual and family psychotherapy, groups, educational classes and reading materials, as well as systems for providing assessment and treatment information from behavioral health providers to primary care physicians. While traditional medical cost savings programs were often based in hospital settings, a new generation of research has targeted the primary care milieu. Primary care based programs typically work with patients on stress management (relaxation, exercise, daily scheduling) and problem solving strategies for addressing life stresses (parenting a hyperactive child, reducing social isolation, addressing a marital conflict). Such programs also educate the patient in how unresolved stress can produce a variety of physical symptoms and a feeling of poor general health. One program designed for patients with distressing physical symptoms and significant psychosocial problems showed that patients reported less physical and psychological discomfort while averaging two fewer health care visits, compared to a no treatment control group. The estimated net savings of the intervention were $85 per participant (Hellman, et al., 1990).

Most of the early cost offset research examined the impact of individual psychotherapy on subsequent medical service use and cost (Cummings and VandenBos, 1981). Since then a variety of interventions targeting psychosocial needs have been shown to produce medical cost savings. Diverse strategies such as brief behavioral health consultation (Smith, Rost & Kashner, 1995, Drisbow, Bennett, & Owings, 1993), videos (Robinson, Schwartz & Magwene, 1989), printed materials and "bibliotherapy" (Kemper, Lorig & Mettler, 1993; Lorig, et al., 1994) psychoeducational classes and groups (Caudill, et al., 1991) and support groups (Lorig, Mazonson & Holman, 1993; Kennell, et al., 1991) have been associated with medical cost savings. This suggests that the mechanisms for delivering effective services may not have to be time intensive and expensive (i.e., individual psychotherapy). Rather, medical patients may be receptive to many different, and far cheaper, methods for learning to manage the behavioral issues in their lives. This discovery is especially significant when one considers the magnitude of behavioral health need in general medicine. The traditional method of behavioral health service delivery simply does not have the capacity to address both the volume and heterogeneity of behavioral health demand in general medicine.

An excellent example of this new generation of primary care based programs was reported by Kent & Gordon (2001), regarding a group care clinic for patients with unstable essential hypertension. The program involved weekly meetings co-led by an internal medicine physician and a psychologist. The focus was on integrating medical and behavioral medicine strategies for the management of hypertension. Results indicated not only increased patient adherence to hypertension self-management strategies, but also produced a large decrease in emergency room visits.

Identifying and Capitalizing on Medical Cost Savings Pathways

The previous section examining the huge economic potential of integrated behavioral health primary care services leads to one pre-eminent question. How can we identify primary care populations that represent "cost savings pathways" and then design affordable and effective programs to capitalize on these economic opportunities? It is important to realize that the segregation of medicine and behavioral health is so complete that it will require a redesign of healthcare to fully capitalize on the economic and clinical benefits of integrated care. This suggests that the process of developing a "mature" integrated delivery system will not take months; it will take years. While it is possible to develop a single program which generates economic benefits, the usual scenario is that the rest of the health care system is still failing to manage the costs associated with other cost pathways. In other words, the amount of "bleeding" in a typical healthcare system is so extensive that a single effective program is just a "drop in the bucket". The task at hand is to develop a panoply of programs and services that, collectively, begin to match the service response to what the patient needs. Practically speaking, this means that healthcare systems that anticipate quick and massive cost shifting as a result of providing a minimal array of behavioral health services are likely to be seriously disappointed. This is not a one-year investment, but a lifetime investment. With this caveat in place, there are several principles that must be fully understood in order for healthcare systems to be successful in this endeavor. These principles help determine the selection of target populations, define the drivers of medical service use within a target population, identify how interventions will target drivers and develop general guidelines for program structure.

Medical Cost Savings Potential Varies Among Populations

The potential for economic benefit in any integrated behavioral health program is heavily dependent upon the population that is targeted and the types of medical services and service delivery processes that will be affected. For example, a early meta-analysis of the cost offset literature suggested that maximum cost offset potential exists among the elderly and primarily is accrued through a reduction of in-patient costs, whereas cost savings were modest in younger adult out-patients (Mumford, et al., 1984). A more recent meta-analysis showed the largest medical cost returns existed in pre-surgical interventions in the hospital setting (Chiles, Lambert, & Hatch, 1999). These findings suggest that the greatest economic and clinical benefits will be achieved through programs and services that target specific conditions and specific patient populations. In essence, a prerequisite for effective program design is to employ the following parameters when attempting to identify whether a population "of interest" is likely to function as a medical cost pathway.

Is the target a high prevalence or high financial impact condition?

Is the target a prime candidate for risk prevention?

What are the drivers of health care costs associated with this target?

What are the estimated controllable medical costs associated with this target, including lost cost effectiveness, lost productivity and unnecessary medical utilization?

Is there a gap in the process of service delivery that perpetuates health care seeking?

Are there logistically feasible, affordable strategies available to correct process of care gaps?

What are the estimated costs of developing and delivering new services and what is the estimated return on investment?

When these parameters are systematically applied in the initial phase of program design, there is a much higher likelihood that the clinical and economic benefits of integrated behavioral health services will be fully realized.

Understand the Psychosocial Drivers of Health Care Seeking

In an earlier section, healthcare seeking was described as a complicated phenomena determined by patient, provider, system and cultural characteristics. This picture becomes significantly more complicated when one analyzes the major psychosocial drivers of healthcare seeking. The concept of "driver", as used here, means a psychological process that motivates the patient to seek medical services. To efficiently manage the medical encounter, to insure the best clinical outcome and to reduce the likelihood of subsequent medical requests requires that the medical provider understand and address the driver of the visit. There are several nuances worth noting before going on to examine the major psychosocial drivers.

First, a psychosocial driver is never defined by a single condition or diagnosis. This suggests that healthcare seeking is not so much determined by a specific diagnosis, but rather by a psychosocial process that is triggered by the occurrence of a set of functional or clinical symptoms. For example, depressed patients don't utilize more medical services because of their depressed mood. Rather, they are stimulated by a host of functional and symptomatic problems ranging from insomnia to work, family or marital problems. However, these concerns also afflict patients with anxiety disorders or other mental disorders.

Second, the concept implies that there is an "ideal" response that is capable of removing the driver. This might involve interventions to reduce physically or psychologically unpleasant symptoms, to educate the patient, to manipulate aspects of the patient's environment. The task in developing effective integrated behavioral programs is to determine what interventions have the best likelihood of removing or neutralizing the driver.

Finally, many patients seek healthcare because of multiple psychosocial drivers. At the point of assessment, it is always important to determine which driver(s) are implicated in the patient's health care requests. Addressing the requirements of one driver while ignoring others is likely to lead to disappointing results. There are several comprehensive papers on the psychosocial drivers of healthcare that the interested reader may consult (Friedman et. al, 1995; Sobel, 1995; Strosahl & Sobel, 1996). For present purposes, the major psychosocial drivers will be only briefly described.

Information and Support

When people lack information about a disturbing symptom or event, or cannot gain an acceptable level of reassurance from natural supports, many patients seek out health care providers because of very simple and basic information needs. Why is it that a significant number of patients with a common cold still insist on seeing a physician or nurse? It is to be reassured by a credible source that they just have a cold, not the early stage of pneumonia or an even rarer disease. This reassurance alleviates the sense of suffering that develops when information is not available. Many patients present in primary medicine with behavioral health concerns that can be addressed by providing them with information and, in some cases, referring the patient to a community resource.

Stress-somatization Response

The link between stress, somatic complaints and medical utilization has been extensively analyzed both at the theoretical and empirical level. At this point, one can say with complete certainty that living with enduring stress is a very unpleasant experience, both physically and psychologically. Stress not only affects one's subjective sense of health and well being, it has a pernicious effect on objective physical health. When one examines the top 10 complaints seen in primary medicine, what is striking is that nearly every presenting complaint could be a symptom of stress (i.e., headache, insomnia, fatigue, nausea, gastro-intestinal distress). These symptoms aren't some manifestation of psyche, they are real, uncomfortable and a reason to see a medical provider. However, the patient may or may not be able and willing to see the link between a stressful life and these physical manifestations. Nevertheless, that patient with somatic complaints will seek medical evaluation and treatment for these uncomfortable physical symptoms.

Social Disenfranchisement

For a shamefully large group of people, life is a daily battle against social isolation and alienation. Whether it is homelessness, serious mental illness or the social isolation of aging, the stop of last resort is the general medical setting. Not only are such patients at extreme health risk, they also lack any meaningful social contacts in their daily lives. An example is the disenfranchised elderly, who tend to receive virtually all of their psychosocial services in primary care (Unutzer, Katon, Sullivan & Miranda, 1997; Unutzer, et al., 1996). For many such patients, their primary social support network consists of the medical providers at the local primary care center. Socially disenfranchised patients have poor perceptions of subjective health status in addition to hungering for social support. These factors in combination lead to a pattern of elevated medical service use, often with poor clinical outcomes. Medical providers spend extraordinary amounts of practice time delivering these disguised social support visits.

Health Risk and Lifestyle Management

Many patients seek medical services because they are justifiably concerned about physical and/or lifestyle factors that subject them to an elevated level of health risk. This includes patients who seek medical advice about smoking, exercise, sexual practices, weight control, diet and so forth. In the world of population-based healthcare, this type of visit driver is increasingly common. Patients are either asking for help to make these difficult changes or being asked by their medical provider to do so. However, these are largely behavioral interventions delivered by providers with less exposure to the evidence-based techniques of behavioral medicine and behavior modification. Once these changes become the "target" of the patient's healthcare, the success or failure of the behavior change directly predicts the visit burden of managing the health care needs of that patient.

Mental Disorders

The most common reason sited for the integration of primary care and behavioral health services is the relatively high prevalence of mental disorders in primary care settings. For example, a recent study determined that approximately 26% of a large cohort of primary care patients had some type of depressive disorder (Spitzer, et al., 1994). Further, approximately 50% of patients randomly selected in primary care waiting rooms will report clinically elevated levels of depression or anxiety (VonKorff, et al., 1987). As we have discussed, there is also a very well established link between mental disorders and increased medical service use (Simon, 1992; Simon, VonKorff & Barlow, 1995; VonKorff & Simon, 1996). The underlying process between this link is probably multi-dimensional. Many patients with mental disorders will seek treatment for the mental disorder from their general medical provider. However, mental disorders also are linked to both increased somatic complaints and somatic sensitivity, as well as to poor perceptions of subjective health. Doubtless, many patients present for medical care because they believe they are physically ill or at risk for some type of disease. These patients are more complicated to manage because they may reject the notion that their health complaints are manifestations of mental health problems and insist on expensive tests and procedures to rule out all medical causes.

Another source of increased medical utilization may be the tendency of general medical providers to first rule out the presence of a primary mental disorder. For example, Ballenger (1987) demonstrated that the single most common diagnosis among consecutive patients referred to a cardiology clinic was panic disorder. This classic study showed that the average panic disorder patient will see multiple medical specialists at imputed costs well in excess of $10,000 before the initial diagnosis of panic disorder is made.

Substance Abuse and Chemical Dependency

The elephant is not only in the living room; it is in primary care as well. Alcoholism and drug abuse collectively are more common in primary care patient than either depressive or anxiety disorders, occurring in approximately 26% of primary care patients (Fleming & Barry, 1992). Patients with substance abuse problems are also heavy utilizers of healthcare because of the social, psychological and physical effects of substance use (Holder & Brose, 1986). They are not only coming in because of the life unraveling stresses associated with addictive behaviors, but also because their objective general health status is deteriorating due to the effects of long term substance abuse. There is a laundry list of health complaints that addicted patients bring to their primary medical provider including gastrointestinal distress, pancreatitis, ulcers, hypertension, sleep disorders and anxiety attacks. Like patients with mental disorders, patients with chemical dependency issues are generally going to seek symptom relief treatment from a medical provider and will not accept a referral to a specialty chemical dependency treatment program. General medical providers have very little exposure to such strategies as motivational interviewing or stages of change intervention. Therefore, it is hard to shift the dialogue in the medical visit to drinking or drug related issues without alienating the patient or engendering a confrontation that damages the working relationship. Eventually, a pattern of symptom management develops that is essentially a reaction to the addictive disorder rather than a treatment of it. Interestingly, studies suggest that even very brief 10 minute interventions delivered by medical providers can result in a significant reduction in drinking behavior in up 15% of primary care patients receiving the intervention. (Wallace, Cutler & Haines, 1988)

Chronic Pain

While chronic pain is not extremely prevalent in the general population (2-3%), such patients are heavily over-represented in primary care populations. The medical expense in primary care and specialty care associated with chronic pain is so great that many health care systems have established chronic pain programs simply to control the delivery of unnecessary medical services. Of course, pain and suffering are major drivers of health care seeking in this, or any group of patients. What is unique about chronic pain is the iatrogenic effect of many pain management strategies leads to increased medical service use. A good example is the use of opioid analgesics, which are extremely addictive and can contribute to the patient's sense of pain, disability and suffering. As tolerance develops, the patient requires greater and greater doses of medicine and therefore is closer to withdrawal at any given point in time. This leads to secondary mental health complaints and physical health problems. Another classic driver is the over-reliance on neurosurgery instead of teaching the patient pain management and pain tolerance strategies.

Chronic Disease

There are many chronic progressive disease states such as diabetes and cardio-vascular disease that require significant lifestyle changes and self-management strategies to control the risk of relapse and mortality. These demands are often juxtaposed with the psychological trauma associated with having a chronic disease. The psychology of adjusting to chronic disease, while simultaneously making lifestyle changes is notoriously difficult. One well established result is the problem of non-adherence to medical self-management regimes, a pervasive problem in healthcare. For example, less than 10% of diabetic patients reliably adhere to their self-management regime over time (Jacobson, 1996). The truth of the matter is that medical providers may understand what lifestyle changes have to occur to manage the process of a chronic disease, but they do not understand how to help patients make these difficult behavior changes. Again, taking the example of diabetes, in a matter of minutes, a person goes from being healthy to discovering the presence of a very unpleasant, progressive disease. At the same time, the patient is ordered to stop smoking, lose weight, start exercising, overhaul diet and engage in daily monitoring. Any one of these changes might be the target of an entire behavior regime in a behavioral medicine clinic or psychotherapist's office! A second driver is the effect of the disease state itself on the patient's general psychological functioning. There is a strong association between having a chronic disease and having a co-occurring mental disorder. For example, the co-occurrence of depression and diabetes is observed in roughly 25% of patients, but the single most common co-morbidity is generalized anxiety disorder (Gavard, Lustman & Crouse, 1993; Lustman, 1988).

Guidelines for Designing Programs to Capitalize on Medical Cost Savings Pathways

In previous sections, the major considerations involved in identifying and evaluating the economic benefits of integrated behavioral care have been examined. It is now possible to develop a template for designing programs to capitalize on these potential benefits. Although there are always nuances in any type of programmatic initiative, there are also general guidelines that apply in almost every case.

Table 1. The following table illustrates a set of parameters for designing cost savings programs. As can be seen, the first consideration is to identify the psychosocial driver (s) that is being targeted. The second objective is to determine how to "attack" this driver in ways that promote the three primary economic outcomes: increased cost effectiveness, increased productivity through leveraging and increased medical cost offsets. The reader will note that the tactics and strategies used vary considerably based upon which economic benefit is being sought. For example, cost effectiveness generally involves finding a way to deliver evidence-based interventions that are appropriate for the pace of primary care and increase the clinical outcome (cf., Robinson, in press, for an excellent treatment of these strategies). In contrast, leveraging will often require patient management protocols that shift patient care away from the physician to other providers or encourage the use of more time efficient service delivery. Medical cost offset strategies look specifically to identify and reduce the short and long term medical service delivery profile for a particular target population.

With these principles in mind, it will be useful to pick two sample conditions that are reflective of two cost savings pathways: depression (i.e. mental disorder pathway) and acute back pain (i.e., chronic pain pathway). There are many other potential targets for medical cost savings within these two pathways. For example, anxiety, panic, tension headache, migraine headache to name a few. For present purposes, depression will illustrate how to attack a more behavioral phenomenon, while acute back pain will demonstrate the application of the same principles to physical health complaints.

Psychosocial Driver	Underpinning Processes	Cost Effectiveness	Productivity Leveraging	Cost Offset
Information and Support	Lack of information or normalizing response produces worry and uncertainty; medical setting a natural contact point to seek information	Provide accurate, easy to use information through pamphlets and electronic media in lieu of medical visit	Shift patient to community health worker, community resource manager, clinic case manager, or consulting nurse line	Matching information distributed and community resource linkages to patient need will reduce information seeking
Stress-Somatization Response	Prolonged stress effects biochemistry and sense of well being; produces alarming somatic symptoms	Link stress and somatic symptoms; offer evidence based classroom program such as Sobel & Ornstein (1996)	Shift patient from individual medical visits to classroom program; have care managed by BH consultant	Effective stress management skills reduces somatic symptoms, increases subjective sense of health
Social Disenfranchisement	Social isolation effects subjective sense of health; increases risk for depression and somatic pre-occupation; increases health risk factors; patients seek social connections in medicine	Create social support buffers and community resource connections; help patients develop effective natural support networks and stable community resource linkages	Manage patients in group care medical clinics; use community outreach and social work services instead of medical services; form clinic based support groups; refer to nurse or BH provider	Linking patient to natural social supports and community resources reduces dependency on medical providers, creates more stable resource picture; social support buffers stress
Lifestyle change & health risk factor management	Health and wellness medicine creates need for medical services to assist with change; lack of	Use evidence based behavioral medicine & health psychology interventions; focus on	Shift patient to BH provider for individual or classroom services; use nursing based phone support in lieu of visits;	Increased success at behavior change reduces sense of health risk, increases self efficacy, improves

	success becomes motivation for medical care seeking	identifying and removing obstacles to behavior change	use interactive education methods to promote home based practice	subjective sense of health
Psychiatric Disorders	Patients seek treatment of primary disorders from medical provider; disorders create unpleasant somatic symptoms, decrease subjective and objective health status	Deliver evidence-based integrated care interventions (Robinson, 2002); protocols increase clinical response rates and improve functional outcomes; reduce unnecessary treatment costs due to non-adherence, lack of relapse prevention focus, provider variability, etc	Shift majority of management to BH consultant within care protocols; consider use of nurse telemedicine support (Hunkeler et. al., 2000) or depression case manager; use home based practice and self management in lieu of clinic management	Effective treatment reduces presentations for care, decreases number and intensity of somatic symptoms, increases subjective sense of health; early diagnosis prevents expensive medical testing
Chemical Dependency	Patients present with wide variety of health complaints; may seek counseling or Antibuse treatment; drug seeking behavior; present for help with mood and behavioral effects of addiction & withdrawal	Use patient education and intervention based in stages of change analysis and motivational interviewing concepts; avoid confrontations that may alienate patient; educate in relationship of substance use and unpleasant somatic and behavioral symptoms	Shift patient to BH provider or primary care based drug & alcohol services; connect patient with community resources such as AA or NA; involve family to help deflect patient to appropriate community care	Reduction in drug or alcohol abuse reduces medical risk factors, improves subjective sense of mental and physical health; decreases likelihood of drug seeking behavior; decreases risk for secondary mood disorder

Chronic Disease	Psychological impact of chronic disease increases sense of vulnerability; anxiety related to self management failures, difficulty with mandated disease management behavior change leads to non-adherence, increased rate of physical and psychological symptoms	Use patient education models such as diabetes education; focus on teaching self controlled behavior modification strategies; increase emphasis on managing the psychological effects of disease	Shift patient to disease management program for education and goal setting; involve BH provider to assess risk for mood disorder & non-adherence; offer group care clinics for high prevalence conditions (i.e. unstable hypertension)	Improved management of physical components of disease increases general health, reduces adverse medical outcomes; effective behavior change management increases self efficacy, reduces risk of secondary mood disorders
Chronic Pain	Pain motivates medical visits to find a diagnosis and seek relief; incentives of disability system may promote non-adherence, search for a miracle cure; drug dependence generates secondary use pattern	Use aggressive risk profiling at "front door" to identify high risk patients; use evidence based protocols that encourage physical exercise, behavioral management strategies, return to work planning; decrease reliance on pain medicines; aggressively manage disability risk	Shift patient to management by BH provider in pain control protocol. Deflect disability seeking behavior by establishing clear temporal parameters for return to work, use of medicine; refer to case manager or outreach worker to create links to support groups, workman's compensation	Effective management of pain reduces medical visits and drug seeking visits; reduces referrals for neuro-surgery; decreases disability driven medical complaints; reduces likelihood of secondary mood disorders; decreases addiction management visits

Major Depression

When addressing patients with depressive symptoms, it is absolutely essential to walk through the set of target population analysis steps described in an earlier section. There are many different types of depressive complaints seen in primary care and it is important to determine how the costs and clinical outcomes of each subgroup vary (i.e., major depression, minor depression, dysthmia, chronic depression). Further, the interventions designed for these sub-groups might also be very different. For example, one might have medication adherence as a primary focus (i.e., major depression), while another might focus on teaching goal setting, problem solving and other activating self-management skills (i.e., minor depression or dysthymia). This would probably result in the decision to screen potentially depressed patients at the front end to be able to place them in the appropriate program track. The cost effectiveness strategy would be to improve the clinical response of depressed primary care patients without adding inordinate cost. This might involve focusing on key process of care targets: early, accurate detection, medication adherence, key self-management skills and relapse prevention planning (cf. Robinson, In Press). To keep the treatment costs down, the treatment might be protocol driven and based in patient education and self-management principles (Robinson, Wischman & Del Vento, 1996). From a leveraging perspective, the management protocol might involve shifting responsibility for follow-up care from the treating physician to a team based behavioral health provider. The behavioral health provider would assess clinical response, side effect problems and provide "curbside" feedback to the treating physician. The behavioral clinician would also teach the patient self-management skills and help develop a medication tapering and relapse prevention program. Alternatively, a medically trained nurse might take on some of these responsibilities. A further leveraging strategy would be to leverage the behavioral clinician's time by conducting classes in depression management skills. From a medical cost offset perspective, the protocol might have a strong education component on the somatic symptoms of depression and how these can be managed without requiring ongoing medical management. This might involve teaching the concepts of sleep hygiene (for insomnia), encouraging regular exercise (for fatigue) and pain management (for headaches). Alternatively, if the depressed patient also had a chronic disease, the focus would be on how depression can effect disease management behaviors with the aim of avoiding disease "flare-ups" that could drive increased hospital costs.

Acute Back Pain

An analysis of acute back pain would start with an assessment of the percentage of acute pain patients that go on to become chronic pain patients. Additionally, one would want to create a typology of the acute back pain patients that seem to be most at risk for developing chronic pain syndrome (cf. Turk & Rudy, 1988). As in the depression example, an attempt would be made to "profile" the costs and outcomes of any identified pain sub-groups in an effort to target the group most likely to produce medical cost returns. This would probably lead to the conclusion that the best strategies for realizing the economic benefits of integration will be to prevent acute back pain patients from becoming chronic back pain patients. From a cost effectiveness perspective, the focus would be conducting an early risk assessment for chronic pain syndrome (i.e., prior history of pain complaints, past difficulties with depression or substance abuse, work history and work satisfaction), creating a consistent message about the role of and time frame for opioid medications, and immediately placing the patient in a program teaching behavioral techniques for pain management as well as exercise/stretching. The protocol might involve an immediate contact with a team based behavioral clinician following the index medical visit with a back pain complaint. A leveraging perspective would overlap in that preventing chronic back pain from developing would leverage a massive number of physician visits. In addition, short and intermediate term management visits might be shared between the behavioral clinician and the medical provider. A medical cost offset approach would emphasize strategies designed to prevent the development of chronic pain syndrome and, in addition, would set very stringent guidelines for referral for neurosurgery. This might involve a mandatory requirement that the patient has gone through a pain management and exercise program first and secondly, has participated in alternative physical treatments with efficacy equal to that of neurosurgery (i.e., chiropractics).

Key Characteristics of Medical Cost Savings Programs

The previous examples highlight several key features that characterize successful medical cost savings programs. Regardless of the type of target selected, the more of these features that are incorporated in a program, the more likely it is that cost effectiveness, leveraging and medical cost offset outcomes will be obtained.

Emphasize Screening, Detection and Deflection

In well-designed programs, there is an emphasis on early screening and detection, which results in the patient being assigned to the appropriate intervention. This permits early identification of a condition that, if allowed to worsen, may not only drive up medical utilization but may also be more expensive to treat. It also makes it more likely that the patient is appropriate for the intervention program. Often, the effect of accurate early screening is to deflect that patient away from unnecessary or poorly targeted treatments. An excellent example of this is the case of panic disorder. Many patients with panic first present to the emergency room with Tachycardia and dramatically elevated blood pressure. After stabilization, they are referred back to primary care. If they are not screened for panic disorder at that point, there is a very good chance that a series of subspecialty referrals will be generated to hunt for the medical cause of the Tachycardia. These specialty workups are very expensive and generally fail to identify a primary medical etiology. Preventing these referrals can mean thousands of dollars in medical cost savings.

Deliver an Aggressive Initial Response

Effective programs deliver an aggressive multi-modal intervention, often involving the close coordination of medical and behavioral health providers. At the same time, the goal is to shift a portion of the burden of patient management to the behavioral health provider to create leveraging and, in cases where the behavioral health provider is best suited to deal with the problem, to increase cost effectiveness.

Match the Level of Service With the Level of Need

The best chance for maximizing cost effectiveness occurs when the intervention program is supported by assessment and treatment protocols that match the level of patient need with the type and intensity of service provided. Based upon the patient's profile, the contents, methods and even the provider of the intervention may vary. This acknowledges the fact that not all patients will require every intervention and that each patient will have an individually tailored service profile. The goal is to put the right provider, with the right intervention, in front of the patient at the right time.

Use Evidence-based Interventions

One can design excellent screening protocols, deliver a very aggressive initial response that is matched to the patient's type of problem, and still be ineffective if the interventions are not clinically effective. It is imperative that medical cost savings programs incorporate evidence-based interventions that result in low patient attrition (a form of treatment failure) and marked clinical response. An excellent example is the Integrated Care Program for Depression (Robinson, Wischman & Del Vento, 1996). It utilizes depression self-management models that are derived from empiracally validated treatments for depression.

Use Flexible Intervention Methods

As noted earlier, a variety of intervention methods have been shown to produce effective clinical and cost outcomes with behavioral health conditions. Well designed programs offer a variety of intervention methods such as patient education pamphlets, educational videos, internet kiosks, support groups, group care clinics, phone call support and psychoeducational classes. The emphasis on multiple methods of delivery increases the probability of finding a way to present information that is acceptable to the patient. This, in turn, leads to the reduced likelihood of patient attrition or an insignificant clinical response.

Prevent Relapse in Recurrent Conditions

A legitimate focus of medical cost savings programs is to prevent relapse in conditions that are known to be recurrent. For example, it is impossible to predict a first episode of major depression. However, once the index episode has occurred, the patient is known to be at risk for a relapse. Interventions that have the effect of preventing relapse can greatly reduce the medical expenses associated with treating recurrences. This is a classic disease management concept that can be directly applied to many behavioral health conditions.

Prevent Iatrogenic Treatments

Some pernicious behavioral health conditions are the unintended by-product of a well intentioned but inappropriate treatment. An excellent example is chronic pain. There is no chronic pain patient alive that didn't start out as an acute pain patient. Many experts in chronic pain argue that commonly employed treatment strategies for acute back pain, such as the indiscriminate prescribing of pain killers or placing patients on unconditional disability leave from work, promote the core features of chronic pain syndrome. Thus, well designed medical cost savings programs attempt to control or eliminate iatrogenic interventions by developing early stage treatment protocols.

Guidelines for Implementing Medical Cost Savings Programs

In the previous section, we examined the core features of well-designed medical cost savings programs. However, these programs do not exist in a vacuum. They must be implemented within the complicated environment of a healthcare delivery system. A critical determinant of success is how these programs are deployed and linked to various components within the primary care setting. The following guidelines are designed to help systems initiate medical cost savings programs in the most effective way possible.

Anticipate Consumer Preferences

The eventual population effectiveness of a program is largely determined by how acceptable it is to the consumer. A clinically effective intervention that results in a 30% patient drop out rate is probably not as valuable as a less effective intervention that has a 10% drop out rate. With this in mind, before implementation, it is important to expose consumers to assessment and intervention protocols in medical cost savings programs and solicit feedback about the acceptability of these methods. Typically, interventions for primary care patients need to be brief and oriented around patient education and home based practice. Interventions that require the patient to attend multiple individual, class or group care sessions are more likely to lead to attrition. We need to recognize that while an individual visit may only require 15-30 minutes of the provider's time, it will require 2-3 hours of the patient's time. Further, interventions need to be tailored to fit the skills and abilities of patients. This is a common source of failure in program implementation; the intervention concepts are nice but they far exceed the typical patient's interest or capacity. Other considerations need also to be addressed, such as how to serve monolingual patients, ethnic or racial subgroups or populations with lower literacy levels.

Seek Medical Provider Involvement and Buy-In

Effective medical cost savings programs require the "good will" of the medical providers who will refer patients and reinforce the messages of the intervention.

When programs are designed and implemented without the full participation of medical providers, there is an increased likelihood that this "buy-in" will not occur. As is the case with consumers, it is important to pilot test any screening devices, patient care materials or protocols in the context of typical primary care practice. Primary care providers are basically stretched to the breaking point in terms of work requirements and they share a common concern about the "new work" associated with a new program. Practically speaking, the goal of the program should be to reduce, not increase, the medical provider's workload. If a program increases workload without some tangible benefit, primary care providers will not use it. A very common failing in well intentioned medical cost programs is that the benefit does not accrue to the medical provider, it accrues to some other point in the system (i.e., increased time assessing depression leads to reduced pharmacy costs for anti-depressants). From the perspective of the treating medical provider, there is not much immediate incentive to change practice style, unless the change is enforced externally.

Nest Behavioral Health and Primary Care Services

In general, programs that are implemented "seamlessly" as part of routine primary care are much more likely to be acceptable to patients and to medical providers. From the patient's perspective, receiving these services in the context of routine primary care is not only more convenient (it allows for the "one stop shopping"), but it also is less stigmatizing. From the medical provider perspective, having such behavioral health services within the immediate practice area makes referring the patient easier, creates better real time communication between providers and allows the medical provider to monitor and reinforce core interventions during medical visits. In most cases, the best place to start is to simply place a behavioral health provider on the medical team to provide generic consultation and brief co-management services (Strosahl, 1997). This familiarizes medical providers with the way behavioral health services can benefit the general process of primary medicine. Once this "platform" is established, it is easier to get buy in for medical cost savings programs that may require more activity on the part of the medical provider. Prior experience with team based integrated behavioral health makes it easier to add more sophisticated medical cost savings treatment protocols.

Phase-In Programs

To fully capitalize on the economic benefits of behavioral health integration, systems will need to implement not one, but perhaps many medical cost savings initiatives targeted at different pathways and target populations. One very successful medical cost savings program may engender political support for integration, but it is unlikely to affect the "big picture" of runaway medical costs. This should be no surprise, given the complexity of medical service systems and the numerous drivers of health care seeking. To actually achieve the promise of behavioral health integration will take a longer period of time and this should be reflected in the program implementation plan. At the same time, it is usually a good idea to keep things simple and focus on implementing one program at a time. This may call for the development of a master plan that establishes a schedule of cost savings targets as well as a strategy for phasing in programs over time.

Guidelines for Demonstrating Medical Cost Savings

One of the more daunting tasks in this whole area is to demonstrate that medical cost savings have actually been realized. This requires that a program evaluation component be attached to any medical cost savings initiative. This is easier said than done in most systems. In the contemporary health information environment, it is deceptively difficult to track costs, not to mention cost savings. In the struggle to design and implement medical cost savings programs, there is a tendency to exert so much energy that the initiative "runs out of gas" at the point where performance measurement must be conducted. To combat this system fatigue, it is wise to identify program evaluation benchmarks and association measurement strategies at the point of initial program design. It will be useful to examine the three different types of medical cost savings in relation to the strategies that will be required to evaluate them.

Measuring Cost Effectiveness

As discussed earlier, cost effectiveness is the measure of value added to "usual care" through the addition of a new test or procedure. It is a mathematical relation between the cost of the new procedure and what the new procedure adds in clinical value relative to the costs and value of usual care. There are many different approaches to the determination of cost effectiveness and the interested reader is encouraged to seek additional knowledge in this area (Levin & McEwan, 2001). There are some general strategies for generating the best demonstrations of cost effectiveness.

First, because cost effectiveness is essentially a comparison between usual care and a new form of care, it is important to be able to compare the two in some type of control group design. For example, one health care site may initiate an experimental program to evaluate the cost effectiveness of an integrated care package for panic disorder. Another site in the same system does not participate in this initiative and has a very similar patient population. All other factors being equal, the outcomes and cost of the new procedure can be compared between the "experimental" and "control" sites.

Second, cost effectiveness analysis requires fairly exact estimates of the costs of treatment in usual care and experimental care. Notice that this does not include some costs that would be measured in cost offset analyses (i.e., general medical service use not related to the treatment of panic per se). The variables of interest in cost effectiveness studies are direct treatments costs generated by medical providers, pharmacy, behavioral health services and so forth.

The primary advantage of the cost effectiveness model is that it gives information about the benefits of both acute and long-term care, if so desired. Rather than requiring a long waiting period to see results, cost effectiveness figures can be generated as soon as the first outcome is known. In some medical savings programs, this information might be available within 2-3 months of a patient's entry into the program. On the other hand, cost effectiveness could be measured at various intervals over time in a long-term intervention program to determine how long treatment should continue in order to achieve maximum cost effectiveness.

Measuring Increases in Productive Capacity

Although there are many ways to define the capacity of a healthcare system, the best unit of measure is quite straightforward: it is the average number of medical encounters by a medical provider in a workday. The leveraging effect of adding a behavioral health provider to the medical team is determined by evaluating any increase in the average number of daily encounters by a medical provider on the same team. A second, related measure would be the average Relative Value Unit (RVU) associated with a typical medical visit. Recall that one goal of leveraging is to divert less difficult patients out of medical encounters. If this effect occurred, it would tend to drive up the percentage of patients seen with more significant medical issues. This approach to measuring leverage also allows a control group design to be put in place. Medical providers on a team without a behavioral health provider can be compared to medical providers with a behavioral health team member. The outcomes of interest are the average number and medical complexity of medical encounters per day.

Medical Cost Offset

As noted earlier, medical cost offset is a result of a reduction in medical service use by a patient after exposure to a behavioral health intervention. A cost offset is a net result: Total medical costs prior to an intervention – total medical costs after an intervention + the costs of the behavioral health intervention. Basically, this requires that we can establish a baseline medical cost in a specific time frame and that current and subsequent medical and behavioral health costs can be tracked and computed. In practice, medical cost offsets are very difficult to demonstrate because there are often multiple cost and utilization data sets within one health care system. Often, data sets are specific to a type of healthcare service (i.e., pharmacy, ambulatory medical services, home health and outreach services, mental health and substance abuse, emergency room). Patching together these disconnected pieces of information can be an overwhelming task, even for experienced software programmers. This makes it extremely difficult to capture all sources of medical cost in a health care system. A second, related problem is that a cost needs to be imputed to each service. Generally, this requires a software program capable of attaching a specific cost to a dizzying array of medical services. In some cases, this information can be extracted from a claims and billing data set. Assuming that the informatics solutions can be found, there are several points about medical cost offsets that are often ignored or overlooked. The result can be misleading or even erroneous results.

First, medical cost offsets can be substantial, but tend to accrue over time. It is not unusual to observe cost offsets two to three years after an index intervention.

A common problem is that the fate of integrated behavioral health interventions is often tied to a rather immediate demonstration of medical cost offsets, when in fact that is rather unlikely to happen. The risk is that well-designed medical cost offset interventions might be "mothballed" prematurely, allowing skeptics to conclude that the cost offsets are not forthcoming, when in fact they might have been had the program been allowed to operate for a sufficiently long period of time. It is important to have medical administrators understand that programs focused on achieving medical cost offsets need to operate for 2-3 years before meaningful conclusions can be drawn. A related consideration is that a sufficiently large number of patients need to be enrolled in the evaluation to detect a variable range of effects. If a cost offset effect is small but consistent, it will require that more patients be enrolled in the program and evaluation project to detect the effect.

Second, cost offsets have been demonstrated with medical patients, but also in their immediate family members. Often, the magnitude of cost offsets in family members is greater than in the index patient (McDonnell-Douglas Corporation, 1989). This means that well designed cost offset evaluations need to track the medical costs of dependents as well as patients.

Third, it is important to track both the direct and indirect costs of healthcare. Cost offset formulations need to include such factors as institutional overhead in computing the unit value of services. Certain types of services such as behavioral health have a much lower institutional overhead associated with them. Failure to anticipate this factor could lead to an overestimate of the costs of behavioral care and an underestimate of general medical costs. This would have the effect of systematically understating the magnitude of a cost offset effect.

Fourth, certain types of cost offset evaluations require a matched control group strategy. A good example of this principle is the evaluation of cost offset programs for high utilizers of medical services. By definition, high utilizers are at the far end of the normal curve of medical utilization. Over time, an untreated high utilizer will typically show a reduction in service utilization, a statistical effect known as "regression to the mean". Studies of this kind require two groups of similar high utilizing patients to be formed. One group will be exposed to the cost offset intervention. The other group will function as a control group. Without a control group in place, one might conclude that a program produced massive reductions in medical service use, when in fact what occurred was a naturally occurring change that would have also been observed in a group of untreated patients.

Summary

In this chapter, the potential economic benefits of integrated behavioral health care have been described and analyzed in detail. We are faced with an unprecedented opportunity to change the face of health care and, ultimately, make it an affordable human service. Capitalizing on the economic benefits of integrated behavioral care will require a complicated blend of strategic vision, scientific acumen and an arsenal full of program development, implementation and evaluation skills. Most of all, it will require a consistency of belief that providing healthcare to the whole human being is the only way out of our contemporary healthcare conundrum. Rather than viewing integrated behavioral health care as a minor modification to the current system of care, it is more accurate to describe this as a re-engineering of health care. Hopefully, the concepts provided in the chapter will provide one possible blueprint for achieving the quality of healthcare that is desired by everyone.

References

Ballenger, J. (1987). Unrecognized prevalence of panic disorder in primary care, internal medicine and cardiology. *American Journal of Cardiology, 60,* 39J-47J.

Beardsley, R, Gardocki, G, Larson D., & Hidalgo, J. (1988). Prescribing of psychotropic medication by primary care physicians and psychiatrists. *Archives of General Psychiatry, 45,* 1117-1119.

Berkanovic, E., Telesky, C., & Reeder, S. (1981). Structural and social psychological factors in the decision to seek medical care for symptoms. *Medical Care, 21,* 693-709.

Caudill M., Schnabel R., Zuttermeister P., Benson H., & Friedman R. (1991) Decreased clinic use by chronic pain patients: Response to behavioral medicine interventions. *Clinical Journal of Pain, 7,* 305- 310.

Chiles, J., Lambert, M., & Hatch, A. (1999). The impact of psychological interventions on medical cost offset: A meta-analytic review. *Clinical Psychology: Science and Practice, 6,* 204-220.

Coffey, R., Mark, T., King, E., Harwood, H., McKusick, D., Genuardi, J., Dilonardo, J., & Buck, J. (2000). *National estimates of expenditures for mental health and substance abuse treatment, 1997.* SAMHSHA Publication No. SMA-00-3499. Rockville, Md: Sustance Abuse & Mental Health Services Administration.

Cummings, N. (1995). Impact of managed care on employment and training: A primer for survival. *Professional Psychology: Research and Practice, 26,* 10-15.

Cummings, N., & VandenBos G. (1981). The twenty years Kaiser-Permanente experience with psychotherapy and medical utilization: Implications for national health policy and national health insurance. *Health Policy Quarterly, 1,* 159-175.

Drisbow E., Bennett H., & Owings J. (1993). Effect of preoperative suggestion on postoperative gastrointestinal motility. *Journal of Western Medicine, 158,* 488-492.

Fawzy, F., Fawzy, N., & Hyun, C. (1993). Malignant melanoma: Effects of an early structured psychiatric intervention, coping, and affective state on recurrence and survival 6 years later. *Archives of General Psychiatry, 50,* 681-689.

Fleming, M., & Barry, K. (1992). Clinical overview of alcohol and drug disorders (pp.3-21). In M. Fleming & K. Barry (Eds.), *Addictive disorders.* Chicago: Mosby Yearbook.

Frasure-Smith, N. (1991). In-hospital symptoms of psychological stress as predictors of long-term outcome after acute myocardial infarction in men. *American Journal of Cardiology, 67,* 121-127.

Friedman, R., Sobel, D., Myers, P., Caudill, M., & Benson, H. (1995). Behavioral medicine, clinical health psychology and cost offset. *Health Psychology, 14*, 509-518.

Fries, J., Koop, C., & Beadle, C. (1993). Reducing health care costs by reducing the need and demand for medical services. *The New England Journal of Medicine, 329*, 321-325.

Gavard, J., Lustman, P., & Clouse, R. (1993). Prevalence of depression in adults with diabetes: An epidemiological evaluation. *Diabetes Care, 16*, 1167-1178.

Holder, H., & Blose, J. (1986). Alcoholism treatment and total healthcare utilization and costs: A four-year longitudinal analysis of federal employees. *Journal of the American Medical Association, 256*, 1456-1460.

Hellman, C., Budd, M., Borysenko, J., McClelland, D., & Benson H. (1990). A study of the effectiveness of two group behavioral medicine interventions for patients with psychosomatic complaints. *Behavioral Medicine, 16*, 165-173.

Hunkeler, E., Meresman, J., Hargreaves, W., Fireman, B., Berman, W., Kirsch, A., Groebe, J., Hurt, S., Braden, P., Getzell, M., Feigenbaum, P., Peng, T., & Salzer, M. (2000). Efficacy of nurse telehealth and peer support in augmenting treatment of depression in primary care. *Archives of Family Medicine, 9*, 700-708.

Jacobson, A. (1996). The psychological care of patients with insulin-dependent diabetes. *The New England Journal of Medicine, 334*, 1249-1253.

Katon, W., Robinson, P., Von Korff, M., Lin, E., Bush, T., Ludman, E., Simon, G., & Walker, E. (1996). A multifaceted intervention to improve treatment of depression in primary care. *Archives of General Psychiatry, 53*, 924-932.

Katon, W., Von Korff, M., Lin, E., Bush, T., Lipscomb, P., & Russo, J. (1992). A randomized trial of psychiatric consultation with distressed high utilizers. *General Hospital Psychiatry, 14*, 86-98.

Kemper, D., Lorig K., & Mettler, M. (1993). The effectiveness of medical self-care interventions: A focus on self-initiated responses to symptoms. *Patient Education and Counseling, 21*, 29-39.

Kennell, J., Klaus, M., McGrath, S., Robertson, S., & Hinkley C. (1991). Continuous emotional support during labor in a US hospital: A randomized controlled trial. *Journal of the American Medical Association, 265*, 2197-2237.

Kent, J., & Gordon, M. (2001). Programmatic approaches to care and outcomes: The medical co-management group appointment (pp. 77-90). In N. Cummings, W. O'Donohoe, S. Hayes & V. Follette (Eds.). *Integrated behavioral healthcare: Positioning mental health practice with medical/surgical practice.* New York: Academic Press.

Kessler, R., Nelson, C., McGonagle, K., Liu, J., Swartz, M., & Blazer, D. (1994). Lifetime and 12 month prevalence of DSM-III-R psychiatric disorders in the United States. *Archives of General Psychiatry, 51*, 8-19.

Kroenke, K., & Mangelsdorff, A. (1989). Common symptoms in ambulatory care: Incidence, evaluation, therapy and outcome. *American Journal of Medicine, 86*, 262-266.

Levin, H., & McEwan, P. (2001). *Cost-effectiveness analysis, 2nd edition.* Thousand Oaks, CA.: Sage Publications

Lorig, K., Holman, H., Sobel, D., Laurent, D., Gonzalez, V., & Minor, M. (1994). *Living a healthy life with chronic conditions.* Palo Alto, CA: Bull Publishing Co.

Lorig, K., Mazonson, P., & Holman, H. (1993). Evidence suggesting that health education for self-management in patients with chronic arthritis has sustained health benefits while reducing health care costs. *Arthritis and Rheumatology, 36,* 439-446.

Lustman, P. (1988). Anxiety disorders in adults with diabetes. *Psychiatric Clinics of North America, 11,* 725-732

Lynch, W. (1993). The potential impact of health promotion on health care utilization: An introduction to demand management. *Association for Worksite Health Promotion Practitioner's Forum, 8,* 87-92.

McDonnell-Douglas Corporation. (1989). *Employee Assistance Program Financial Cost Offset Study,* 1985-1988.

Mumford, E., Schlesinger, H., & Glass, G. (1984). A new look at evidence about reduced cost of medical utilization following mental health treatment. *American Journal of Psychiatry, 141,* 1145-1158.

Narrow, W. Regier, D., Rae, D., Manderscheid, R., & Locke, B. (1993). Use of services by persons with mental and addictive disorders: Findings from the National Institute of Mental Health Epidemiologic Catchment Area Program. *Archives of General Psychiatry, 50,* 95-107.

Pallak, M., Cummings, N., Dorken, H., & Hanke, C. (1995) Effect of mental health treatment on medical costs. *Mind/Body Medicine, 1,* 7-12.

Regier, D. A., Narrow, W. E., Rae, D. S., Manderschied, R. W., Locke, B. Z., & Goodwin, F. K. (1993). The de facto US mental and addictive disorders service system: Epidemiologic Catchment Area prospective 1 year prevalence rates of disorders and services. *Archives of General Psychiatry, 50,* 85-94.

Richardson, W . (chair) (2001). *Institute of Medicine Report: Crossing the quality chasm: A new health system for the 21st century.* Washington, DC: Institute of Medicine.

Robinson, J., Schwartz, M., & Magwene, K. (1989). The impact of fever health education on clinic utilization. *American Journal of Disabled Children, 143,* 698-704.

Robinson, P. (in press). Adapting evidence-based treatments for the primary care setting: A template for success. In W. T. O'Donohue (Ed), *Treatments that work in primary care.* New York: Allyn & Bacon.

Robinson, P., Wischman, C., & Del Vento, A. (1996). *Treating depression in primary care: A manual for primary care and mental health providers.* Reno, NV: Context Press.

Shapiro, S., Skinner, E., & Kessler, L. (1984). Utilization of health and mental health services: Three epidemiologic catchment area sites. *Archives of General Psychiatry, 41,* 971-978.

Simon, G. (1992). Psychiatric disorder and functional somatic symptoms as predictors of health care use. *Psychiatric Medicine, 10,* 49-60.

Simon, G., VonKorff, M., & Barlow, W. (1995). Health care costs of primary care patients with recognized depression. *Archives Of General Psychiatry*, *52*, 850-856.

Smith, G., Rost, K., & Kashner, T. (1995). A trial of the effect of a standardized psychiatric consultation on health outcomes and costs in somatizing patients. *Archives of General Psychiatry*, *52*, 238-243.

Sobel, D. (1995). Rethinking medicine: Improving health outcomes with cost-effective psychosocial interventions. *Psychosomatic Medicine*, *57*, 234-244.

Sobel, D., & Ornstein, R. (1996). *The healthy mind, healthy body handbook*. Los Altos, CA: DRx Publishing, 1996.

Spitzer, R.L., Williams, J.B., Kroenke, K., Linzer, L., deGruy, F. V., Hahn, S.R., Brody, D., & Johnson, J.G. (1994). Utility of a new procedure for diagnosing mental disorders in primary care: The PRIME-MD 1000 Study. *Journal of the American Medical Association*, *272* (22), 1749-1756.

Strain, J., Lyons, J., Hammer, J., & Fahs, M. (1991). Cost offset from a psychiatric consultation-liaison intervention with elderly hip fracture patients. *American Journal of Psychiatry*, *148*, 1044-1049.

Strosahl, K. (1994). New dimensions in behavioral health primary care integration. *HMO Practice*, *8*, 176-179.

Strosahl, K. (1996a). Primary mental health care: A new paradigm for achieving health and behavioral health integration. *Behavioral Healthcare Tomorrow*, *5*, 93-96.

Strosahl, K. (1996b). Confessions of a behavior therapist in primary care: The Odyssey and the ecstasy. *Cognitive and Behavioral Practice*, *3*, 1-28.

Strosahl, K. (1997). Building primary care behavioral health systems that work: A compass and a horizon. In N. Cummings, J. Cummings & J. Johnson (Eds.), *Behavioral health in primary care: A guide for clinical integration* (pp. 37-68). Madison, CN: Psychosocial Press.

Strosahl, K. (1998). Integration of primary care and behavioral health services: The primary mental health care model. In A. Blount (Ed.), *Integrative primary care: The future of medical and mental health collaboration* (pp. 43-66). New York: Norton Publishing.

Strosahl, K., & Sobel, D. (1996). Behavioral health and the medical cost offset effect: Current status, key concepts and future applications. *HMO Practice*, *10*, 156-162.

Turk, D., & Rudy, T. (1988). Toward an empirically derived taxonomy of chronic pain patients: Integration of psychological assessment data. *Journal of Consulting and Clinical Psychology*, *56*, 233-238.

Unutzer, J., Katon, W., Sullivan, M., & Miranda, J. (1997). *The effectiveness of treatments for depressed older adults in primary care*. Paper present at the meeting, Exploring Opportunities to Advance Mental Health Care for an Aging Population. John A. Hartford Foundation, Rockville, MD.

Unutzer, J., Patrick, D., Simon, G., Grembowski, D., Walker, E., & Katon, W. (1996). *Depression, quality of life and use of health services in primary care patients over 65: A four-year prospective study*. Paper presented at the American Psychiatric Association, 148th Annual Meeting.

Von Korff, M., Shapiro, S., Burke, J., Teitlebaum, M., Skinner, E., German, P., Turner, R., Klein, T., & Burns, B. (1987). Anxiety and depression in a primary care clinic: Comparison of Diagnostic Interview Schedule, General Health Questionnaire and practitioner assessments. *Archives Of General Psychiatry, 44*, 152-156.

Von Korff, M., & Simon, G. (1996). The prevalence and impact of psychological disorders in primary care: HMO research needed to improve care. *HMO Practice, 10*, 150-155.

Wallace, P., Cutler, S., & Haines, A. (1988). A randomized controlled trial of general practitioner intervention in patients with excessive alcohol consumption. *British Medical Journal, 297*, 663-668.

Wells, K., Steward, A., Hays, R.., Burnam, M., Rogers, W., Daniels, M., Berry, S., Greenfield, S., & Ware, J. (1989). The functioning and well being of depressed patients: Results from the Medical Outcomes Study. *Journal of the American Medical Association, 262*, 914-919.

Yingling, K., Wulsin, L., Arnold, L., & Rouan, G. (1993). Estimated prevalences of panic disorder and depression among consecutive patients seen in an emergency department with acute chest pain. *Journal of General Internal Medicine, 8*, 2315.

Roles for Psychological Procedures, and Psychological Processes, in Cost-Offset Research: Cost →Procedure → Process →Outcome Analysis

Brian T. Yates
American University

As researchers, therapists, and policy-makers, we ought to be able to answer these Cost →Procedure →Process →Outcome Analysis (CPPOA) questions:

What types and amounts of *resources* (valued as costs) do we need...

... to implement what mixture of treatment *procedures*?

... that will produce the changes in which biopsychosocial processes?

... that will cause the targeted outcomes? (Linden & Wen, 1990).

At present, we cannot answer these questions for most therapies.

Answering these questions well, from a foundation of theory buttressed by research, requires all our previous research in psychotherapy, and more. Basic research has examined the strength and direction of relationships between biological, psychological, or social processes that occur inside the brains or bodies of people, and how they behave (a type of outcome). Applied research has examined relationships between use of treatment procedures and processes, or procedures and outcomes, and sometimes all three. Evaluation research examines relationships between procedures and outcomes. Cost-effectiveness research describes how the monetary value of resources used to implement treatment procedures compares to outcomes. Cost-benefit research describes how the monetary value of resources used to implement treatment procedures compares to the monetary value of those outcomes. Each of these types of research assembles important parts of the picture of treatment, but the findings of each type of research need to be integrated into a whole that is both cohesive and comprehensible. This is the challenge of Cost → Procedure →Process →Outcome Analysis (CPPOA; cf. Yates, 1980a, 1996, 1999).

And what is the purpose of all this analysis – this compounding of research upon research, study upon study? What is the benefit of examining each possible linkage of cause and effect between the many resources that go into treatment, and the many outcomes that can result from it? Moreover, is it likely that this benefit is worth the cost of examining intermediary steps between resources "in" and outcomes "out?" Our research suggests it can be, even when a program does not achieve the outcomes that were targeted. Several of our studies illustrate how measuring the strength and direction of relationships between costs, procedures, processes, and outcomes can show why a program has negative outcomes, and how to change the program so that it has a better likelihood of succeeding. We describe one of these program analyses after discussing common problems and misunderstandings in research that examines the costs and benefits of psychotherapies.

How the Cost-Savings Produced by Therapy Can Exceed the Cost of Therapy (and How We Can Measure This)

Cost-Savings (Cost Offset) Produced by Therapy

Psychological problems range from depression, anxiety, and schizophrenia to substance abuse, suicide, and violence against other people. Psychological problems are prevalent, costly – and sometimes treatable, at a cost that could be less than what would be spent if the problems continued untreated. Therapies for psychological problems range from intensive psychoanalysis to brief cognitive-behavioral therapy, sometimes assisted by prescribed drugs. This potential positive difference between the costs of therapy and the savings generated with therapy can be caused by (a) the relatively low costs of some therapies, and (b) the high costs to society of allowing psychological problems to go untreated.

Usually, researchers define and measure the savings potentially produced by therapies as reduced criminal justice costs (e.g., arrests, incarceration, trials) and reduced health care expenditures (e.g., for emergency room visits and hospitalizations, for both health and mental health problems). This may be due to these researchers' focus on therapies for substance abuse problems (e.g., Finigan, 1996; Jones & Vischi, 1979; Yates, 1984), which often result in high criminal justice costs prior to treatment (cf. Hubbard & French, 1991). For example, the Center for Substance Abuse Treatment (CSAT) (1999) found that of the total savings produced by substance abuse treatment for criminal offenders, over 90% was reduced criminal justice costs, while reduced health care costs were less than 10%.

For many consumers and funders of mental health services, however, maintaining productivity in the workplace may be a more substantial outcome of therapy for psychological dysfunction. In advanced economies, such as the United States, mental illness ranks second only to cardiovascular conditions in the burden it places on workers (measured as Disability Adjusted Life Years or DALYs; Murray & Lopez, 1996). The same study found that mental illnesses are responsible for more of a decrement in DALY for workers than all cancers combined. Furthermore, in the United States alone, between 5 and 6 million employees "...lose, fail to seek, or cannot find employment as a result of mental illness..." each year (p. 21, Marcott & Wilcox-Gök, 2001). Furthermore, those who do continue to work while mentally ill make $3,500 to $6,000 less than they would if they were healthy (Marcott & Wilcox-Gök, 2001). Ettner, Frank, and Kessler (1997) estimate that being mentally ill reduced women's changes of employment 11%, and reduces a woman's income by one-fifth to one-half. Clearly the potential cost-savings that can be produced by effective therapy are considerable – but are they worth the cost of that therapy?

Money Spent to Make Therapy Happen

It is both easy and common to confuse the cost-savings produced by some therapies for some psychological problems with the costs of those therapies. If one is not particularly enamored of the notion of including costs among the variables measured in research, it is tempting to simply lump all costs together in one group – and then to ignore them as much as possible, to delay measuring them as long as possible, or to finally decide that they are too difficult (or costly) to measure well (cf. Yates, in progress). It is more acceptable to think about costs in terms of outcomes, especially money saved. A variety of participants in the research process will endorse measuring money saved as a result of treatment (some because those funds then could be used to provide therapy for additional people, some because those funds then could be reallocated to other works). Once the actual cost of treatment is held up as a variable to be measured, however, concern often becomes acute, and confusion as well as anxiety and even resistance can result.

Input Cost, Output Cost, and Cost-Offset: Definitions

It can be helpful to draw a distinction between input cost and output cost. Input cost is the monetary value or total "price" of all resources that make therapy possible. Examples of input costs would be therapists' time, space used for therapy sessions, liability insurance, and many other resources (including therapy administrators' time, clients' time, client transportation expenses; cf. Yates, 1996). Output cost is the sum of all funds that other programs did not have to spend, because of positive effects of therapy, plus all funds generated because of therapy. Examples of the first type of output costs would be (a) criminal justice services that were no longer required because the individual no longer stole goods or prostituted to obtain cash to buy drugs, and (b) health care costs that were no longer required because the person stopped engaging in self-destructive behaviors such as smoking and overeating. Examples of the second type of output cost include (c) income generated from employment and (d) profits gained from licit entrepreneurship that was begun or enhanced because of therapy. The hope of many therapists, clients, researchers, funders, and policy-makers is that these "output" costs of therapy will more than offset the "input" costs of therapy, i.e., that the monetary benefits of therapy will exceed the expenditures made in order to provide therapy.

The magnitude of this *cost-offset* needs to be considerable, given (a) the uncertain nature of the amount of benefits (cost-savings and income generation) that may accrue as a result of therapy, and (b) the certain nature of the immediate costs of providing (and receiving) therapy. Several quantitative methods have been developed to measure the magnitude of this cost offset, and to take into account the difference in time and certainty with which therapy costs and potential cost-savings and other benefits occur. Statistical methods can be used to decide whether the differences between costs and benefits found for a small sample of clients are the result of chance variations in costs, benefits, and the measures used to quantify them, or are the result of systematic effects of therapy (cf. Kazdin, 1998). The magnitude of these effects also can be measured, within a range of certainty that can be further discerned with measurable degrees of confidence (cf. Smith, Glass, & Miller, 1980). Finally, the delayed nature of benefits can be compared more precisely to the immediate nature of costs by a variety of discounting formulae (Yates, 1996).

Cost-Offset or Cost-Effectiveness ... or Something Else?

What is more challenging to incorporate into contrasts of these benefits and costs are the increases in use of services that may – and sometimes should – result from therapy. As noted above, while a common outcome of therapy is the eventual decreased need for future health and mental health services, individuals receiving therapy may become sufficiently knowledgeable and assertive to more actively seek and use health care services to which they are entitled, but which they have not used before. The result can be a temporary increase in service utilization (and service costs), followed by a decrease in service utilization below (a) pre-therapy levels of service utilization, and possibly (b) below levels of service utilization that would have occurred if therapy had not been provided.

Some mental health services view the increased use of health care services as a desirable outcome, and not necessarily one that should be transient. Critics of cost-benefit analyses also note that not all of the desirable outcomes of therapy can be measured in monetary units or transformed into money saved or money generated (e.g., Book, 1991). To incorporate these and related considerations into research on the effects of psychotherapy, researchers have turned to *cost-effectiveness analysis* as an additional, and sometimes as an alternative and preferable, way of comparing the value of resources invested in therapy to the value of outcomes produced by therapy. While a variety of studies show that the cost-savings and income enhancement benefits that typically result from therapy exceed the cost of that therapy (e.g., Cummings, 1997; Cummings & Follette, 1968), we pursue in the remainder of this manuscript a form of cost-effectiveness analysis that explores the observable and inferable events that between costs "in" and outcomes "out," i.e., Cost →Procedure → Process → Outcome Analysis, or CPPOA for short.

Cost → Procedure → Process → Outcome Analysis (CPPOA)

A major challenge to integrating information on costs and outcomes into treatment research is, surprisingly, not mastering the rather basic quantitative skills for describing relationships between costs and outcomes but accepting what might be called the "multi-variable" nature of cost-outcome relationships. While some accountants and economists are trained to focus the types and amounts of resources used in service enterprises, such as therapy, most psychologists and other social scientists (including some economists) are trained to focus on the types and amounts of outcomes that occur during and after therapy. To focus simultaneously on measurement of costs and outcomes is so difficult that it can seem impossible (cf. Yates, 1998). To not only measure, but value in monetary terms, both the resources used in therapy and the outcomes produced in therapy – well, most social scientists throw up their hands and let someone else do it. That, however, is not necessary and not in the best interests of the providers or consumers of therapy.

When therapy works, we need to know what makes it work. When it works especially well, we really need to know why it worked so well. And, when therapy fails, or even hurts – and it does, at times, for some clients – we very much need to know why, and how to prevent that failure for future clients. Finally, even when therapy works extremely well, we need to know how much it costs and how to keep the costs as low as we can. We cannot understand this by measuring and comparing only the beginning and ends of the psychotherapeutic process, i.e., only the value of resources consumed and outcomes generated. We need to measure, find, and understand the nature of the critical paths between resources put into therapy and outcomes resulting from therapy.

What CPPOA Is Not

Research on or evaluation of the outcomes of psychotherapy is not CPPOA; it is typically only "OA" (Outcome Analysis). Knowing the cost-savings or effectiveness of therapy can be very useful when choosing which type of therapy to pursue, but it is not the whole story. If only the outcomes of therapy are measured, we do not know what it costs. Essentially, measuring the outcomes but not the costs of therapy implies that we can assume that the costs of therapy do not matter, or will not change, or must be paid regardless of the how effective therapy is. This may be the case if therapy is considered an entitlement, or if no substantial variation in therapy can be considered. If, however, the type or amount of therapy can be changed, not measuring costs amounts to assuming that we consider the costs of each type or amount of therapy to not be significantly different.

Research on or evaluation of the costs of therapy also is not CPPOA; it is only "CA." Knowing the cost per client per month for different types of therapy can be useful, but it is not the whole story either. If only the costs of therapy are measured, then we are saying that the effects of therapy do not matter, or will not change, or will occur regardless of the amount of resources spent on therapy. Again, this may be the case if the therapies under consideration are not significantly different in effectiveness, or if no real change in the type or amount of therapy is possible. If therapy can be changed, however, not measuring effectiveness implies that we consider all therapies under examination to be similar in effectiveness. Alternatively, perhaps it is thought that the effects of therapy cannot be measured reliably or validly. (Interestingly, the same is unlikely to be said for costs.)

Finally, research or evaluation regarding the cost-effectiveness or cost-benefit of therapies also is not CPPOA, but only "COA." ("CEA" is cost-effectiveness analysis, "CBA" is cost-benefit analysis.) If only the effects and costs of therapy are measured, and nothing that may occur between resources and outcomes is measured, we are implying that we cannot measure the intervening therapeutic activities. By focusing exclusively on cost and outcomes in research, one also calls into question whether there are any biological, cognitive, and behavioral processes that causally link resource expenditure and outcome attainment. Alternatively, perhaps it is believed that there is no use in measuring these linkages, because the same activities will be performed in therapy regardless of research findings.

What CPPOA Is

If, however, it is possible to measure the costs, therapist activities (procedures), biopsychosocial processes, and outcomes of therapies, and if the procedures of therapy can be modified substantially based on findings of the analyses, CPPOA can systematically improve the effectiveness or cost of therapy (or both). The following section summarizes advice for measuring each class of cost, procedure, process, and outcome variables; the next section describes some basic types of CPPOA and basic types of findings generated by CPPOA for therapy.

Advice for Measuring Costs, Procedures, Processes, and Outcomes

Measuring Costs: The Value of Resources Consumed

"Cost" can be defined in two notably distinct manners, as it is in the American Heritage Dictionary of the English Language:

1. "An amount paid or required in payment for a purchase; a price."
2. "The expenditure of something, such as time or labor, necessary for the attainment of a goal."

The first definition is what most researchers and policy makers understand "cost" to be. The monetary definition of cost allows critics to dismiss it as "only money," with the implication that it is something somehow degrading. The second definition is what is more useful when trying to understand relationships between resources consumed, procedures exacted, processes engendered, and outcomes produced. Certainly, cost is the value of resources used – time, space ... even "overhead." It is important to not let the negative associations that most of us have with "cost" distract us from the importance of measuring and understanding the types and amounts of resources that are needed to provide therapy, i.e., certain amounts of time of certain professionals, specific amounts of space in certain areas, insurance coverage, and much more.

Time. The time of therapists, supervisors, and support staff are very likely the most important and most expensive resources used in most therapies. In addition to managing their time, the value of that time needs to be determined. Usually, the value of that time can be calculated by multiplying local pay scales for persons with education and experience similar to the persons providing therapy, supervision, or support by the amount of time directly spent in therapy activities. In addition to this direct service, time spent by therapists in other activities (from supervision to staff meetings) needs to be measured and, the value of this indirect service calculated. Methods of monitoring staff time accurately and with minimum negative reactivity have been developed (cf. Yates, 1999). Finally, an analysis that seeks to understand why the value of time devoted by clients to receiving therapy – including "direct" time (in therapy sessions, for example, or doing "homework" readings or record-keeping related to therapy) and "indirect" time (getting to and from sessions, for example). The amount of time that clients are asked to spend in therapy and therapy-related activities may be a primary determinant of whether they persist in or drop out of therapy, which in turn may well determine whether therapy is or is not successful for them. Time required of third parties because of therapy, from employers of clients to members of clients' families and clients' friends, also could be important to both the success of therapy and the comprehensive measurement of what it takes to provide therapy.

Space. Office space typically is consumed at the rate of several hours per week of access to rooms that measure 8 feet by 10 feet or larger (including space used for therapy, for supervision, and for record-keeping). "Square-foot hours" can be measured, and multiplied by the cost of the lease per square foot-hour (which, itself, is the total lease cost divided by total square feet), to calculate the spatial cost of therapy (cf. Yates, Haven, & Thoresen, 1979). Virtual therapy may consume less space for sessions, as most communication is conducted via computer, but space is nevertheless consumed (for the computer as well as the therapeutic agent, and for supervisors and support personnel). If large expenditures are borne by the therapy provider for renovation, and are not captured in the lease cost, those costs should be distributed over the estimated lifetime of the renovation. (Otherwise, the cost of a therapy may be exaggerated.)

Equipment and materials. Computers used to communicate with clients need to be included in costs, of course. (Everything needs to be included in costs – at least everything that you would want to include in a replication of the therapy.) Telephones, copiers, office supplies, biofeedback apparatus ... all of those items need to be included, too. Monthly costs are calculated easiest from leases; the cost of equipment that is purchased needs to be spread out over the estimated lifetime of the equipment.

What about "overhead" expenses? "Overhead" can includes the time of a great many people, from administrators to janitors, as well as a high percentage of space in therapy office areas (e.g., hallways, staff lounges, closets, waiting rooms, administrator's offices) and sometimes a great deal of equipment, supplies, and other resources. Accountants, lawyers, security ... all are paid and need to be included. The cost of each of these needs to be distributed over individual clients (consumers). The fairest way to do this usually is to distribute overhead costs in proportion to the total of the costs that can be attributed directly to the client – usually the time spent by the therapist, and any office space and supplies devoted to therapy for that client.

What about furniture? Furniture such as desks, lamps, file cabinets, and chairs usually is best considered overhead, too. If inequities exist in the value of furniture in different therapists' offices, the value of their furniture can be distributed over the anticipated lifetime of that furniture and then over the time that different clients spend in the office receiving therapy.

What about volunteers? ...donated equipment and supplies? Resources that are donated, whether the time of volunteers or fruit or office materials, are used in therapy, so they should be included in any description of what it takes (and took!) to offer the therapy. Externs, unpaid interns, and undergraduates working at a clinic or hospital to get experience, all are volunteers whose time is valuable – and should be valued! The best way to value this volunteer time, and other donated resources, is according to what money would have to be spent to obtain similar resources if they were not available freely – this is sometimes called *replacement cost*. Another approach to measuring the cost of donated resources is figuring out what the next best use of that resource would be, e.g., what the extern could have done with that time to earn money. If the extern could have done computer programming, their donated time was quite valuable. If the extern was otherwise qualified only to sweep floors, their donated time might be somewhat less valuable. This is the *opportunity cost* of the donated resource. To avoid the appearance of penalizing programs for their use of donated resources, it can be helpful to note separately in reports the value of donated resources as opposed to those resourced purchased with money.

What about research expenses? Generally, research expenses should be excluded from cost estimations. Only if the research is a routine, integral part of the program, e.g., for periodic managerial decision-making or supervision, or for making regular reports to funding agencies, should it be included in costs. Research costs typically include the time of researchers, as well as time spent by administrators and staff in meetings and other activities related to research. Separating out these expenses can be challenging. If research costs are incurred as a method of recruiting externs and interns, who then use research data for theses and dissertations, those costs should be included as recruitment costs – and, possibly, subtracted from the estimated monetary value of the time donated by those externs and interns.

What about the time of clients and third parties? Clients may spend a great deal of time in therapy and in activities related to therapy, including getting to and from sites at which therapy is delivered. This time may have an opportunity cost, if the client otherwise could have been working or providing valued services, e.g., in child care. Third parties whose time is consumed in therapy-related activities, such as administering procedures or medications at home or on the job, also need to be included in cost assessment.

Additional advice. Avoid double-counting in cost assessment. If the office lease includes janitorial and security services, those services should not be costed separately and added to the lease. Also, avoid spending a great deal of time measuring trivial costs. Paperclips may be necessary, but probably do not need to be counted. Do not exclude resources that are important, however. Financial services, for example, may be essential to the therapy organization.

Psychological resources. Tolerance for change, and ability to withstand potentially stigmatizing actions, are resources that clients do not always bring to therapy but that may be key determinants of whether clients stay in therapy and succeed at it. The presence or absence of social skills and skills for self-control also may be important resources for therapy, along with social support networks. These resources may seem like the least monetizable of all, but they do have clear opportunity costs: if a resource such as a basic set of social skills for daily interactions with others is lacking, time may have to be spent instilling those skills before additional therapeutic work can commence. That time, for professionals who train clients in basic social skills, has considerable value that may well have to be paid for in dollars and cents. Other psychological resources, such as the capacity to cope with major life events, still can be measured and monetized. Some therapy may, in fact, have as its goal the teaching of these skills. For those therapies, what is a resource for other therapies is an outcome. Those therapies do, of course, themselves consume resources – the time of the skills trainer and of the client, at the very least.

Keeping down the cost of cost measurement. It is not too much to considering measuring and constraining the *cost of measuring costs*; in fact, it would be hypocritical not to! Unfortunately, accounting records rarely are sufficient or even adequate to quantify relationships between expenditures of specific resource and, eventually, attainment of specific outcomes via certain procedures and changes in some processes. Therapists can be asked to report the time they spend in different therapeutic activities with different clients, and may have incentives to do so well if they are reimbursed based on these reports. The same incentive system can produce exaggerated reports, unless other data are collected at least occasionally and compared to self-reports (cf. Yates, 1999). Client self-reports could provide possible corroboration, as could "passive systems," such as computer networks that remind therapists of client appointments, produce client records and therapist notes, and in the process collect data on occurrence and duration of therapy sessions.

Measuring Procedures

Paydays and hiring practices, as well as budgets and lease-signings, make it abundantly clear that there is a relationship between funding and the availability of resources. It is the hope of most therapy researchers, as well as the belief of most therapists, many clients, and at least some funders, that there also is a relationship between what the therapist does in sessions and the outcomes of therapy. "What the therapist does" may, for some, mean the changes that the therapist (hopefully) produces inside the client, such as an awareness of problematic behavior, for example, or the instillation of new insights, certain skills or repertoires, or increased self-efficacy expectancies about the performance of specific routines. Those, however, are (ideally) the results of the only things the therapist directly controls: the observable acts that the therapist performs during the sessions, including what the therapist says as well as nonverbal behavior. Those observable, and hopefully therapeutic, activities are procedures, and are distinct from the changes they are designed to produce within clients (which we will call processes).

Basic procedure measurement issues, such as who reports the occurrence, and other characteristics, of which procedures, how and how often, are covered in a variety of texts (e.g., Kazdin, 1998), and are commonly taught in graduate courses and are learned experientially in graduate research. There are several distinctions between different types of procedures, and between procedures and other components of the Cost → Procedure → Process → Outcome Analysis model, that can be drawn with potential benefit to the evaluation enterprise.

Procedures versus processes. It is common in evaluation research to term as "processes" whatever occurs between the investment of resources in a social change effort and the outcomes of that effort. However, psychological training and findings suggest that the distinction between what one does as a therapist to produce change in clients, and what changes actually occur in clients, may be an important one. This distinction often is ignored until, as described in an example detailed later in this chapter, commonly accepted practices lead to outcomes that are not what one intended. Then, attempts to explain what went wrong typically inspire a closer look at what goes on between the implementation of "standard accepted practices" and the occurrence of unwanted outcomes.

Meta-procedures. Procedures can be measured at different levels of specificity. The extent to which a type of therapy is implemented, as well as its simple occurrence or nonoccurrence, can be called meta-procedures. These can be measured both as nominal values (occurred or did not occur) as well as continuous values (degree of occurrence, analogous to "dose"). In addition to the amount of therapy provided, the fidelity of that therapy in terms of adherence to specified activities or theory also could be assessed. Treatment also might be separated into two types of meta-procedures: intervention and maintenance. Prevention could be viewed as yet another meta-procedure.

At a more specific level, the duration of individual sessions could be measured. Fidelity could be measured for each session separately, too, perhaps as the percent of activities covered in a session that were listed in a manual or specified by a supervisor. These activities could be weighted for importance to form more global indices for the dose or fidelity of treatment procedures.

Extra-program procedures. Although the measurement of the occurrence of specific therapy procedures and of regimen adherence seems straightforward enough, the comprehensive approach to program operationalization that often accompanies CPPOA reminds one that the therapist is not the only agent of change in the client's environment. Spouses and ex-spouses, employers and ex-employers, colleagues in licit and illicit operations, and many other people may be attempting to engage the client in any number of procedures that are hoped to be therapeutic – or at least are hoped to accomplish specific goals held by that third party alone. These extra-program activities, as they might well be called, can amplify, diminish, nullify, or even reverse the intended outcomes of procedures enacted by the therapist; they, arguably, should be measured. While it probably is impossible to measure all extra-program activities, it seems possible to hypothesize and measure a few extra-program procedures that might interact positively or negatively with the therapy program.

Potentially cost-saving and effectiveness-retaining procedures. There are, of course, therapy procedures that one really hopes will occur: things you can say or do that make a client so much better, and that take no more time or effort than other procedures that would have been so much less positively impactful. Perhaps it is an entirely different procedure than the standard accepted practice, as behavioral therapy was in the era dominated by dynamic therapy. Perhaps it is less, or more, of a procedure already in practice, e.g., briefer-term therapy, or outpatient rather than inpatient therapy. Possibly there is an augmentation of therapy, by involving consumer-operated services along with traditional services, or a continuation of therapy beyond the usual period, as in the "booster sessions" proposed by Kiesler and Morton (1988). Or, perhaps the new procedure whose costs, outcomes, and effects on processes are being examined could be more politically acceptable, e.g., education about risky behavior.

Whatever the alternative procedures being examined, some variation of clinical research design (cf. Kazdin, 1998) should be implemented to rule out as many alternative explanations of the findings as possible. Ideally, procedure measurement is integrated with a plan for procedure implementation so that statistical analyses can show beyond a reasonable doubt which procedures are responsible for which changes in which processes (and outcomes), using which resources of what value (i.e., at what cost).

Measuring Processes

Processes are internal to the client. They are the inside-the-skin biological, psychological, and social processes that are supposed to be affected by therapy procedures. Examples of processes targeted by some forms of therapy include specific self-efficacy expectancies, and formulation and adaptation of self-management plans for a limited range of situations. Other examples of processes are reduced depression, anxiety, or hostility, increased readiness to change stage (à la Prochaska, DiClemente, & Norcross, 1992), movement to a new stage of readiness to change, improved social support systems, and more accurate self-efficacy expectancies regarding treatment effects and relapse prevention.

These and other biopsychosocial processes may or may not occur in program settings. Possibly as the result of what was said and done in therapy, processes may be created or enhanced later, after the sessions, in the community or home or work environments. Also as a possible result of the execution of therapy procedures, processes may be diminished or eliminated later in community, home, or employment environments.

The measurement of biopsychosocial processes has been the focus of most measurement efforts in the past century of psychology. A variety of measures for many internal states, from depression to anxiety to self-monitoring, is available. Issues of reliability and validity (and cost) of these measures have been the focus of intense research for much of this time. It is outcomes that have had far less attention paid to them, and which typically are measured by methods developed on an ad-hoc basis by researchers.

Measuring Outcomes

Outcomes that matter to funders. The behavioral revolution in the later half of the twentieth century focused attention on some outcomes of therapy, and fostered the development of strategies for measuring the outcomes of diverse therapies with reliability and validity (cf. Bandura, 1969, 1977; Mischel, 1968). The cognitive-behavioral revolution of the later quarter of the twentieth century revisited internal processes, and made the hypothesizing, measuring, and testing of them again legitimate in the eyes of many researchers (as noted in the preceding *Processes* section; cf. Mahoney, 1974). What psychotherapy researchers are still coming to terms with, however, is the need to measure outcomes that are esteemed not only by the consumers of therapy, but by the funders of therapy: the "real world" outcome variables of responsible health behavior, responsible sexual behavior, taking responsibility for child care, gainful employment and income, minimal interaction with criminal justice services and use of social services, and appropriate use of health services. In the era of third-party payment for health and mental health services, whether the payments come from government or private sources, funders fund therapy in the hopes that one or more of these variables will change, and in ways that increase revenues or decrease expenditures or both (Yates, 1994).

Outcomes can be conceptualized as the "pay-off" of processes, and less directly of the procedures that made those processes possible, and even less directly of the resources that made it possible to perform those procedures. Outcomes are not what traditional psychotherapy researchers measured. Most psychologists continue to be more interested in changing internal states, such as depression or anxiety. If the externally observable behavior that should change as a result of alleviated depression does change, that's the way it should be. If the behavior does not change, despite the change in depression, then the attitude too often is that "it can't be helped." I have heard very noteworthy therapists state that they should be held responsible only for the implementation of standard and accepted practices (i.e., procedures); if the processes that were supposed to change did not, the therapist was not responsible. And, certainly, if the desired outcomes were not achieved, that was even more removed from the therapist's realm of responsibility.

Now the responsibility of therapists and the goals of therapy have been extended to the realm of income enhancement and cost-savings. In terms of the CPPOA model, outcomes are observable events or acts. A distinction can be drawn between short-term or *proximal* outcomes, such as increased drug-free days and decreased visits to the doctor's office, and longer-term or more *distal* outcomes such as enhancement of productivity and of licit income through gainful employment and ethical enterprise and the decrement of public and private expenditures for health care services. There can, of course, be effects beyond these; at some point the therapy researcher determines that attempts to measure even more distal outcomes should cease because the uncertainty of whether therapy contributed to the occurrence of an outcome is sufficiently high, or that the cost of measuring more removed outcomes is sufficiently prohibitive, or both.

The trick in measuring outcomes well is to find those immediately (and inexpensively) observable behaviors and events that are reliable, valid predictors of more delayed but more important behaviors and events. Measuring drug-free days may predict improvements in future employment, decreased use of criminal justice services, and eventually decreased use of social and health care services. The key here is to have good research already done that supports these assumptions (e.g., Ball & Ross, 1991; Manning, Keeler, Newhouse, Sloss, & Wasserman, 1991). Some changes in behavior (e.g., self-reports of reduced HIV-risky behaviors, reduced use of drugs) can even be verified by biological or chemical measures (e.g., HIV or proxy STD infection tests, urinalyses for drug metabolites).

Calculating the monetary value of these outcomes is challenging, but certainly can be done – and is estimated, subjectively at least, in the minds of policy makers on a rather routine if imperfect basis. Adding the objectivity of solid research and reasoned estimation will likely help reduce the perpetuation of biases by overly subjective estimation of the monetary value of therapy outcomes. Gold, Siegel, Russell, and Weinstein (1996), provide guidelines, and Manning et al. (1991) detail methods, for making these monetary estimations. In some cases, behaviors or events can be monetized by simply multiplying the behavior or event by a fixed rate of cost. For example, the monetary value of not using drugs for a day has been estimated (Ball & Ross, 1991) and can be multiplied by the number of drug free days produced by a therapy for a client, to approximate one of the possible benefits of therapy for substance-abusing clients. In other instances, projected lifetime earnings can be used (e.g., Yates, 1986; cf. Nas, 1996; Thompson, 1980). In other cases, the actual monies generated and saved can be measured for a representative period, and extrapolated. More delayed benefits need to be discounted (as do more delayed expenditures of resources) using one of several available formulae (cf. Yates, 1996).

The Place of "Demographic Variables" in CPPOA

A major set of variables that commonly are investigated in psychotherapy research, and were missing from initial formulations of CPPOA, are gender, socioeconomic status, ethnicity, and other "demographic" variables. These could be used to decide who would benefit most from different forms or administrations of therapy, a possibility which could recommend to some that these variables *not* be investigated, to avoid possible denial of entitlements to persons of a particular gender, socioeconomic status, ethnicity, and so on. These sorts of variables are included in CPPOA as *interaction terms* with one or more of the sets of variables in CPPOA.

The effects of gender, for example, might be evidenced as one or more of the following:

1. the availability of certain amounts of certain *resources* for one gender but not the other, or
2. the performance of certain *procedures* for one gender but less for another, *or*
3. the greater (or opposite) effects of a procedure on a biopsychosocial *process* for one gender, or
4. the increased production of certain *outcomes* more for one gender than the other.

Although the interaction of demographic variables and *processes* probably is a natural process, the interaction of demographic variables and resources, procedures, or outcomes could be evidence of discrimination.

Methods for Analyzing Relationships between Costs, Procedures, Processes, and Outcomes

The following are very brief reviews of topics detailed in a variety of sources, including Gold et al. (1996), Levin and McEwan (2001), and Yates (1980a, 1996).

Cost Rates

"Cost per client" is, at first glance, a valuable measure of cost ... cost *what?* There is no measure of outcome in "cost per client;" it is only one side of the cost → ... → outcome equation. Nevertheless, program managers find it useful to know the cost per client or, more often, the amount they are reimbursed for a client "slot." That single figure can determine much of their budget. For the present purposes, the most important thing to note is that cost per client provides no information about the relationship between cost and outcome – unless, again, outcomes either can be assumed to be fixed, or cannot be measured or are not important.

Differences and Ratios

The simplest comparison of costs and outcomes is the simple difference between costs and benefits. Costs (monetary units) are subtracted from benefits (outcomes measured in monetary units), and if the difference is positive, the relationship is positive. The size of the difference between costs and benefits can be calculated for alternative procedures, but the number of clients who participate in the alternative procedures need to be very similar. If not, higher benefit-cost differences could simply be caused by more clients. Calculation of average net benefit per client is rarer but more useful. When therapy is continued over long periods of time, i.e., several years, the more delayed costs and benefits are discounted prior to benefit-cost calculations. A related comparison of benefits to costs is the amount of time that it took for benefits to exceed costs (sometimes called "time to return on investment").

Comparing benefits to costs by division rather than subtraction seems inherently more sophisticated, but introduces assumptions that often are untenable. It seems logical, for example, that all procedures that produced benefits that exceed costs should be implemented; that, however, is tenable only if one has an unlimited budget. Dividing benefits by costs, and then comparing the benefit/cost ratios for different therapeutic procedures, suggests that the best procedure can be chosen by simply finding the highest benefit-to-cost ratio. The ratios encourage one to assume, however, that the more funds that are spent on a procedure, the more benefit one will attain. That rarely is the case; more often, diminishing returns result, and the benefit-to-cost ratio declines as the duration of treatment (or, possibly, the number of people treated) increases (cf. Yates, 1996, 1999). The same problems apply to ratios of effectiveness divided by cost (e.g., drug free days produced per $1,000 investment) or cost by effectiveness (e.g., cost of procedure per drug free day produced by that procedure).

These differences or ratios can be calculated per client, although they often are calculated for the program as a whole by summing benefits, summing costs, and then subtracting total costs from total benefits. Individual variation is better captured by calculating benefit-to-cost ratios or differences for each client, and then calculating averages for clients.

Ratios, and differences, can be useful first approximations to descriptions of relationships between costs and outcomes for different procedures, but they involve hidden assumptions that can be unwarranted and, in any case, do not include information on biopsychosocial processes at all.

Graphing

The manner in which outcomes may vary as a function of costs can be examined more closely, and possibly with more accuracy, by graphing outcomes against costs (with outcomes on the vertical axis and costs on the horizontal axis; cf. Siegert & Yates, 1980). Cumulative outcomes can be graphed against cumulative costs for individual clients, and averages can be calculated and graphed as well. Cumulative cost-outcome graphs can be compared for different procedures, and for different resources, to allow a variety of possible insights into how different types of resources, procedures, and processes can moderate cost →outcome relationships (cf. Siegert & Yates, 1980; Yates, 1999).

Matrix Analyses

As detailed in Yates, Delany, and Dillard (2001), relationships between each consecutive pairing of variables in Cost →Procedure →Process →Outcome Analysis can be investigated pair-by-pair using matrices. For example, different types of resources can be listed in rows, and different procedures in columns, as shown in the upper portion of Figure 1. The amount of each resource consumed to implement each procedure can be entered in the cells of the Resource →Procedure matrix for each client, and averaged for all client to describe the typical Resource →Procedure relationship. The monetary value of resources spent can be totaled for total cost, of course. Similar matrices can be formed for each remaining step, i.e., Procedure → Process and Process → Outcome matrices. Examples of these are provided, without cell entries, in the remainder of Figure 1 (cf. Yates et al., 2001).

Path Analyses, Structural Equation Modeling

As detailed in Yates (1980a, 1996), relationships between different types of resources, various procedures, numerous possible processes, and probably outcomes, can be depicted most completely in a network diagram that shows the

Process Outcome		Outcomes		
		Drug Use	Employment	Services Use
Processes	Addiction	↗	↗	↗
	Consequation Expectancies	↗	↗	↗
	Social Support	↗	↗	↗

Resource Procedure		Procedures		
		Therapy	Drugs	Self-Help
Resources	Personnel	↗	↗	↗
	Facilities	↗	↗	↗
	Equipment, Supplies	↗	↗	↗

Procedure Process		Processes		
		Addiction	Consequation Expectancies	Social Support
Procedures	Therapy	↗	↗	↗
	Drugs	↗	↗	↗
	Self-Help	↗	↗	↗

Figure 1. Matrices for Cost → Procedure → Process → Outcome Analysis.

significant paths of causality that therapy forges between these variables. If the sample size studied is sufficiently large, path analysis and structural equation modeling can be used to find the most substantial, common, statistically significant paths from resources through procedures and processes to outcomes. Smaller samples encourage use of more finite and focused statistical analyses. Kissel and Yates (in progress) and Ansari and Yates (in progress) used a series of multiple regressions to find which relationships were the most common to clients.

The resource, procedure, process, and outcome variables investigated by Kissel and Yates are listed in Figure 2. An initial round of simple multiple regressions treated each outcome variable in turn as the dependent variable, with each process variable being a possible independent variable. In the next round of multiple regressions, those process variables that were found to be significantly associated with one or more outcome variables were treated individually as dependent variables, and the procedure variables serviced as independent variables. Finally, the average amount of each type of resource used to enact each procedure was calculated per client. The result of these analyses by Kissel and Yates is detailed below.

Participant Characteristics	Resources	Procedures	Processes	Outcomes

• Risk
• Gender
• Age
• Race
	• Prevention Specialists
	• Project Director
	• Evaluation
	• Clerical
	• Travel
	• Supplies
	• Other
		• Student Small Group Meetings
		• Individual Student Meetings
		• Field Trips
		• Camping Trips
		• Home Visits
		  Mother
		  Father
		Parent Groups
		  Mother
		  Father
			Family Bonding
			• Communication with *Mother*
			• Communication with *Father*
			• *Parent-child* communication
			School Bonding
			• Feelings about School Climate
			Societal Bonding
			• Social Responsibility
				Willingness to Use Gateway ATODs
				• Tobacco cigarettes
				• Chewing tobacco
				• Beer, Wine or Wine coolers
				• Liquor
				• Marijuana
				Willingness, Use of All ATODs *Add to above:*
				• Cocaine or crack
				• "Serotin" (bogus)

Figure 2. Resource, Procedure, Process, and Outcome Variables investigated by Kissel and Yates (in progress).

Operations Research, Linear Programming

A final type of CPPOA is the use of all the information collected on costs, procedures, processes, and outcomes, along with data on budget constraints for each resource, to decide which procedures to implement to maximize the effectiveness or benefit possible with a particular set of resources. These *linear programming* analyses are described with hypothetical examples in Yates (1980a, 1980b, 1998). Other forms of linear programming can be used to decide, systematically, how to minimize the costs of achieving particular types and levels of outcomes (cf. Yates, 1980a).

Some Relationships Found Between
Costs, Procedures, Processes, and Outcomes

The most common findings anticipated in cost-outcome analyses are that you get what you pay for, and that more therapy produced better outcomes. Indeed, careful psychotherapy outcomes research (e.g., Howard, Kopta, Krause, & Orlinksky, 1986; Newman & Howard, 1986) shows that, generally, there is a positive dose-response relationship between number of sessions of psychotherapy and outcomes of psychotherapy, with diminishing returns after a number of sessions. These are not, unfortunately, the present author's most common findings (cf. Yates, 1994).

Outcomes Can Be a Function of Procedure, Not Cost

Bandura, Blanchard, and Ritter (1969) found that the most effective treatment for snake phobia was not the most expensive, i.e., most time-consuming. Participant modeling, which took an average of about 2.25 hours of client and therapist time in direct service, was 90% effective in helping clients achieve the "terminal" behavior in a snake approach repertoire: keeping one's hands at one's sides while a three-foot snake (nonpoisonous) rested in one's lap. The standard procedure of systematic desensitization required an average of almost twice that much client and therapist time to execute, and was only 25% effective. (For a more complete CPPOA of the Bandura et al. findings, see Yates, 1995).

Outcomes Can Be a Negative Function of Procedure, and Cost

Kissel and Yates (in progress) found that a comprehensive program for preventing substance abuse in fourth grade girls and boys actually *increased* subsequent reports of willing to use gateway drugs, and actual use of some of these drugs. Because Kissel and Yates conducted a Cost → Procedure → Process → Outcome Analysis, however, they could say with reasonable confidence (a) which procedures were responsible for these iatrogenic outcomes, (b) which clients were most harmed by the procedures, which led to ready suggestions on how to modify the program to reduce or eliminate its iatrogenic effects.

The CPPOA path diagram describing the findings of iterative multiple regressions (performed as described earlier in this manuscript) is shown in Figure 3. Willingness to use both gateway drugs and alcohol, tobacco, and other drugs (ATODs), and even actual use of ATODs, were significantly, and negatively, related to the process variable of Social Responsibility. Other process variables that had been hypothesized as related to drug use and willingness to use drugs, including communication with parents and feelings about school, were neither positively nor negatively related to drug use and willingness to use drugs (see Figure 3).

The negative relationship between Social Responsibility and drug use was as predicted (more Social Responsibility was associated with less drug use and less willingness to use drugs). What was not predicted and not desired was the negative relationship found between prevention program procedures and Social Responsibility. A series of multiple regressions showed that the more the boy or girl participated in the program, the *less* their Social Responsibility, and the more their drug use and willingness to use drugs. The program seemed to decrease Social Responsibility especially well for girls (an interaction between procedure, process, and demographic variables, of the sort alluded to earlier). Fortunately, more procedure-specific analyses showed that one particular procedure, i.e., student groups, was the only procedure that was significantly associated with lowered Social Responsibility and increased drug use and willingness. Retrospective consideration of this

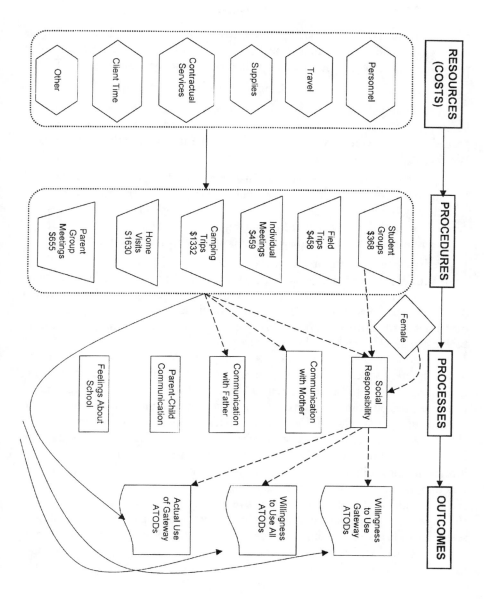

Figure 3. Cost →Procedure →Process →Outcome Analysis network produced by iterative multiple regressions (Kissel & Yates, in progress).

component suggested that placing students who were at some risk of using drugs together in small groups might actually not have been a procedure with a high probability of decreasing subsequent willingness to use, or actual use of, ATODs.

Conclusion

Almost all psychotherapy research to date is not CPPOA, but only a partial, incomplete version of it. Often processes are measured, such as depression, and procedures may be measured if only to check on the adequacy of the manipulation. We can, and must, go further. We need to

"... integrate research on basic mechanisms underlying the disorder with applied research. At first glance, such research may seem irrelevant to therapy outcome, but ... basic research may provide clues as to what is potentially inhibiting change from taking place, which may, in turn, suggest techniques that can provide a greater cost-benefit" (Newman, 2000).

Perhaps the most important and yet most neglected area in which we need to work is education – of ourselves and of our students in the sorts of analyses described in this chapter. We have training and experience in measuring outcomes, although not usually cost-related ones. We have little experience transforming nonmonetary outcomes into monetary units. Some of us are especially willing to measure biological, psychological, and social processes occurring with the client, and some of us are good at this. Some of us know the importance of measuring the degree to which different specific procedures are implemented in different therapies. Some of us have training, and experience, in analyzing relationships between procedures, processes, and outcomes, which can translate readily into the CPPOA once we add the measure of the value of diverse and specific resources used in therapy.

What remains absent in most of our curricula for graduate and post-graduate training as well as continuing education is an awareness of the importance of integrating these different measures and research skills for our profession. It is very much in our interest to teach our students (and ourselves) to measure, understand the determinants of, and attempt to improve costs, and cost-related outcomes. Given the importance of costs and cost-related outcomes to policy and funding, we should seek education about costs and related outcomes with at least the same enthusiasm and determination that accompanies our efforts to teach our students to measure, understand the determinants of, and systematically improve traditional outcomes.

References

Ansari, G., & Yates, B. T. (in progress). *A program for mothers' of children with emotional or behavioral disorders: an evaluation of cost, procedure, process, and outcome relationships*. Thesis proposal submitted to the Department of Psychology, American University, 4400 Massachusetts Ave., N.W., Washington, DC 20016-8062.

Ball, J. C., & Ross, A. (1991). *The effectiveness of methadone maintenance treatment: Patients, programs, services, and outcome*. New York: Spring-Verlag.

Bandura, A. (1969). *Principles of behavior modification*. New York: Holt, Rinehart and Winston.

Bandura, A. (1977). *Social learning theory*. Englewood Cliffs, NJ: Prentice-Hall.

Bandura, A., Blachard, E. B., & Ritter, B. (1969). Relative efficacy of desensitization and modeling approaches for inducing behavioral, affective, and attitudinal changes. *Journal of Personality and Social Psychology, 13*, 173-199.

Book, H. E. (1991). Is empathy cost efficient? *American Journal of Psychotherapy, 45*, 21-30.

Center for Substance Abuse Treatment (CSAT). (1999). *The costs and benefits of substance abuse treatment: Findings from the National Treatment Improvement Evaluation Study (NTIES)*. National Evaluation Data Services (NEDS): http://neds.calib.com/products/pdfs/cost-ben.pdf.

Cummings, N. A. (1977). Prolonged (ideal) versus short-term (realistic) psychotherapy. *Professional Psychology: Research and Pratice, 8*, 491-501.

Cummings, N. A., & Follette, W. T. (1968). Psychiatric services and medical utilization in a prepaid health plan setting. *Medical Care, 5*, 31-41.

Ettner, S. L., Frank, R. G., & Kessler, R. C. (1997). The impact of psychiatric disorders on labor market outcomes. *Industrial and Labor Relations Review, 5*, 64-81.

Finigan, M. (1996). Societal outcomes and cost savings of drug and alcohol treatment in the state of Oregon. *Report to the Office of Alcohol and Drug Abuse Programs, Oregon Department of Human Resources and the Governor's Council on Alcohol and Drug Abuse Programs.*

Gold, M. R., Siegel, J. E., Russell, L. B., & Weinstein, M. C. (Eds.) (1996). *Cost-effectiveness in health and medicine*. New York: Oxford University Press.

Howard, K. I., Koptas, S. M., Krause, M. S., & Orlinsky, D. E. (1986). The dose-response relationship in psychotherapy. *American Psychologist, 41*, 159-164.

Hubbard, R. L., & French, M. T. (1991). New perspectives on the benefit-cost and cost-effectiveness of drug abuse treatment. In W. S. Cartwright & J. M. Kaple (Eds.), *Economic costs, cost-effectiveness, financing, and community-based drug treatment* (pp. 94-113). Research monograph 113, DHHS Publication No. (ADM)91-1823. Rockville, MD: National Institute on Drug Abuse.

Jones, K. R., & Vischi, T. R. (1979). Impact of alcohol, drug abuse, and mental health treatment on medical care utilization: A review of the research literature. *Medical Care, 17* (Supplement), 1-82.

Kazdin, A. E. (1998). *Research design in clinical psychology (third edition)*. Boston: Allyn and Bacon.

Kiesler, C. A., & Morton, T. L. (1988). Psychology and public policy in the "health care revolution." *American Psychologist, 43*, 993-1003.

Kissel, A. V., & Yates, B. T. (in progress). *Effectiveness and costs of school-based drug abuse prevention for preadolescents: a multi-year trial yields unexpected results.* Thesis accepted by the Department of Psychology, American University, 4400 Massachusetts Ave., N.W., Washington, DC 20016-8062.

Levin, H. M., & McEwan, P. J. (2001). *Cost-effectiveness analysis (second ed.)*. Thousand Oaks, CA: Sage.

Linden, W., & Wen, F. K. (1990). Therapy outcome research, health care policy, and the continuing lack of accumulated knowledge. *Professional Psychology: Research and Practice, 21,* 482-488.

Mahoney, M. J. (1974). *Cognitive and behavior modification.* Cambridge, MA: Ballinger.

Manning, W. G., Keeler, E. B., Newhouse, J. P., Sloss, E. M., & Wasserman, J. (1991). *The costs of poor health habits.* Cambridge, MA: Harvard University Press.

Marcott, D. E., & Wilcox-Gök, V. (2001). Estimating the employment and earnings costs of mental illness: Recent developments in the United States. *Social Science & Medicine, 53,* 21-27.

Mischel, W. (1968). *Personality and assessment.* New York: Wiley.

Murray, C. J. L., & Lopez, A. D. (Eds.). (1996). *The global burden of disease. A comprehensive assessment of mortality and disability from diseases, injuries, and risk factors in 1990 and projected to 2020.* Cambridge, MA: Harvard School of Public Health. Nas, T. F. (1996). *Cost-benefit analysis: Theory and application.* Thousand Oaks, CA: Sage.

Newman, M. G. (2000). Recommendations for a cost-offset model of psychotherapy allocation using generalized anxiety disorder as an example. *Journal of Consulting and Clinical Psychology, 68,* 549-555.

Newman, F. L., & Howard, K. I. (1986). Therapeutic effort, treatment outcome, and national health policy. *American Psychologist, 41,* 181-187.

Prochaska, J. O., DiClemente, C. C., & Norcross, J. C. (1992). In search of how people change: Applications to addictive behaviors. *American Psychologist, 47,* 1102-1114.

Siegert, F. A., & Yates, B. T. (1980). Cost-effectiveness of individual in-office, individual in-home, and group delivery systems for behavioral child-management. *Evaluation and the Health Professions, 3,* 123-152.

Smith, M. L., Glass, G. V., & Miller, T. I. (1980). *The benefits of psychotherapy.* Baltimore: Johns Hopkins University Press.

Thompson, M. S. (1980). *Benefit-cost analysis for program evaluation.* Beverly Hills, CA: Sage.

Yates, B. T. (1980a). *Improving effectiveness and reducing costs in mental health.* Springfield, IL: Thomas.

Yates, B. T. (1980b). The theory and practice of cost-utility, cost-effectiveness, and cost-benefit analysis in behavioral medicine: Toward delivering more health care for less money. In J. Ferguson & C. B. Taylor (Eds.), *The comprehensive handbook of behavioral medicine* (Vol. 3) (pp. 165-205). New York: SP Medical & Scientific.

Yates, B. T. (1984). How psychology can improve the effectiveness and reduce the costs of health services. *Psychotherapy, 21,* 439-451.

Yates, B. T. (1986). Economics of suicide: Toward cost-effectiveness and cost-benefit analysis of suicide prevention. In R. Cross (Ed.), *Non-natural death: Coming to terms with suicide, euthanasia, withholding or withdrawing treatment.* Denver, CO: Rose Medical Center.

Yates, B. T. (1994). Toward the incorporation of costs, cost-effectiveness analysis, and cost-benefit analysis into clinical research. *Journal of Consulting and Clinical Psychology, 62,*729-736.

Yates, B. T. (1995). Cost-effectiveness analysis, cost-benefit analysis, and beyond: Evolving models for the scientist-manager-practitioner. *Clinical Psychology: Science and Practice, 2,* 385-398.

Yates, B. T. (1996). *Analyzing costs, procedures, processes, and outcomes in human services: An introduction.* Thousand Oaks, CA: Sage.

Yates, B. T. (1998). Formative evaluation of costs, cost-effectiveness, and cost-benefit: Toward cost →procedure →process →outcome analysis. In L. Bickman & D. Rog (Eds.), *Handbook of applied social research methods* (pp. 285-314). Thousand Oaks, CA: Sage.

Yates, B. T. (1999). *Measuring and improving cost, cost-effectiveness, and cost-benefit for substance abuse treatment programs: A manual.* Bethesda, MD: National Institute on Drug Abuse. NIH Publication No. 99-4518. Also available at the NIDA Internet site: http://165.112.78.61/IMPCOST/IMPCOSTIndex.html.

Yates, B. T. (in progress). *Resistances to measuring, analyzing, and understanding costs in mental health services research: Why cost(s), why now, and why me?* American University, Washington, DC: Manuscript in preparation, Fall 2001.

Yates, B. T., Delany, P. J., & Dillard, D. L. (2001). Using cost →procedure →process →outcome analysis to improve social work practice. In B. A. Thyer (Ed.), *Handbook of social work research* (pp. 207-238). Thousand Oaks, CA: Sage.

Yates, B. T., Haven, W. G., & Thoresen, C. E. (1979). Cost-effectiveness analysis at Learning House: How much change for how much money? In J. S. Stumphauzer (Ed.), *Progress in behavior therapy with delinquents* (pp. 186-222). Springfield, IL: Thomas.

Measuring Medical Cost

Jeanne Wendel
University of Nevada, Reno

If psychological interventions lead to improved management of chronic diseases, the cost of the psychological care may be offset by reductions in medical care costs. Accurate measurement of these medical cost savings will require careful planning. Eight planning issues are discussed here.

What Do You Want to Measure?

Specifying the appropriate measure requires thoughtful analysis of several issues. There are no global answers to these questions – each issue must be addressed in the context of the specific goals of individual studies.

First, whose costs will be measured? If the psychological intervention is conducted within a managed care organization, will the study focus solely on costs incurred by that organization? If the intervention impacts costs incurred by patients (for home care) or employers (due to the amount of missed work), are these costs relevant to the study?

Second how do these costs relate to incentive structures? If the managed care organization enjoys cost savings as a result of the psychological intervention, will the psychologist's physician-colleagues share some of the benefit? Alternately, will the physicians be impacted negatively by reduced demand for their services as psychological services substitute for physician services? Answering this question will depend on analysis of the organization's compensation system and physician contracts. Whether analysis of these impacts should be included in the medical cost offset study depends on the study's purpose.

Third, does "cost" fully capture the impact of the intervention on the managed care company? Firms do not generally minimize total cost; they maximize profit, which is equal to the difference between revenue and cost. The intervention's impact on revenue is just as important as the impact on cost. Interventions that impact patient satisfaction, for example, may impact revenue by affecting enrollee turnover or employer willingness to contract with the organization. Some large employers and employer-purchasing coalitions conduct regular surveys to assess patient satisfaction with managed care organizations and providers. It might be useful, therefore, to document the impact of the intervention on patient satisfaction.

It is also important, in this early planning stage, to consider whether the intervention will impact measures of patient health. A cost-saving intervention that improves, or does not impact, health is quite different from a cost-saving innovation that is associated with negative health impacts.

Will You Focus on Intermediate Process Variables or Final Health Outcome Measures?

The next question that must be addressed is whether the targeted impacts will be measured directly or indirectly. Consider, for example, a program aimed at increasing compliance with a medical instruction. Assume, for example, that studies reported in the medical literature show that compliance with this instruction significantly reduces adverse health outcomes. Assume further that the medical literature provides estimates of the cost reduction associated with reduced incidence of the adverse outcomes. Will you measure compliance with the medical instruction, and rely on evidence from the medical literature to estimate the associated cost reduction, or will you measure the actual cost savings in your organization? Both approaches have advantages and disadvantages. Directly measuring actual cost savings offers the advantage of explicit consideration of costs relevant to your organization. The disadvantage of this approach lies in the sample size questions. If the adverse health outcomes occur infrequently (but with very high cost per occurrence), a large sample may be required to obtain a statistically significant result. If the required sample size is large relative to the annual number of patients, the data collection period may be unreasonably long.

In deciding how to specify the outcome measures, it may be useful to step back from this issue, and consider the level at which your planned intervention addresses an identified problem. Consider, for example, a business process intervention designed to reduce waiting time in a busy emergency room. A level 1 solution to the waiting time problem would accept the basic structure and functioning of the emergency room as given. The intervention might focus on streamlining the clerical tasks to speed up the process of preparing new patient charts. A level 2 solution to the waiting time problem would accept the basic mission of the emergency room as given, but might attempt to restructure the patient triage system. Perhaps non-emergent patients could be identified upon entry to the waiting room and shifted to an adjacent clinic for treatment. This solution would not alter the numbers of emergent and non-emergent patients, but would separate them for treatment in facilities appropriate to each type of patient. A level 3 solution to the waiting time problem might work to narrow the emergency room's mission to focus on patients requiring emergency care. The problem-solving team might accomplish this by working to create an alternate source of care for uninsured non-emergent patients.

If the problem targeted by this intervention is the length of time emergent patients wait for treatment, the direct measure of patient wait time is clearly applicable for assessing the level 3 solution. It may be too global, however, for assessing a level 1 solution. Because new patient chart preparation represents only one potential cause of emergency room waits, it might be better to measure the impacts of these improvements by focusing specifically on chart-production time.

How Will You Measure Your Target Variable?

An appropriate statistic must be specified to measure the target variable. Two initial questions are relevant here. Is the data qualitative or quantitative? Is the intervention designed to change the "typical" outcome or to reduce the variability of outcomes? The average is generally used to measure impacts on the data's central tendency for quantitative data, while proportion measures these impacts for qualitative data. The average may not be a sound measure, however, if the data is bimodal, is highly skewed, or includes outlier observations.

If the intervention in designed to decrease variability within the data, the study might focus on standard deviation or the proportion of observations that lie within an acceptable range.

If the data includes outlier observations, careful consideration must be given to the treatment of these observations. Do they appear as outliers in this dataset because they really do not belong in this data set (perhaps because these patients have significant comorbidities)? If so, they should be excluded from the study. Alternately, outlier observations may present data on patients who do not violate any of the criteria for inclusion in the study. Complete exclusion of these data points from the study might not be wise, because these data points extend the range of variation available for study. They may present valuable opportunities to analyze the causes of variability within the data.

Are You Committed to the Use of Statistical Significance as a Decision Criterion?

This may seem like an odd question. Requiring statistical significance before drawing a conclusion is standard operating procedure for scientific investigations. This decision criterion is receiving increased emphasis as organizations implement total quality management principles that focus data-driven decision making based on statistically rigorous data analysis. In addition, courts are responding to recent Supreme Court decisions that emphasize judicial responsibility to ensure that expert testimony is based on scientifically sound analysis. Commitment to this decision criterion requires consideration of two issues.

First, it might be worthwhile to consider the position taken by some plaintiff attorneys, who argue against reliance on the standard of statistical significance at the traditional .01, .05 or .10 levels. They argue that this standard focuses exclusively on the Type I error of potentially rejecting a null hypothesis that is true. This approach ignores the Type II error of potentially accepting a null hypothesis that is false. These plaintiff attorneys focus on situations such as health impacts of chemical exposure. The null hypothesis in such a situation may be that a specific chemical exposure did not cause the observed health impacts. Rejection of this null hypothesis would result in compensation to the plaintiffs; failure to reject the null hypothesis would impose no penalty on the defendants. The plaintiff attorneys who argue for relaxed significance criteria emphasize the potential for large values of b, the probability of accepting a null hypothesis when it is false. In the context of this example, b is the probability of failing to compensate victims when the chemical exposure actually did cause their adverse health outcomes. This argument focuses attention on possible reasons that data might fail to support rejection of a false null hypothesis, such as inadequate sample size or lack of precision in the available measures. Essentially, they are arguing that the statistical significance criterion (at traditional levels of significance) favors inaction when the development of scientific knowledge is in a preliminary stage. When the cost of making a Type II error is substantial, relative to the cost of making a Type I error, these attorneys argue that this is not a balanced approach. Opponents of this view dismiss these arguments with the term, "junk science."

While few health outcome researchers would seriously argue that statistical significance is not important, individuals who propose to base business decisions on this criteria should recognize that they may face similar dilemmas. One study team member posed the dilemma with this question: "I realize that the decrease in waiting time is not statistically significant, but don't you think it is still practically significant?"

If the study outcome indicates a decrease in costs, but the decrease is not statistically significant, will the intervention be discontinued? What decision will be made if the impact is not statistically significant, but the intervention appears to be potentially promising? What criteria will be used to assess "potentially promising"? If the psychologist's compensation is dependent on demonstration of medical cost offsets, will the contract specify that the results must be statistically significant?

Second, a decision that statistical significance will be used as a decision criterion may influence degree of effort and expense that should be allocated to data specification, collection, and analysis. If psychological care decisions will be data-driven, with statistical significance as a major decision criterion, rigorous statistical methodology is required. This requires careful attention to sample size determination before the study is launched. It may also require funding for consultation with a statistician, development of an appropriate computer infrastructure, and development of a detailed cost accounting system (see items 7 and 8 below).

The sample size issue is particularly important if the intervention is designed to prevent infrequent but high-cost adverse health outcomes. Sample sizes required to obtain statistically significant results may be sizeable in such cases.

How Will You Control for Confounding Variables?

Linkages between interventions and outcomes may be influenced by an array of potentially confounding variables. Two major strategies address this issue. The issue may be addressed at the experimental design stage. Randomized controlled trials, for example, attempt to eliminate confounding variables by defining eligibility criteria and then matching participants in the treatment group and the control group. If patient age, for example, is expected to exert a confounding influence, patients in the two groups will be matched on this variable.

Alternately, regression analysis accounts for the influence of confounding variables by including these variables directly in the statistical analysis. This approach broadens the potential to utilize administrative data sets to study the impacts of interventions of samples of patients, where the samples were not created for the purpose of conducting a study. Drawing valid conclusions from regression analysis may require statistical expertise to ensure that issues raised by specific data characteristics are addressed appropriately.

Will You Continue to Measure the Intervention's Impact to Provide a Foundation for Continued Improvement?

If one goal of measuring medical cost offset is to provide a foundation for continued improvements, control charts may provide a useful tool for assessing the data. Control charts were developed initially for industrial quality management. These charts provide an efficient method to monitor an ongoing process and determine whether a statistically significant change has occurred. Suppose, for example, that an intervention has produced a statistically significant cost reduction and is adopted as an ongoing process. Managers may want to monitor this process to ensure that process problems are identified and addressed quickly. A control chart provides a strategy for differentiating between routine outcome variations that result from expected variations in week-to-week patient characteristics and outcome variations that signal a statistically significant change. Developing a control chart requires initial estimates of the process mean and standard deviation, as illustrated in Figure 1, along with determination of the appropriate interval for measuring outcomes. (Whether outcomes should be measured on a daily, weekly, or monthly basis depends on patient volume and the sample size required to achieve the desired level of precision.) The initial control chart includes three horizontal lines. The middle line indicates the historic mean. The upper and lower lines indicate the boundaries of the region of acceptance of the null hypothesis of no significant change from the historic mean.

As the periodic observations are recorded as points on the control chart, quick visual inspection will indicate whether new observations fall in the region of acceptance of the null hypothesis if the mean is still equal to the historic mean. When the mean of a sample falls outside this acceptance region, managers must consider whether this constitutes evidence that the null hypothesis should be rejected. Rules of thumb have been developed for assessing observations that lie outside the acceptance region. Assuming the control chart is based on an a=.05, this implies that 5% of the observations are expected to lie outside the acceptance region, so a single observation outside the acceptance region is not generally viewed as an indication that action is needed. A run of several such observations or a clear trend in the observations, however, would signal that the null hypothesis of no change should be rejected, and investigation is warranted.

Is the Data Readily Available?

Two issues concerning data availability are important. Is accurate and relevant data available in an electronic format? Is the relevant data available within your managed care organization, or does some of it reside elsewhere?

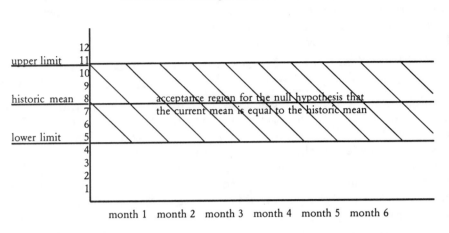

Figure 1. Control charts like this one can be a useful tool for assessing medical cost offset data.

Ongoing collection and analysis of electronic data is potentially more cost-effective than collection and analysis data from patient charts. Relevant electronic data may be housed in the patient billing system (was the patient charged for a specific medication?), an electronic patient medical record, if such records are stored electronically, or subsystems housed within departments or within provider offices. This potential fragmentation of data systems raises the immediate question of whether the data in these disparate systems can be linked in a meaningful way. Experience with prenatal care clinic records and birth certificate records (which include the mother's statement of the trimester in which prenatal care was initiated) present a cautionary tale. An attempt to match the names included in these two separate data systems yielded a sizeable number of names that could not be matched, either by computer or visually. Mary Jenny Smith, for example, who normally uses Jenny as a primary name, might be listed as Mary J Smith in one database and as Jenny Smith in a second unrelated database. In addition, Mary Jenny Smith might have married or divorced (and changed her last name) before providing data to the second database.

Use of administrative record systems for a research study also raises questions about accuracy of the data. When data is used for a new purpose such as a medical cost offset study, the researcher may be using fields in the database that are not widely used, and may therefore contain undetected errors. Advocates of more extensive use of administrative record systems for ongoing process improvement argue that this is not a valid reason to eschew use of these records. Instead, they argue that more intensive use of these databases will gradually improve data accuracy as errors are identified and corrected. Nonetheless, the researcher must assess potential data accuracy before deciding to rely on the electronic field.

A second major issue presented by use of administrative databases is cost. While electronic databases offer the promise of cost-effective data analysis once a system is established, developing the system needed for a new study may be costly. Extracting data from electronic data systems and linking stand-alone databases may require significant computer expertise. Efficient use of these resources may also require investment in the hardware and software infrastructure. Decisions to fund such efforts may require evaluation of more than one proposed study. Computer systems experts argue that investments that do not appear to be cost-effective for a single project may be fiscally sound when the larger universe of potential users is considered.

The importance of electronic clinical information systems for facilitating efficiency improvements has been explicitly highlighted in the Department of Justice guidelines for antitrust assessment of physician networks. These guidelines address the question: how can antitrust enforcement officials differentiate between physician networks formed for the purpose of exerting market power in negotiations with managed care organizations and physician networks formed for the purpose of increasing the efficiency and quality of care? The guidelines identify investment in an integrated clinical information system as an indication that the network intends to increase efficiency and should not be questioned by antitrust enforcement personnel.

Which Types of Costs are Relevant?

Clear thinking about cost is fundamental to a study of the cost impacts of an intervention. Economists emphasize the importance of differentiating between fixed and variable costs. Variable costs increase when service volume increases, while fixed costs are unaffected by service volume changes. If the intervention reduces the volume of services required to treat a group of patients, variable costs are relevant, but fixed costs are not. Because fixed costs, or overhead costs, are frequently included in accounting summaries describing department or service delivery costs, care must be taken to identify specific costs that are relevant.

Analysis can be simplified by focusing on marginal cost and asking the question, "precisely which costs will be affected by the reduction in services?" Analysis of an intervention that reduces hospital length of stay following a specific type of surgery provides an example. Assume three things for this example:

1. the intervention will reduce the average length of stay by one day, from 5 days to 4,
2. average cost for this hospital stay is $10,000
3. the focus of our study is the impact of the intervention on the hospital's cost.

While it might be tempting to calculate the average cost per day (\$10,000/5 = \$2,000) and conclude that the intervention's medical cost offset is \$2,000, this conclusion is probably erroneous. Examination of the pattern of costs incurred during the 5-day stay would probably indicate that a substantial portion of that cost was incurred on the first day, during and immediately following the surgery. Actual costs incurred on the fifth day (which has been eliminated by the intervention) were substantially less than the average daily cost. The high cost of the surgery is a fixed cost in this example because it does not vary when the length of stay is reduced. Only the actual costs of services provided to the patient are relevant variable costs. If the normal daily charge includes allocated overhead (i.e. each hospital inpatient typically helps pay for equipment whether the patient uses the equipment or not), the daily charge does not provide a good basis for estimating cost savings.

Estimation of these savings requires addressing several questions. First, which services are no longer provided to the patient, now that the length of stay is shorter? Of the services that were traditionally provided on the fifth day, which services have been eliminated, and which (perhaps patient education) are now provided earlier in the patient's stay?

A more difficult, but equally relevant, question is: what happens to the resources that are no longer needed to provide the services that have been eliminated? If the eliminated services save .5 FTE of a nurse's time, has staffing been adjusted accordingly? If a bed is now empty for an extra day, is that bed immediately filled by a revenue-generating patient who would have been delayed prior to the intervention? Does the bed sit empty? If the bed is empty, has staffing been reduced?

Four cost issues are illustrated in this example:

1. Average costs are likely to be misleading. Instead, it is important to examine marginal costs.
2. Accounting cost summaries often combine fixed and variable costs. Only variable costs are relevant for identifying the marginal cost impact of the intervention. If the intervention leads to a saving in nurse time, but that saving is distributed over so many nurses that it is not feasible to reduce staffing, then there is no cost-saving. There may be, instead, a different type of benefit – each nurse now has more time to spend with other patients.
3. Identification of marginal costs is situation-specific and must focus on answering the question: precisely which costs will no longer be incurred as a result of the intervention?
4. Opportunity costs are relevant and should be measured and included in the estimated medical cost offset. The term, opportunity cost, refers to foregone opportunities. If occupancy is high, all beds are filled, and patients desiring discretionary surgery must wait for a bed to become available, then the marginal cost of permitting patient X to occupy a bed for a fifth day is the foregone opportunity to admit a new patient on that day. (This may be an important opportunity if surgery is more

profitable than post-surgical care.) In contrast, if occupancy is low and beds do not constrain new admissions, then the marginal cost of permitting patient X to occupy a bed for a fifth day is only the direct cost of services provided on that day.

If the intervention leads to significant and complex medical cost offsets, this type of analysis may require in-depth understanding of the organization's accounting practices, as well as computer expertise to extract the relevant data. In fact, this computer expertise may be invaluable if the relevant data is embedded in proprietary software that was designed for another purpose. Suppose, for example that an intervention leads to reduced use of prescription medications. The pharmacy medication ordering system may contain the data needed to measure this reduction. When the researcher asks this question, however, he may be asking a question that was not considered when the software was developed. Computer expertise may be needed, therefore, to extract this data.

Conclusion

Measuring medical cost offset is both straightforward and complex. The concept is straightforward: the researcher wants to measure the cost savings that result from an intervention. Actually measuring the cost savings, however, is complex for three reasons. First, implementing this concept requires careful consideration of issues that are situation-specific; hence simple cookbook prescriptions may not be helpful. Second, most of these issues should be considered, at least with preliminary analysis, before implementing the intervention, to assure that appropriate data is collected before and after implementation. At this point, however, the actual cost impacts may be difficult to predict. Some of the issues may be revisited, therefore, as data becomes available. Third, it is clearly possible to estimate medical cost offset with varying degrees of precision. Obtaining precise estimates may require significant investment of time and expense. Whether this precision is worth that investment will depend on the purpose of the study, the expected magnitudes of the cost impacts, and the strength of the computer and accounting infrastructure that is already in-place.

Psychopharmacology and Medical Cost Offset

Janet L. Cummings
President, The Nicholas & Dorothy Cummings Foundation

In the 1950s, Kaiser Permanente physicians discovered that 60% of physician visits were by patients who had no physical disease (Cummings, 1997a; Cummings & VandenBos, 1981), as these "somatizers" were experiencing the translation of their emotional problems into physical symptoms or the exacerbation of physical disease by emotional factors (Cummings, 1997a). This information prompted research in which Kaiser Permanente Health Plan enrollees who were thought to be somatizers were given behavioral healthcare services, which led to the discovery that the inclusion of a behavioral healthcare benefit could bring about savings on medical and surgical costs far in excess of cost of the behavioral services (Cummings, 1997a; Cummings, Kahn, & Sparkman, 1962). This "medical cost offset phenomenon" remains the most important argument for the inclusion of behavioral healthcare services in health benefits packages (Cummings, 1997a; Cummings & Follette, 1968; Cummings, Kahn, & Sparkman, 1962; Follette & Cummings, 1967).

In order to be meaningful, the savings in medical utilization must exceed the cost of the behavioral healthcare services provided (Cummings, 1997a). Although traditional long-term psychotherapy generally brings about an increase in medical and surgical costs, brief, focused psychotherapy can significantly reduce medical and surgical costs in somatizing patients. The savings is often in excess of 60% over the 5 years following the application of the psychotherapeutic interventions (Cummings, 1997a; Follette & Cummings, 1967). During the 1980s and 1990s, a number of managed care companies became adept at providing behavioral healthcare services in a "carve-out" model and were able to achieve impressive medical cost offset savings (Cummings, 1997a).

In the New Millennium, however, new challenges demand a new body of research on medical cost offset. Advances in the pharmaceutical industry during the past decade have resulted in the availability of psychotropic medications with improved safety and efficacy over their older counterparts, as well as an increasing number and variety of available agents from which to choose (Cummings, 2001; Gitlin, 1996). The result has been a dramatic, in some cases 10-fold or more, increase in the number of prescriptions written for psychotropics compared to 10 years ago (Cummings, 2001; Joseph, 1997).

Clearly, many patients benefit from these changes. As safer psychotropics are developed, many physicians become willing to prescribe medications to patients who may benefit from them but who do not demonstrate the severe pathology that was often necessary to warrant the use of the older medications (Cummings, 2001;

Joseph, 1997; National Alliance for the Mentally Ill, 2001a; National Alliance for the Mentally Ill, 2001b). As drugs with less severe side effect profiles and drugs with varying side effect profiles become available, medication compliance increases in a number of patients who formerly found the side effects of their psychotropics to be intolerable (Cummings, 2001; Lehman & Steinwachs, 1998; National Alliance for the Mentally Ill, 2001a).

However, the dramatic advances in the pharmaceutical industry during the past decade also have brought some challenges for both providers and third-party payors. For example, many third-party payors are now spending more money on psychotropic medications than on behavioral care. As a result, some payors are finding it necessary to limit access to psychotropics by classifying the newer, more expensive drugs as non-formulary (Huttin & Bosanquet, 1995; National Alliance for the Mentally Ill, 2000; Nganele, 2001; Sakurai, 1996). If the physician and consumer decide upon a non-formulary drug, the consumer is then required to pay a substantially higher co-pay or, in some cases, the entire cost of the drug.

In order to overcome such challenges, a new body of research is needed which will focus on the impact of the appropriate management of psychotropic medications on patients, providers, and third-party payors. Because many new medications have been introduced within the past 5 to 10 years and because the escalating drug benefit is also fairly recent, most of this research is yet to be conducted.

The remainder of this chapter will outline some issues in the area of psychopharmacology which necessitate a new body of research and will summarize the research available to date. The author will then propose a model for managing psychotropic medications which is patterned after the original model developed at Kaiser Permanente in the 1960s and the refinement of the original model used by American Biodyne during the 1980s. The model to be proposed is applicable for use in both "carve-in" and "carve-out" systems. Although there is no guarantee that this model will lead to medical cost offset, it is very likely that such a model will lead to the best care for the patient, which may in turn produce a medical cost offset effect.

Some Current Issues in Psychopharmacology

Medication vs. Behavioral Intervention

In general, the research comparing medication to psychotherapy concludes that medication and psychotherapy are about equally effective for a number of conditions, and that medication and psychotherapy combined often have a slight advantage over either alone (Cummings, 2001; Cummings & Sayama, 1995). However, there are some methodological difficulties associated with much of this research.

Depression, for example, is not a single homogeneous category, even though it is generally treated as such in the research literature. Rather, there are at least five distinct types of depression and the treatment of choice is different for each one (Cummings, 1985; Cummings & Sayama, 1995). Endogenous depression may be influenced by external events, but is primarily determined by biological factors and is best treated with antidepressant medications. Exogenous depression (reactive or neurotic depression), on the other hand, is best treated with psychotherapy. Antidepressant medication can actually interfere with the resolution of the problem. Chronic depression originating in childhood is best treated with a combination of antidepressant medication and supportive psychotherapy. Anniversary depression, or postponed bereavement, is best treated with psychotherapy to discover the anniversary. Antidepressant medication will generally interfere with this process. Although simple bereavement is not depression, it resembles depression and is therefore often misdiagnosed as depression. Antidepressant medications will usually inhibit and prolong the bereavement process, so psychotherapy which encourages the patient to go through the process of mourning is the treatment of choice for uncomplicated bereavement (Cummings, 1985; Cummings, 2001; Cummings & Sayama, 1995).

When these types of depression are studied separately, a pattern emerges that is much different from that presented in most of the research which treats depression as a homogeneous category. It becomes apparent that medication is significantly more effective than psychotherapy in some cases, that psychotherapy is significantly more effective than medication in other cases, and that some cases require both medication and psychotherapy for optimal results (Cummings, 1985; Cummings & Sayama, 1995).

The available body of well-designed outcomes research demonstrates that, for many conditions, behavioral interventions are both less costly and more effective than medications (Cummings, 1985). Antonuccio, Danton, and DeNelsky (1995) and DeRubeis, Gelfand, Tang, and Simmons (1999) cite a body of research demonstrating that most acute depressions, even the most severe, respond well to behavioral interventions. These interventions generally produce lasting results. They also cite studies suggesting that behavioral interventions are effective in the prevention of depression, whereas antidepressant medications leave the patient vulnerable to relapse following their withdrawal. Because cognitive-behavioral therapies for depression can be delivered in time-limited psychoeducational groups or via bibliotherapy and provide long-lasting results (Smith, Floyd, Scogin, & Jamison, 1997), they can be highly cost-effective compared to pharmaceutical treatments.

Reactive (neurotic) depression can be effectively treated in an average of six sessions of focused psychotherapy (Cummings, 1985; Cummings & Sayama, 1995). On the other hand, treatment with antidepressants would typically require several weeks of treatment before any therapeutic effect could be expected, followed by a minimum of six months of treatment (Cummings, 2001). Since it is unlikely that antidepressant medication would allow resolution of the underlying problem (in this case, internalized rage or introjection), the depression would likely recur following withdrawal of the medication. In the case of psychotherapy, it is possible (even likely) that the patient would learn some skills to prevent recurrence (Cummings, 1985; Cummings & Sayama, 1995).

Panic disorder with agoraphobia is another example of a condition for which focused psychotherapy is superior to medical treatment for most patients. The Biodyne group protocol, which can also be used effectively in individual therapy, is effective in treating over 95% of agoraphobics in 16 to 20 group sessions combined with a small number (usually about three or four) individual sessions. Because the protocol addresses the underlying dynamic in agoraphobia that is often missed in strictly behavioral protocols, namely the presence of one or more ambivalent relationships, the relapse rate is quite low (less than 5%) (Cummings, 1985; Cummings & Sayama, 1995). On the other hand, many patients presenting with agoraphobia came to Biodyne with long histories of treatment with benzodiazepines which masked the panic symptoms but did not treat the phobias. In this author's clinical experience, it is not uncommon for patients to have received benzodiazepines for ten years or more to treat their panic symptoms while continuing to suffer from phobias. These same patients typically have histories of frequent emergency room visits during panic attacks, as well as costly EKGs and echocardiograms which have been repeated many times due these patients' constant need for reassurance. Patients who received treatment using the Biodyne group protocol not only had low relapse rates, but also significantly reduced overall medical costs because they no longer demanded expensive cardiac tests and no longer frequented hospital emergency rooms during panic attacks (Cummings, 1985; Cummings & Sayama, 1995).

Antidepressant medications have become the most common treatment for depression, and antidepressants are now among the most prescribed psychotropics in the U.S. (Antonuccio, Danton, & DeNelsky, 1999). The Selective Serotonin Reuptake Inhibitors (SSRIs) have become particularly popular, and are frequently chosen over less invasive behavioral approaches for the treatment of depression (Pincus, et al., 1998). Many authorities are concerned about this trend and believe that many patients who are given medication instead of psychotherapy are getting short-changed, as their treatment is both more expensive and less efficacious than behavioral interventions would be (Cummings & Wiggins, 2001; Emslie, Walkup, Pliska, & Ernst, 1999; Fisher & Fisher, 1996; Greenhill, 1998; Minde, 1998; Safer, Zito, & Fine, 1996; Zito, et al., 1998, 2000)

Much research is needed to determine the savings that could be obtained by providing psychotherapy instead of psychotropic medications or in addition to medications with the goal of discontinuing the medications. It is very likely that such research will demonstrate that a cost offset effect is attained when psychotropics are properly managed, which in many cases means providing psychotherapy instead of psychotropics or providing psychotherapy to patients already taking psychotropics with the goal of eventually tapering and withdrawing the medications. The costs of the psychotropic medications themselves, physician visits and laboratory tests to monitor the medications, emergency room visits and other services used to manage patients whose problems are not being effectively treated with medications all added together will likely prove to be significantly higher than appropriate, effective psychotherapeutic interventions for many patients.

The Non-Psychiatrist Physician Factor

Approximately 70 to 80% of psychotropic medications are currently prescribed by non-psychiatrists, including primary care physicians, internists, and gynecologists (Beardsley, Gardocki, Larson, & Hildalgo, 1988; Cummings, 2001; Pincus, et al., 1998). Because most of these physicians have received little training in psychiatry, they are not adept at accurately diagnosing mental and emotional problems. They are generally not trained to be able to determine when medication would be most appropriate and when psychotherapy would be most appropriate and, as physicians, tend to opt for medical treatment even in cases where behavioral treatment would likely be superior (Beardsley, et al.).

Because non-psychiatrists tend to be less skilled at using psychotropic medications, they tend to prescribe psychotropics in only very low dosages and to give those same low dosages to all their depressed patients. These dosages are so low as to be sub-therapeutic for many patients, particularly those with moderate to severe depression who would likely need larger dosages in order to be effective. Many patients who do need psychotropic medications often do not receive them in dosages likely to be helpful. In fact, some managed care companies have documented that about 40% of depressed patients receive sub-therapeutic doses of medication, have too few medication management visits, and receive inadequate long-term monitoring of their medications (National Alliance for the Mentally Ill, 2001b). Thus, the money spent on those medications is essentially wasted (Cummings & Wiggins, 2001; Beardsley, et al., 1988).

Although much research is needed to determine the magnitude of savings which can be obtained by properly managing psychotropic medications, some principles are apparent. First, a significant amount of money is being wasted on psychotropic medications for patients who really do not need them, but whose physicians do not know how to help them. Second, a significant amount of money is also being wasted by providing only sub-therapeutic dosages of medications to people who need the medications, but in therapeutic levels.

PCPs and other non-psychiatrists are seldom able to effectively monitor whether or not their patients are taking the psychotropic medications as prescribed (Antonuccio, et al., 1999; Beardsley, et al., 1988), and there is some evidence that adjunctive behavioral interventions can significantly increase compliance (Cummings, 1985; Cummings, 2001). In many cases, money is spent on psychotropic medications which then are used inconsistently, improperly, or not at all. Patients who could benefit from the medications are not able to receive maximum benefit in the absence of behavioral interventions aimed at increasing medication compliance (Cummings, 1985; Cummings, 2001; Cummings & Sayama, 1995). Although there certainly is some cost involved in providing these behavioral interventions, they are likely to save significant amounts of money in many cases. In the Biodyne experience and this author's own clinical experience, adjunctive psychotherapy (often occurring as infrequently as once a month or once every several months) can greatly increase medication compliance in chronically mentally ill patients and thus reduce the need for very costly psychiatric hospitalization.

Over-Medication

Although over-medication likely occurs in a number of populations, two populations seem to be most seriously affected: children (Kaplan & Sadock, 1993) and the elderly (Hartman-Stein, 1997). A number of physiological changes in the elderly make them more sensitive to medications, thus requiring less medication to achieve a therapeutic effect (Cummings, 2001; Kaplan & Sadock, 1993). These changes include slower absorption rates, increases in the volume of distribution for fat-soluble medications, decreases in the volume of distribution for water-soluble drugs, decreased liver metabolism (resulting in increased amounts of unmetabolized medication and increased potential for toxicity), prolonged half-lives of medications, and greater receptor sensitivity. The result is that the elderly are commonly given dosages of medications which are much higher than nececessary.

Furthermore, the elderly are commonly medicated for conditions which should not require medication, such as uncomplicated bereavement (Cummings, 2001; Hartman-Stein, 1997). In the elderly, such unnecessary medication can produce symptoms which mimic psychiatric disturbances (Cummings, 2001; Kaplan & Sadock, 1993). For example, the sedation caused by benzodiazepines, sedating tricyclic antidepressants, and sedating antipsychotics is commonly mistaken for depression in the elderly. The confusion which can be caused by over-sedation or anti-cholinergic side effects may be mistaken for dementia. Unfortunately, once these medication effects are misdiagnosed, they are often "treated" with more medications (Cummings, 2001; Hartman-Stein, 1997; Kaplan & Sadock, 1993), resulting in costly, ineffective, and often unnecessary treatment.

A number of physicians and mental health professionals have warned in recent years that children are being overly and unnecessarily medicated (Moore, 1998; Jensen, 1998; Zito, et al., 2000). According to Kaplan (1999), the use of both stimulants and antidepressants in children has increased dramatically in recent years. Stimulants are now the most commonly used psychotropics in children, with SSRIs being the next most commonly prescribed psychotropic (Jensen, 1998).

Cummings and Wiggins (2001) quote a number of studies which challenge the use of antidepressants in children. For example, an evaluation of 13 double-blind placebo controlled studies concluded that antidepressant medications are no more effective than placebo in children (Fisher & Fisher, 1996). Johnson and Fruehling (1994) see no evidence that antidepressants are effective in children, yet recommend their continued use nonetheless. Pellegrino (1996) cautions physicians that it may be unethical to prescribe antidepressant medications to children in the absence of scientific data supporting their efficacy, and Vitiello (1998) outlines some possible serious side effects of antidepressants in children, including damage to the developing brains of very young children. Although these and other authorities challenge the safety and usefulness of antidepressant medications in children, the warnings issued by Zito, et al. (2000) have attracted widespread attention from the public and the U.S. government.

In response to the warnings from Zito, et al. (2000) and others, Cummings and Wiggins (2001) looked at 168,113 episodes of children and adolescents who received behavioral interventions through Biodyne following their having been prescribed psychotropic medications. The data cover a four-year period, 1988-1992. For each child and adolescent in the study, there was an average treatment length of 17.2 sessions (an average of 6.3 for the identified patient and an average of 10.9 for the parent or parents). This was nearly three times the average number of sessions (6.2) for episodes of treatment for adults who were seen for problems unrelated to their children or adolescents during the same time period.

During the period from 1988 to 1992, children and adolescents were prescribed antidepressants and/or antipsychotics only infrequently, with the exception of Imipramine for nocturnal enuresis (Foxman, Valdez, & Brook, 1986; Jensen, 1998). Most of the psychotropics prescribed to children and adolescents were stimulants, primarily methylphenidate (Ritalin) and pemoline (Cylert), given for Attention Deficit Disorder and Attention Deficit Hyperactivity Disorder (ADD/ADHD).

The study showed that behavioral interventions (which included parenting skills training and provision of male role models for those children who lacked adequate male role models) dramatically reduced the use of medications by the conclusion of treatment. Among 5- to 6-year-olds, medication usage was reduced by 95%. The 17- to 18-year-olds had the least reduction in medication usage, but still experienced an impressive 92% reduction. Interestingly, the decision to reduce or discontinue medication was always made by the physician (usually a PCP or pediatrician) who had originally prescribed the medication as the result of feedback about the patient's progress in psychotherapy, and only with the agreement of the "point of friction" (complainant or referral source, such as the school in the case of an ADD/ADHD child).

On entering treatment, 61% of boys and 23% of girls in the study had been diagnosed with ADD/ADHD by their PCPs or pediatricians and had been prescribed medication accordingly. At the conclusion of behavioral treatment, only 11% of boys and 2% of girls retained these diagnoses. Thus, only one-fifth of boys and one-tenth of girls retained the ADD/ADHD diaganoses. The study also indicated a possible trend toward medicating younger and younger patients instead of understanding their needs and managing their behavior with behavioral interventions (Cummings & Wiggins, 2001).

The decline in medication usage shown in this study parallels the Biodyne experience with adults on medication (Cummings & Wiggins, 2001; Wiggins & Cummings, 1998). Like the children and adolescents in the 2001 study, most adults who entered Biodyne treatment already taking psychotropic medication were able

to discontinue their medication following brief (average of 6.2 sessions) psychotherapy. Only those with chronic mental disorders, such as schizophrenia and
bipolar, were continued on medications (Wiggins & Cummings, 1998).

This research on the medication usage of Biodyne patients (Cummings &
Wiggins, 2001; Wiggins & Cummings, 1998) does not put a precise dollar amount
on the savings obtained by proper management (which in many cases meant
discontinuation) of psychotropic medications.

However, the 2001 study does conclude that, even though the treatment
necessary to stabilize the behavior of the children and adolescents in the study was
significantly greater than the expenditures needed to stabilize adults in the same
setting, the expenditures were still less than the resources that would have been
necessary to maintain these patients on psychotropic medication over extended
time (Cummings & Wiggins, 2001).

Newer Medications and Cost Savings

Some recent research indicates that some newer, more expensive drugs used for
various medical conditions actually save money by reducing the need for other
costly procedures (Kleinke, 2001). Despite the high cost of some newer prescription
drugs, they have been shown to shorten hospital stays and prevent the need for costly,
invasive procedures. In fact, Kleinke (2001) considers pharmaceuticals to be the
cheapest weapon against rising medical costs. While pharmaceutical spending rose
from 5.5% to 8.5% of the total medical spending during the 1990s, hospital
expenditures dropped from 37% to 33% during the same time period (Kleinke,
2001). In describing how pharmaceutical spending may lower overall medical costs,
Kleinke (2001) divides prescription medications into six categories:

1. *Fast pays.* These are expensive drugs that lower short-term medical costs.
   For example, anticoagulant therapy for a stroke costs about $1,095 per
   year, while the lifetime cost of a severe stroke averages about $100,000.
2. *Slow pay.* These are drugs which take several years to lower medical
   spending. For example, hormone replacement therapies may reduce
   osteoporosis (thus preventing costly hip fractures) and may reduce the
   risk for cardiovascular disease (with its associated medications,
   procedures, and hospitalizations) in women. However, in order to be
   effective, the medications must be taken years before symptoms
   actually appear.
3. *Narrow pays.* These are drugs which lower costs for some narrow clinical
   subpopulation but do not decrease medical spending overall. Ex
   amples include cholesterol-lowering drugs and vaccines.
4. *Diffuse pays.* These treatments actually increase medical costs while
   lowering non-medical costs. For example, non-sedating allergy medications treat inexpensive medical conditions while keeping patients
   productive in the workplace.

5. *Pay-me-laters*. These treatments improve health and short-term costs, while guaranteeing higher aggregate costs in the long-term. Examples include treatments for cystic fibrosis, multiple sclerosis, and possibly HIV/AIDS.

6. *No pays*. These drugs do not save money, but they do improve the quality of human life. Examples include treatments for acne, toenail fungus, or overactive bladder.

Although the research on psychotropics is still in its infancy, there is some evidence that some of the newer psychotropic medications can actually save money, even though they are more expensive than their older counterparts. About 90% of what is currently known about both normal and abnormal brain structure and function has been discovered in the last 15 years (National Alliance for the Mentally Ill, 2001b). However, a large number of people with mental illnesses have yet to benefit from these discoveries in neuroscience because they are using medications which pre-date these advances (National Alliance for the Mentally Ill, 2001b). A significant percentage of the psychiatric population needs the newer drugs, in sufficient dosages, in order to avoid more costly interventions such as psychiatric hospitalizations.

According to the National Depressive and Manic-Depressive Association (NDMDA) (2000), many patients taking antidepressant medications are non-compliant with their treatment regimen because of side effects. NDMDA statistics suggest that nearly half of patients taking antidepressant medications report having medication side effects, and 55% of these patients stop taking their medication because of the side effects. The NDMDA suggests that compliance can be greatly increased by minimizing the side effects. In fact, less than 47% of patients who have bothersome side effects are satisfied with their treatment, while 68% of patients who do not have bothersome side effects are satisfied.

Because the newer antidepressants like Serzone, Effexor, and Remeron are at least as effective as the older antidepressants and generally have fewer bothersome side effects than even the SSRIs, compliance tends to increase with these drugs (Cummings, 2001; National Alliance for the Mentally Ill, 2000; Simon, VonKorff, & Heiligenstein, 1996) and some authorities believe they are major steps toward the treatment of depression and should be first-line pharmaceutical treatments for depression (Crisman, Trivedi, & Pigott, 1999; Munoz, 2000; National Alliance for the Mentally Ill, 2000). Furthermore, they are generally safer if taken in overdose (National Alliance for the Mentally Ill, 2000) and, therefore, may avoid medical costs associated with toxicity and overdose.

Although these newer antidepressants may be "no pays" in patients with milder depression, they may very well prove to be "fast pays" in patients with more severe illnesses who are likely to need hospitalization or who are at risk for the development of somatization disorder if their depression is not effectively treated. The National Alliance for the Mentally Ill's meta-analysis of available research has concluded that the total treatment costs of older and newer antidepressants are about equal.

Although medication costs are higher with the newer agents, costs of office visits and other medical care are reduced because dosage adjustment is simpler and side effects are less problematic (National Alliance for the Mentally Ill, 2000; Simon, et al., 1996).

As is the case with antidepressants, the newer antipsychotic medications show improved effectiveness and reduced side effects when compared to their older counterparts (Cummings, 2001; National Alliance for the Mentally Ill, 2000). These newer medications, including Clozaril, Risperdal, Zyprexa, and Seroquel, have fewer annoying side effects, such as dry mouth and constipation. They also have fewer serious side effects, such as tardive dyskinesia and neuroleptic malignant syndrome (Keck & McElroy, 1997; McEvoy, Scheifler, & Frances, 1999; National Alliance for the Mentally Ill, 2000).

Conventional antipsychotics greatly ease the psychotic symptoms, or "positive" symptoms, of schizophrenia. During the past 50 years, they have allowed countless mentally ill patients to leave the psychiatric hospitals and return to their communities. However, these drugs are limited in their effectiveness in that they do not target the "negative" symptoms of schizophrenia, which include apathy, withdrawal, and lack of emotion. Furthermore, they fail to target the cognitive problems and mood disturbances that often accompany severe psychotic illness (Carpenter, 1996). They also fail to alleviate psychosis in many "treatment resistant" patients (Kane, Honigfel, Singer, & Meltzer, 1988).

Conventional antipsychotic drugs generally have side effect profiles which many patients find intolerable. These drugs frequently cause debilitating neurological side effects that can be painful, humiliating, stigmatizing, and sometimes permanent, including uncontrollable muscle movements, total rigidity, and difficulty swallowing. Many schizophrenic patients have refused to remain compliant with their medications because they find the side effects to be more bothersome than their illness, thus requiring repeat hospitalizations and other expensive interventions (Hansen, Casey, & Hoffman, 1997). Consider that medication plus supportive therapy can cost as little $150 to $500 per month (or less than $6000 per year) per patient, while inpatient psychiatric hospitalization can cost $45,000 to $80,000 per person per year for severely disabled patients (National Alliance for the Mentally Ill, 2001b).

Most of the newer "atypical" antipsychotic medications have been FDA approved within the past 10 years. These medications have efficacy equal to conventional agents in targeting the "positive" symptoms of schizophrenia, but also are of some benefit to most patients in targeting the "negative" symptoms, cognitive problems, and mood disturbances which often accompany the psychotic features (Keck & McElroy, 1997; McEvoy, et al., 1999). The atypical agents often are effective in treating patients previously thought to be "treatment resistant" (Kane, et al., 1988; Kane, 1995). Because these newer medications have fewer side effects overall, compliance increases in many schizophrenic patients when conventional agents and replaced by newer agents (Keck & McElroy, 1997; McEvoy, et al.; National Alliance for the Mentally Ill, 2000).

McEvoy, et al. (1999) suggest that the newer atypical antipsychotics should be the drugs of first choice in most situations and for most patients. They cite two reasons: (a) they have been shown to be more effective in treating a wider array of symptoms in more patients; (b) the side effects associated with the newer agents cause fewer short-term and long-term problems. However, state Medicaid agencies and managed care companies are considering and implementing cost-cutting measures that deny the newer agents or make access to them more difficult (National Advisory Mental Health Council, 1993; National Alliance for the Mentally Ill, 2000). These measures are of two types: (a) restrictive drug formularies, in which non-formulary drugs must be purchased out-of-pocket or with increased co-pays, and (b) fail-first policies, in which more expensive medications are covered only after less expensive medications have failed. Although these measures make intuitive economic sense, they are likely to produce greater economic burdens in the long run due to the increased costs associated with non-compliance and serious side effects (National Advisory Mental Health Council 1993; National Alliance for the Mentally Ill, 2000). Medications account for only a very small part of the total treatment costs associated with severe mental illness, in some cases as little as 2% (Haveman, 1998). Attempting to save money on antipsychotic medications while increasing other costs will only create an increase in overall costs.

Based on the research available to date, the newer medications are proving to be very cost effective (Fichtner, Hanrahan, & Luchins, 1998). Although atypical antipsychotics cost more, the increased cost is more than recovered in the decreased costs of clinical care, especially decreased hospital days. In one study, the newer antipsychotic drugs produced a net savings of $8,702 per schizophrenic patient per year (National Alliance for the Mentally Ill, 2000). For patients with severe and persistent mental illness, the newer antipsychotics, combined with supportive community services, result in the greatest savings, driven primarily by reduction in number of hospital days (Texas Council of Community MHMR Centers, 1988). Although studies with different patient populations show different levels of savings, none shows increased total costs of treatment with atypical antipsychotics (National Alliance for the Mentally Ill, 2000).

In addition to the direct cost savings, there are other significant financial benefits from returning previously disabled patients to work. Because the atypical agents target "negative" symptoms, cognitive problems, and mood disturbances associated with schizophrenia, they are more likely than the older agents to allow patients to return to work and remain gainfully employed (Keck & McElroy, 1997; National Alliance for the Mentally Ill, 2000).

Furthermore, the use of newer antipsychotics may provide cost savings by reducing liability. There is a potential significant legal cost associated with law suits on behalf of patients who develop tardive dyskinesia or neuroleptic malignant syndrome from older antipsychotics when newer medications are available which are much less likely to cause these serious problems. It is possible that only one or two such lawsuits could offset the cost of the newer agents in a large population of patients (Hansen, et al., 1997; National Alliance for the Mentally Ill, 2000).

Unfortunately, considerable money is being wasted on both conventional and atypical antipsychotic medications. According to the Schizophrenia Patient Outcomes Research Team (PORT) study, funded by the National Institute of Mental Health (NIMH) and the Agency for Health Care Policy and Research (AHCPR), only about 29% of chronic schizophrenic patients receive appropriate medication dosages. About a third of these patients (39%) receive dosages that are too low, thus wasting money on medication unlikely to be effective. About a third of these patients (32%) receive dosages that are too high, thus wasting medication and increasing the likelihood of side effects which may cause non-compliance or serious complications (Lehman & Steinwachs, 1998; National Alliance for the Mentally Ill, 2001a, 2001b).

Proposed Model for the Management of Psychotropics

The proposed model is based on the models that were used at Kaiser Permanente (in the 1950s, 1960s, and 1970s) and American Biodyne (in the 1980s) (Cummings, 1997b; Cummings & Wiggins, 2001; Wiggins & Cummings, 1998). It has a number of elements:

1. It is a collaborative model between physicians (PCPs, pediatricians, internists, ob-gyns, and other physicians) and behavioral healthcare providers.
2. When the PCP or other physician writes a prescription for a psychotropic medication, he/she also notifies the behavioral healthcare provider and refers the patient to the behavioral healthcare provider.
3. If the patient does not follow up on the referral, the behavioral healthcare specialist makes an outreach call to the patient to encourage compliance with the referral.
   There are no restrictions on physicians' exercise of their prescriptive authority.
4. Those physicians who choose to participate in the collaborative model do so voluntarily.
5. Those physicians who choose to participate receive training in the collaborative model.
6. The behavioral healthcare provider initiates appropriate behavioral intervention, and the prescribing physician and behavioral healthcare specialist consult with each other regularly regarding the case.
7. The prescribing physician decides to titrate or discontinue the prescription when the patient's symptoms have sufficiently diminished.
8. The behavioral healthcare specialists are trained in diagnosis and psychopharmacology and are able to provide information for the

physicians to consider if the medication regimen is questionable, in error, or unnecessary.

9. The relationship between the physician and the behavioral healthcare provider remains collegial and in the patient's best interest. The behavioral healthcare providers are trained to skillfully convey psychological information that may impact the medication and dosage selected, while remaining respectful of the physician's prescriptive authority.

10. Psychotherapy is the primary intervention for behavioral health problems, with medication as an adjunct. Exceptions are chronically psychotic patients, bipolar patients, and children with confirmed ADD/ADHD. Even with these conditions, psychotherapy is used in conjunction with medication.

Because only about 10% of patients referred to behavioral healthcare actually follow through on the referral (Cummings, Cummings, & Johnson, 1997), various strategies can be used to increase compliance. If the behavioral healthcare specialist is co-located in the same office as the physician, the physician can introduce the patient to the behavioral healthcare specialist, who initiates his/her assessment and treatment during that same visit. If the behavioral healthcare specialist is not co-located, he/she can make an outreach call to the patient to encourage him/her to comply with the referral. Despite the best efforts on the parts of the physician and behavioral healthcare specialist, not all patients will enter behavioral treatment. However, enough will enter treatment to make a significant difference in overall outcomes and cost savings.

It must be noted that the behavioral healthcare provider never interferes with the physician's medical responsibility and prescriptive authority. He/she never "advises" the physician regarding continuation or discontinuation of psychotropic medication. Rather, he/she asks the physician to "consider" continuing or discontinuing the prescription. Thus, the physician's prescriptive authority is respected.

When the patient has made sufficient progress in psychotherapy, the behavioral healthcare provider calls the prescribing physician and asks him/her to consider titration or withdrawal of the medication. The behavioral healthcare provider must demonstrate to the physician that the medication is no longer necessary. For example, in the Biodyne system, patients were not taken off psychotropic medications unless the prescribing physician and the "point of friction" (referral source, such as the school in the case of an ADD/ADHD child) agreed that the problem was sufficiently resolved. Then, the medication was titrated or withdrawn on a trial basis and would be re-started if the prescribing physician or "point of friction" considered it necessary (Cummings & Wiggins, 2001; Wiggins & Cummings, 1998).

In this model, ongoing medication management and prescription renewals may be performed by the physician who originally wrote the prescription and made the referral to the behavioral healthcare provider. It is also possible to have a psychiatrist who works closely with the behavioral healthcare provider take over these functions. However, if the latter is the case, it is important that the non-psychiatrist physicians understand and agree to the system. Otherwise, they are likely to feel that their prescriptive authority is being challenged.

One problem with this model can arise in carve-out systems. It is possible for physicians to "dump" difficult and problematic patients into the behavioral health carve-out. The carve-out psychiatrist or nurse practitioner then prescribes medications and sends the patient back to the medical system for continued medication management, even in cases where psychotherapy would be the treatment of choice. Thus, the cost of maintaining that patient comes out of the medical system's pocket, and any potential medical cost offset effect is lost. In such cases, the patient gets neither appropriate medications nor behavioral healthcare. Therefore, these patients fall through the cracks and are unable to provide adequate data on how best to select and handle psychotropic medications versus behavioral healthcare.

Although the proper management of psychotropics is likely to produce a cost offset effect, the proposed model is not just about saving money. It is primarily about providing appropriate and optimal treatment for the patients. As was demonstrated earlier in this chapter, providing optimal treatment often results in significant cost offset.

During the 1980s, both physicians and psychotherapists within the American Biodyne system adhered to a specific protocol for medication use. The protocol was designed to provide the best possible care to the patients, but also brought about significant cost savings (Cummings, 2001). The elements of this protocol follow:

1. Through clinical interview, mental status exam, family history, and psychological symptoms, the clinician defines the nature of the disorder. The clinician then decides whether or not the disorder is medication responsive. If so, a referral is made to the psychiatrist who works with the behavioral healthcare specialist.
2. All clinicians must be familiar with classes of psychotropic medications, appropriate uses of medications, adverse reactions, methods and routes of administration, and dosage ranges.
3. The attitude that the clinician portrays is important. It should be one of optimism and hope.
4. Non-medical treatments are used when they are at least as effective as drug treatments. (Examples include behavior therapy for phobias and cognitive or insight therapy for neurotic depression.)
5. Do not deny the patient appropriate medications.
6. Choose the drug with the fewest adverse reactions and greatest potential clinical effects.
7. Administer the lowest effective dose of medication for the shortest period of time.
8. Prescribe the simplest possible drug regimen (such as a single bedtime dose) in order to increase compliance.

9. Whenever possible, avoid polypharmacology. Combinations of drugs are rarely more effective than a single agent. In most cases, it is best to stay at a dosage range that does not require a second medication to treat side effects.

This author suggests that this principle to avoid polypharmacology should be amended in light of recent developments in the area of psychopharmacology where research has shown multiple medications to be the pharmaceutical treatment of choice for some conditions. When polypharmacy cannot be avoided, it is best to use "rational polypharmacology," which entails the following (Kaplan & Sadock, 1993):

1. Use the least number of medications needed to achieve optimal improvement.
2. Combine medications if necessary to treat two or more distinct symptoms (symptoms not attributable to one underlying cause).
3. Exercise special care in medicating children, the elderly, and the medically ill.
4. Administer each drug trial for an appropriate length of time.
5. "Taking the edge off" is of more value to the patient than over-medication.
6. If a medication is likely to cause unpleasant side effects, start with a small dose.
7. Consider the patient's prior experience with this and other medications, his/her attitude toward medications, his/her family's attitude toward and experiences with medications, and his/her PCP's attitude toward psychotropic medications.
8. Be aware that it is not uncommon that patients who want or demand medication do not need it, whereas patients who do need it may be resistant to taking it.
9. Psychotropic medications work best when combined with appropriate psychotherapy. Psychotropics are not used alone, but only in conjunction with psychotherapy. (The psychotherapy does not necessarily need to take place on a weekly basis, but can take place on whatever basis is most appropriate, as long is it is at least once every three months.)
10. If a patient is clearly unwilling to use medication, it is usually best to respect his/her wishes (except in cases of severe mental illness which render the patient incapable of acting in his/her own best interest).

Concluding Remarks

Although research into the area of psychopharmacology and medical cost offset is still in its infancy, the studies to date generally indicate that the proper management of psychotropic medications can produce tremendous medical cost offset savings. The proper management of psychotropics is also necessary to provide the best possible care for our psychiatric patients. Because cost containment and treatment effectiveness are likely to both result from the same set of medication management skills, it is highly probable that future research will continue to demonstrate significant cost savings, and to be able to quantify both the potential cost offset in terms both dollars to be saved and the increased quality of life for the patients.

References

Antonuccio, D. O., Danton, W. G., & DeNelsky, G. Y. (1995). Psychotherapy versus medication for depression: Challenging the conventional wisdom with data. *Professional Psychology: Research and Practice, 26* (6), 574-585.

Antonuccio, D. O., Danton, W. G., & DeNelsky, G. Y. (1999). Raising questions about antidepressants. *Psychotherapy and Psychosomatic Medicine, 68*(1), 3-14.

Beardsley, R. S., Gardocki, G. J., Larson, D. B., & Hildalgo, J. (1988). Prescribing of psychotropic medication by primary care physicians and psychiatrists. *Archives of General Psychiatry, 45,* 1117-1119.

Carpenter, W. T. (1996). Treatment of negative symptoms: Pharmacololgical and methodological issues. *British Journal of Psychiatry, 168* (suppl. 29), 17-22.

Crisman, M. L., Trivedi, M., & Pigott, T. A. (1999). The Texas medication algorithm project: Report of the Texas consensus conference panel on medication treatment of major depressive disorder. *Journal of Clinical Psychiatry, 60*(3), 142-156.

Cummings, J. L. (2001). *Psychopharmacology update.* Scottsdale, AZ: The Nicholas & Dorothy Cummings Foundation.

Cummings, N. A. (1985). *Biodyne training manual.* South San Francisco: Foundation for Behavioral Health.

Cummings, N. A. (1997a). Behavioral health in primary care: Dollars and sense. In N. A. Cummings, J. L. Cummings, & J. N. Johnson (Eds.), *Behavioral health in primary care: A guide for clinical integration.* Madison, CT: Psychosocial Press.

Cummings, N. A. (1997b). Pioneering integrated systems: Lessons learned, forgotten, and relearned. In N. A. Cummings, J. L. Cummings, & J. N. Johnson (Eds.), *Behavioral health in primary care: A guide for clinical integration.* Madison, CT: Psychosocial Press.

Cummings, N. A., Cummings, J. L., & Johnson, J. N. (Eds.). (1997). *Behavioral health in primary care: A guide for clinical integration.* Madison, CT: Psychosocial Press.

Cummings, N. A. & Follette, W. T. (1968). Psychiatric services and medical utilization in a prepaid health plan setting: Part 2. *Medical Care, 6,* 31-41.

Cummings, N. A., Kahn, B. I., & Sparkman, B. (1962). *Psychotherapy and medical utilization: A pilot study.* Oakland, CA: Annual Reports of Kaiser Permanente Research Projects.

Cummings, N. & Sayama, M. (1995). *Focused psychotherapy: A casebook of brief, intermittent psychotherapy throughout the life cycle.* NY: Brunner/Mazel.

Cummings, N. A. & VandenBos, G. R. (1981). The twenty year Kaiser-Permanente experience with psychotherapy and medical utilization: Implications for national health policy and national health insurance. *Health Policy Quarterly, 1,* 159-175.

Cummings, N. A. & Wiggins, J. G. (2001). A collaborative primary care/behavioral health model for the use of psychotropic medication with children and adolescents. *Issues in Interdisciplinary Care, 3* (2), 121-128.

DeRubeis, R. J., Gelfand, L. A., Tang, T. Z., & Simons A. D. (1999). Medications versus cognitive behavior therapy for severely depressed outpatients: Mega-analysis of four randomized comparisons. *American Journal of Psychiatry, 156* (7), 1007-1013.

Emslie, G. J., Walkup, J. T., Pliska, S. R., & Ernst, M. (1999). Nontricyclic antidepressants: Current trends in children and adolescents. *Journal of the American Academy of Child and Adolescent Psychiatry, 38,* 517-528.

Fichtner, C. G., Hanrahan, P., & Luchins, D. J. (1998). Pharmacoeconomic studies of atypical antipsychotics: Review and perspective. *Psychiatric Annals, 28,* 381-386.

Fisher, R. L., & Fisher, S. (1996). Anti-depressants for children: Is scientific support necessary? *Journal of Nervous and Mental Disease, 184,* 99-102.

Follette, W. T. & Cummings, N. A. (1967). Psychiatric services and medical utilization in a prepaid plan setting. *Medical Care, 5,* 25-35.

Foxman, B., Valdez, R. B., & Brook, R. B. (1986). Childhood enuresis: Prevalence, perceived impact, and prescribe treatments. *Pediatrics, 77,* 482-487.

Gitlin, M. J. (1996). *The psychotherapist's guide to psychopharmacology.* NY: The Free Press.

Greenhill, L. L. (1998). The use of psychotropic medicaitons in preschoolers: Indications, safety, and efficacy. *Canadian Journal of Psychiatry, 43,* 576-581.

Hansen, T. E., Casey, D. E., & Hoffman, W. F. (1997). Neuroleptic intolerance. *Schizophrenia Bulletin, 23,* 567-582.

Hartman-Stein, P. E. (Ed.). (1997). *Innovative behavioral healthcare for older adults.* San Francisco: Jossey-Bass.

Haveman, J. K. (1998). "Access to atypical antipsychotics: A public payer's perspective, as reported in *Behavioral Healthcare Tomorrow* (pp. 45-48). Tiburon, CA: CentraLink.

Huttin, C. & Bosanquet, N. (1995). *The prescription drug market: International perspectives and challenges for the future,* Vol. 17. NY: Elsevier Science Publishers.

Jensen, P. S. (1998). Ethical and pragmatic issues in the use of psychotropic agents in young children. *Canadian Journal of Psychiatry, 43,* 585-588.

Johnson, H. F., & Fruehling, J. J. (1994). Pharmacological therapy for depression in children and adolescents. In W. M. Reynolds & H. F. Johnson (Eds.), *Handbook of depression in children and adolescents* (pp. 122-131). New York: Plenum.

Joseph, S. (1997). Symptom-focused psychiatric drug therapy for managed care. NY: The Haworth Medical Press.

Kane, J. M. (1995). Tardive dyskinesia. In F. E. Bloom & D. J. Kuplier (Eds.), Psychopharmacology: The fourth generation of progress (pp. 1485-1495). NY: Raven Press.

Kane, J. M., Honigfel, G., Singer, J., & Meltzer, H. Y. (1988). Clozaril Collaborative Study Group: Clozapine for the treatment-resistant schizophrenic. *Archives of General Psychiatry, 45*, 789-796.

Kaplan, A. (1999, September). Medication prescribing practices for children and adolescents. *Psychiatric Times, 9*, 5, 11.

Kaplan, H. I. & Sadock, B. J. (1993). Pocket handbook of psychiatric drug treatment. Baltimore: Williams & Wilkins.

Keck, P. E. & McElroy S. L. (1997). The new antipsychotics and their therapeutic potential. *Psychiatric Annals, 5*, 320-331.

Kleinke, J. D. (2001). The price of progress: Prescription drugs in the health care market. *Health News, 20* (5).

Lehman, A. & Steinwachs, D. (1998). Patterns of usual care for schizophrenics: Initial results from the Schizophrenia Patient Outcomes Research Team (PORT) client survey. *Schizophrenia Bulletin, 24*, 11-20.

McEvoy, J. P., Scheifler, P. L., & Frances, A. (1999). Expert consensus guidelines series: Treatment of schizophrenia 1999. *Journal of Clinical Psychiatry 60* (suppl. 11), 4-83.

Minde, K. (1998). The use of psychotropic medication in preschoolers: Some recent developments. *Canadian Journal of Psychiatry, 43*, 571-575.

Moore, T. J. (1998). *Prescription for disaster*. NY: Simon & Schuster.

Munoz, R. A. (2000). Psychopharmacologic nihilism. *Psychiatric Times, 17* (8), 25-26.

National Advisory Mental Health Council. (1993). *Health care reform for Americans with severe mental illnesses*. Bethesda, MD: National Institute of Mental Health.

National Alliance for the Mentally Ill. (2000). Access for effective medications: A critical link to recovery. Arlington, VA: author.

National Alliance for the Mentally Ill. (2001a). Schizophrenia PORT study. http://www.nami.org/research/portstudy.html.

National Alliance for the Mentally Ill. (2001b). Omnibus mental illness recovery act. http://www.nami.org/update/omirasec3.html.

National Depressive and Manic-Depressive Association. (2000). *Beyond diagnosis: Depression and treatment*. Chicago: author.

Nganele, D. M. (2001). *Surviving the cost of prescription drugs*. iUniverse.com.

Pelligrino, E. D. (1996). Clinical judgment, scientific data, and ethics: Antidepressant therapy in adolescents and children. *Journal of Nervous and Mental Disease, 184*, 106-108.

Pincus, H. A., Tanielian, T. L., Marcus, S. C., Olfson, M., Zarin, D. A., Thompson, J., & Zito, J. M. (1998). Prescribing trends in psychotropic medication: Primary care, psychiatry, and other medical specialities. *Journal of the American Medical Association, 279*, 526-531.

Safer, D. J., Zito, J. M., & Fine, E. M. (1996). Increased methylphenidate usage for attention deficit disorder in the 1990s. *Pediatrics, 98,* 1084-1088.

Sakurai, M. (1996). *Integrated cost management: A companywide prescription for higher profits and lower costs.* Productivity Press (ppress.com).

Simon, G. E., VonKorff, M., & Heiligenstein, J. H. (1996). Initial antidepressant choice in primary care: Effectiveness and cost of fluoxetine versus tricyclic antidepressants. *Journal of the American Medical Association, 275,* 1897-1902.

Smith, N. M., Floyd, M. R., Scogin, F., & Jamison, C. S. (1997). Three-year follow-up of bibliotherapy for depression. *Journal of Clinical Psychology, 65* (2), 324-327.

Texas Council of Community MHMR Centers. (December 1988). *New generation drug treatment: Upstream help for Texans with schizophrenia and other severe mental illnesses.* Austin, TX: author.

Vitiello, B. (1998). Pediatric psychopharmacology and the interaction between drugs and the developing brain. *Canadian Journal of Psychiatry, 43,* 582-584.

Wiggins, J. G. & Cummings, N. A. (1998). National study of the experiences of psychologists with psychotropic medication and psychotherapy. *Professional Psychology: Research and Practice, 29* (6), 549-552.

Zito, J. M., Safer, D. J., dosReis, S., Gardner, J. F., Boles, M., & Lynch, F. (2000). Trends in prescribing of psychotropic medications to preschoolers. *Journal of the American Medical Association, 283,* 1025-1030.

Zito, J. M., Safer, D. J., Riddle, M. A., Johnson, R. E., Speedle, S. M., & Fox, M. (1998). Prevalence variations in psychotropic treatment of children. *Journal of Child and Adolescent Psychopharmacology, 8,* 99-105.

Treating Depression in Primary Care: What Are the Cost-offset Opportunities?

Patricia Robinson
Mountainview Consulting Group
Moxee, Washington

Depression is highly prevalent in our country, and effective treatment of this disorder may help improve the serious health care budget deficits that have confronted Americans in recent decades. The purpose of delivering health care services to depressed patients assumed in this paper is to improve their health status by using available resources cost effectively (Eddy, 1996). In order to realize this objective, we must develop clinical policies that are based on evidence about treatment benefits, harms, costs, and patient preference for use of the collective health care dollar. Since treatment of an episode of depression is most likely to occur in the primary care setting (Regier, et al., 1993), the primary care setting has fundamental importance for improving the health of depressed adults. In the present paper, I focus on evidence derived from primary care treatment studies because primary care *is* the setting where most depressed patients —medically sick and medically well— are accessible. Additionally, primary care is the setting where health care providers are able to treat the most patients for the least cost.

Provision of mental health services to patients suffering from depression sometimes leads to a decrease in their use of medical services. Health care researchers and medical economists refer to this phenomenon as a "cost-offset effect." The cost of providing mental health services is offset by reductions in the cost of general medical services. "Mental health" cost offsets may be demonstrated when behavioral health services are integrated into the primary setting, with a result of a savings in the cost of delivering mental health services in traditional settings (Von Korff, et al., 1998). Cost offsets are a secondary outcome rather than a primary aim in the delivery of mental health services. The primary purpose for delivery of mental health services in any health care setting is to provide effective treatment for an array of diagnosable disorders that have a negative impact on quality of life. Medical cost-offsets have the potential to occur when use of health care services is driven in part or whole by psychological or psychiatric factors.

Depression is a good choice of a mental disorder for studying economic offset effects. Patients suffering from symptoms of depression want and seek treatment for these symptoms, and several effective treatments are available. Efficacy studies indicate that antidepressant medications and structured psychotherapies improve the outcomes of acute phase treatment of major depression (Public Health Service Agency for Health Care Policy and Research, 1993). Additionally, treatments integrated into the primary care setting may be more effective than traditional treatments delivered in mental health clinics (Katon, Von Korff, et al.; 1995; Katon, Robinson, et al., 1996; Mynors-Wallace, Davies, Gray, Gath, & Barbour, 1997; Mynors-Wallis, Gath, Day, & Baker, 2000; Mynors-Wallis, Gath, Lloyd-Thomas, & Tomlinson, 1995). While there is little research on the cost-effectiveness of treating specific mental disorders, one study suggests that treatment of depression in the primary care setting is a better value than treatment in the mental health clinic setting (Von Korff, et al., 1998). However, a second study suggests that shifting patients away from mental health specialists may worsen functional outcomes while decreasing costs (Sturm & Wells, 1995). Consumers have voted with their feet on the issue of depression. Symptoms of depression are the leading reason for pursuit of mental health services (Zimmerman, M., & Mattia, 2000).

Four factors influence the realization of cost-offsets in treatment of depression. These include the population and health care setting targeted, health care policies, and provider implementation of policies. In this paper, I present information on these factors, including both opportunities for enhancing cost offset effects and obstacles that impede progress. I conclude with recommendations for health care services researchers. Their thoughtful work will build the foundation of the information base needed for generating policies that support effective use of resources for treating depression.

Who: What Groups of Depressed Patients Need Improved Care?

Depression is one of the most costly disorders in the United States (Hirschfeld, et al., 1997). The direct and indirect costs of depression have been estimated at $43 billion each year, not including pain and suffering and diminished quality of life (Finkelstein, Berndt, & Greenberg, 1996). Depression costs include substantial health care costs, as well as workplace costs (Birnbaum, et al., 1999). The literature on cost-offset effects suggests three patient groups with high potential for generating cost-offset effects. These include medical inpatients, medical outpatients with somatization disorder, and alcoholic adults (Olfson, Sing, & Schlesinger, 2001). Additionally, cost-offset effects may appear with improved treatment of stressed adults presenting to primary care with psychosomatic symptoms; older adults (particularly those with significant medical illness burden and those with possibly life-threatening conditions); out-patients with chronic medical conditions; outpatients with conditions that cause depression, and workers disabled by depression. Primary care is the hub of treatment for all of these patient groups, and the setting to which most depressed patients go for care.

Medical Inpatients

Major depression may go undetected among inpatients, as well as outpatients, with medical illness because providers see depression as a normal reaction to serious illness, such as cancer, myocardial infarction, stroke, dementia and Parkinson's disease. In fact, the risk of depression is increased for patients with these disorders, but it is not normal and it may worsen the rate of patient progress (Cassem, 1995). The literature documenting the cost-effectiveness of mental health treatment for general medical inpatients dates back to the early 1970's. Mumford, Schlesinger, Glass, Patrick, and Cuerdon (1984) reviewed 58 controlled trials concerning treatment of general medical patients. Psychosocial treatments used in these studies included educational interventions, development of resource plans, emotional and social support, and brief psychotherapeutic treatment regimes. Collectively, the interventions were associated with an average 10 percent reduction in inpatient medical care costs. Savings tended to be greater for older medical inpatients than for younger medical inpatients. In another early study, patients who experienced an initial myocardial infarction that were randomly assigned to brief supportive psychotherapy left the hospital 2.5 days earlier than their usual care counterparts (Gruen, 1975). More recently, a study of elderly orthopedic surgical patients found that patients who received psychiatric consultations had shorter hospital stays (Levenson, Hamer, & Rossiter, 1992).

Medical Outpatients

Depressed medical outpatients may present with somatic complaints, the most common of which include headaches, gastrointestinal disturbances and recurrent unexplained pain (Diagnostic and Statistical Manual of Mental Disorders, 4th Ed., 1994). These symptoms may complicate diagnosis of depression in the primary care setting. When patients present with vague somatic symptoms over an extended period of time, they may be diagnosed with somatization disorder. The essential feature of somatization disorder is a pattern of recurring, multiple, clinically significant somatic complaints, which often begin by adolescence. Estimates vary from .2% to 2% depending on the gender of the patient and the discipline of the interviewer (Diagnostic and Statistical Manual of Mental Disorders, 1994). As with depression, the prevalence of somatization disorder is higher among women. Somatization disorder is a fluctuating disorder, but it is chronic. These individuals may be at increased risk for depression secondary to medical procedures that may actually put them at risk for development of medical problems with an organic basis. Smith, Rost, & Kashner (1995) found that delivery of psychiatric consultation services to patients with somatization disorder resulted in lowered medical charges. For every patient diagnosed with somatization disorder, there are roughly 100 other adult patients with symptoms of this disorder, and they contribute to excessive utilization of medical services (Robins & Regier, 1991).

Alcoholic Adults

Symptoms of depression and mood instability are among the most common psychiatric symptoms seen in individuals with substance use disorders. Data from the ECA study indicated that among people with any affective disorder, 32% had a co-morbid addictive disorder (Robins & Regier, 1991). Among individuals with major depression, 16.5% had a co-morbid alcohol-use diagnosis. Medical cost savings can be realized by treatment of alcoholic patients, particularly during the early stages of alcohol-use disorders (Holder & Blose, 1986). These savings may be realized only in the long-term in that medical complications develop after years of untreated abuse. Medical complications of repeated intake of high doses of alcohol are numerous. Nearly every organ system, especially the gastrointestinal tract, cardiovascular system, and the central and peripheral nervous systems, suffer. The savings associated with treatment of alcohol use disorders, with or without co-morbid depression, may only be realized in the long-term, and this may dampen managed care interest in pursuing the cost-offset opportunity with this group. However, the medical dollar that funds treatment of medical complications of long-term alcoholism is generated by all of us, and employers are wise to evaluate the impact of untreated alcoholism on worker productivity and disability, particularly when alcoholism is co-morbid with depression. With this particular population, use of intermediate outcomes may facilitate realization of long-term savings. One HMO study found that changes in co-pay structures designed to improve access to an alcohol treatment program were associated with significant intermediate outcomes, including increased use of alcohol treatment services, longer periods of abstinence and greater participation in non-drinking activities (Hayami & Freeborn, 1981).

Stressed Adults

Mild to moderate symptoms of depression are common reactions to psycho-social stressors. The growing discipline of mind-body medicine is defining a causal link between mental / emotional problems and physical illnesses (see, for example, Ornstein & Sobel, 1988; 1990). Pautler (1991) reported that as many as 25 percent of all outpatient visits can be accounted for by psychological factors that cause physiological disturbance with no permanent organ damage (e.g., migraines, functional bowel disease, types of chronic pain). This rate rises to 50% if the definition of psychosomatic illness is broadened to include conditions where actual physiological changes occur (e.g., hypertension, hyperthyroidism, asthma, and chronic skin disorders) (Paulter, 1991). Additionally, patients with psychosomatic illness often require more physician time in visits than medical patients not impacted by psychosomatic illness. Brief psychotherapy reduces patients' stress levels, related physical symptoms, and overall medical costs (Cummings, 1993; Cummings & VandenBos, 1981). Further, "preventive optimism training" appears to prevent depression, reduce physical symptoms of illness, and reduce medical visits (Buchanan, Rubenstein, & Seligman, 1999).

Older Adults

Late-life depression is costly because it has a deleterious interaction with physical health and contributes to excessive disability. Older primary care patients with depression visit the doctor and emergency room more often, use more medication, incur higher outpatient charges, and stay longer when in the hospital (Callahan, Hui, Nienaber, Musick, & Tierney, 1994; Cooper-Patrick, Crum, & Ford, 1994; Callahan & Wolinsky, 1995; Unutzer, et al., 1996). Older adults with symptoms of depression also accrue greater average diagnostic test charges than their non-depressed cohorts (Callahan, Kesterson, & Tierney, 1997). Since depressed patients have greater co-morbid medical illness than their non-depressed cohorts, optimal treatment often requires integrating care for depression with self-management training for medical conditions. Of course, delivery in the primary care setting is more acceptable to older patients than treatment in mental health settings (Robinson, Wischman, & Del Vento, 1996). Integrated medical and behavioral health treatment in a primary care group format may reshape the utilization patterns of frail older adults, and the shift from emergency room utilization to nurse phone calls may create a cost savings (Robinson, Del Vento, & Wischman, 1998).

Herman, Brand-Driehorst, Kaminsky, Leibing, Staats, et al. (1998) reported an association between depression and higher 22-month mortality rates for people who have been hospitalized for a wide variety of problems on a hospital general medical unit. Mortality rates are higher for patients with coronary artery disease (Barefoot & Schroll, 1996; Barefoot, Helms, et al., 1996) and for patients recovering from myocardial infarction when they experience co-morbid depression (Frasure-Smith, Lesperance, Juneau, Jalajic, & Bourassa, 1999; Frasure-Smith, Lesperance, & Talajic, 1993). In a prospective 7-year study of 7,518 white women over age 66, women with 6 or more depressive symptoms had a 2-fold increased risk of death compared with those who had 5 or fewer depressive symptoms (Whooley & Browner, 1998). In study analyses, this association remained constant after adjusting for potentially confounding variables, including numerous health status indicators. It is unclear as to whether depressive symptoms are a marker for, or a cause of, life-threatening conditions. It is clear that depressive symptoms in older women and men, particularly those with potentially life-threatening conditions, can serve as a reminder for health care providers to initiate discussions about patient preference concerning the end of life. Providers can help control unnecessary medical spending and enhance patient self-efficacy by developing living wills and suggesting materials for patients to use in actively planning for the end of life (see for example, Humphry, 1991).

Outpatients with Chronic Medical Conditions

According to Catherine Hoffman of the Henry J. Kaiser Family Foundation (Hoffman, Rice, & Sung, 1996), nearly half the people in the United States are currently living with chronic conditions. Many of these patients struggle with symptoms of depression along with the symptoms of their individual chronic medical problem. Up to 25% of diabetic patients experience clinically significant symptoms of depression. Symptoms of depression compromise patient abilities for successful adherence to disease management plans. Programs that help patients cope with depression symptoms and self-manage chronic conditions need to be delivered in the primary care setting. Four conditions that are ideal for combined depression treatment and self-management support services are diabetes, heart disease, arthritis, and asthma, as these collectively cost the nation an estimated $457.6 billion a year (National Institutes of Health, 1995). Unfortunately, as with alcoholism treatment, purchasers of health care are faced with a disincentive to invest in these interventions, as the benefits of treatment accumulate over a lifetime and patients change health insurance providers relatively often. However, infrequent, single incident costs can add up for this group (for example, hospitalization for a diabetic comma or limb amputation), and timely delivery of depression and self-management programs may support short-term as well as long-term cost savings.

Outpatients with Medical Conditions that Cause Depression

This group includes patients with endocrine disorders (such as hypothyroidism and Cushing's disease) and neurological disorders (such as multiple sclerosis, Parkinson's disease, migraine, and various forms of epilepsy, encephalitis, and brain tumors). Additionally, patients who are taking medications that cause depression need to be screened for early detection of depression symptoms and monitored on an on-going basis. Depressogenic medications include anti-hypertension agents such as reserpine, glucocorticoid, and anabolic steriods.

Workers Disabled by Depression

Depression causes more disability than do many chronic medical disorders (Spitzer, et al., 1995; Hays, Wells, Sherbourne, Rogers, & Spritzer, 1995), and this is felt dramatically in worker productivity, absenteeism and disability claims. Employers pays a significant amount for the health care services that depressed workers use during an episode of major depression. A recent study using employer claims data for over 4,000 patients with a claim for major depression or a depression-related disability in 1997 found these patients to have higher rates of inpatient admissions, outpatient procedures, and office visits than the overall employee population (Birnbaum, et al., 1999). Additionally, the depression group had total medical, pharmaceutical, and disability costs that were 4.2 times higher than those for the typical beneficiary ($8,709 versus $2,059). When the researchers excluded the costs of depression treatment, the remaining annual per capita health care costs (i.e., medical and prescription) of depressed patients were almost three times those of the overall employee population ($5,092 versus $1,790, respectively). Other researchers have suggested that the bulk of health care costs associated with treating depressed patients are spent on care for co-morbid medical conditions (Croghan, Obenchain, & Crown, 1998). In the study by Birnbaum and colleagues (1999), 59% of health care costs of treating depressed employees were spent on non-depression related treatment. Increased attention to management training in recognition of the depression symptoms and referral to employee assistance programs in a timely manner may help create cost savings in both mental health and medical budgets.

Where: What Setting Has an Economic Incentive for Developing Depression Treatment Programs That Are Likely to Demonstrate a Cost-Offset Effect?

From a population-based care perspective, primary care is the optimal platform for treatment of depression. Treatment of an episode of major depression is most likely to be initiated and monitored over time in primary care. Medical cost-offset savings are most likely to be realized by programs that focus service delivery in the primary care setting because all patient groups with potential for realization of a cost-offset effect are primary care patients. Available literature suggests that primary care physicians fail to recognize depression in as many as half of their patients and fail to provide adequate treatment when depression is detected half of the time (Perez-Stable, Miranda, Munoz, & Ying; 1990; Simon & Von Korff, 1995; Miranda, Hohmann, Attkisson, & Larson, 1994; Depression Guideline Panel, 1993). Support from behavioral health consultants working in the primary care setting is likely to help primary care providers make needed improvements (Katon, et al., 1995; Katon, et al., 1996).

Hospital and emergency room settings also have potential for improving recognition and treatment of depression. While the hospital is a difficult setting for addressing depression, delivery of behavioral health consultation services may boost recognition rates, facilitate shorter hospital stays, and result in more comprehensive discharge plans. When provided by primary care behavioral health consultants, follow-up services are more likely to be focused on delivery of appropriate behavioral health treatment in the primary care setting in coordination with the primary care team. In that patients often receive care from physicians other than their primary care physician during a period of hospitalization, use of a primary care behavioral health consultant for these services would support continuity of care and perhaps enhance patient satisfaction. Screening of hospital patients is important because of the high prevalence of depression among hospitalized patients. Kathol and Wenzel (1992) found that one third of 128 patients admitted to a general medicine ward had major depression. While many improve quickly, a policy requiring follow-up screening would help identify patients with persistent symptoms and significant impairments in functioning. The emergency room setting is another setting where primary care behavioral health consultants can provide links between depressed patients and their primary care teams.

The primary care system has tremendous potential for depression prevention activities and on-going clinical monitoring of patients with recurrent depression. Collaborative work between primary care providers and behavioral health providers can result in programs that target high utilizers and shape patient and provider behavior patterns to reduce excessive procedures, prescriptions and hospital days and to prevent depression-related disability. By working with employers, primary care and behavioral health providers may also design detection and intervention programs for the work setting.

What: What Policy for Treating Depression Will Support Realization of a Medical Cost-Offset?

The purpose of health care policy is to influence decisions about interventions. Since policies are designed to fit specific health care settings and since primary care clinics with integrated behavioral health services have the greatest potential for improving outcomes, discussion about policy development will be restricted to policies affecting this setting. While there is ample room for improvement of both recognition and treatment outcomes in primary care, policies must address the barriers to improved recognition and treatment of depression in this setting in order to be successful. These include time, somatization, stigmatization, reimbursement, and co-morbid medical conditions (Kroenke, 1997). Most medical outpatient visits last 15 minutes or less while visits to mental health providers typically last 30 minutes or longer (Schappert, 1993). Further, the primary care patient typically brings physical concerns to the visit and symptoms of depression may be very subtle. Co-morbid medical disorders may also mask symptoms of depression. Providers may assume a stigma concerning depression and avoid asking questions about depression for fear of harming the relationship with the patient. Insurance policies may prohibit reimbursement to providers who are not mental health clinicians, restrict visits or require co-payments.

Efficacy and cost data are available from several studies conducted in the primary care setting (Katon, et al., 1995; Katon, et al., 1996). Procedures and protocols employed in these studies were developed with the intention of minimizing identified barriers to improved outcomes and informing policy development. Both studies resulted in improved clinical outcomes, as well as a mental health cost-offset. Prior to considering this evidence, we will consider important questions concerning patient, purchaser, and payor preferences, as these are also critical to the development of optimal policies.

What Do Patients Want?

Depression is one of the few mental health disorders for which patient preference is available (Katon, 1996; Bennet, Torrance, Boyle, & Guscott, 2000). In a recent study of 400 psychiatric outpatients, 47% obtained major depression as a principal or additional diagnosis, and 98.9% of these patients reported that their symptoms of depression were their reasons for seeking treatment (Zimmerman & Mattia, 2000). Even when these psychiatric outpatients had depression as an additional, as opposed to a principal diagnosis, 95% wanted treatment to address their mood problems. This finding is consistent with results of the Epidemiologic Catchment Area (ECA) study findings. Among the 28.5% of persons with a DSM-III disorder that had received mental health treatment in the prior year, those with mood disorders were treated more frequently than those with other diagnoses (Robins & Regier, 1991; Regier, et al., 1993). More specifically, individuals with mood disorders were treated more often than persons with anxiety disorders, who were treated more frequently than persons with substance use disorders (45.7% versus 32.7 percent versus 23.6 percent) (Robins & Regier, 1991; Regier, et al., 1993). Similar results were obtained in the National Comorbidity Study (36.4 percent versus 26.5 percent versus 22.7 percent) (Kessler, et al., 1994). A recent study applied utility measures to depression symptoms to obtain information about patient preferences concerning treatment. Patient utility rating scores for moderate depression were below those reported for being "blind, deaf or dumb" (Torrance, Boyle, & Horwood; 1982; Bennet, et al., 2000). However, patients, as a group, want to limit health care cost spending, and patients, as well as providers, have evaluated less intensive treatments (such as educational pamphlets) positively (Robinson, et al., 1997).

What Do Payors and Purchasers Want?

Payors and purchasers, like patients, want cost-effective quality treatment for depression. Payors and purchasers, as groups, may be better stationed to appreciate the population management perspective than patients and providers. They focus on economic outcomes, and this focus is more consistent with the population-based care view. Payors and purchasers want effective methods for controlling cost and assuring quality. Payors may employ strategies that draw the cost lines on people (e.g., treatment of major depression, but not minor depression) and/or treatment intensity (e.g., 5 sessions but not 10 sessions). In the case of depression, policies that draw cost lines on treatment intensity may be more likely to support medical cost-offsets. Several reasons suggest this possibility. First, there is potential cost saving associated with treatment of patients with more minor symptoms because patients with minor symptoms may have a greater burden of medical illness relative to that of patients with major depression (Wells, et al., 1989; Von Korff, et al., 1998), and their medical costs tend to be more than those of patients with major depression (Katon, et al., 1996). Secondly, available evidence suggests that patients with major depression that receive an integrated treatment in primary care that is one-quarter of the intensity of traditional mental health psychotherapeutic treatment have equal clinical outcomes (Katon, et al., 1996).

What Do Providers Want?

While payors and purchasers struggle with policy development, patients and providers struggle with policy implementation. Patients protest when effective care is withheld, and providers are uncertain about the ethical and legal consequences of withholding care. In the case of depression, health care systems may choose to recommend treatments that are less efficacious, but more cost-effective in an effort to better serve the large population of depressed patients. At some level, patients clearly share the concern of payors and purchasers. This is the level of analysis where patients, as citizens, object to lowered pay increases, higher employee contributions to medical insurance plans, and substantial tax increases that are required by the out-of-control health care budget. The amount of money we are willing to pay for health care is limited, and policies for treating depression must be developed with the assumptions of (a) a very large patient population and (b) limited resources. Patient and provider collaboration with payors and purchasers in policy development is critical. With this understanding, we can look at the evidence available concerning development of health care policies for primary care treatment of depression. After considering efficacy and cost data, we will turn briefly to the "by whom" questions related to policy development.

Cost Effectiveness Evidence

Several studies have found that primary care treatment of depression can be improved by models of care involving on-sight behavioral health care (Miranda, et al., 1994; Mynors-Wallace, et al., 1997; Mynors-Wallis, et al., 2000; Mynors-Wallis, et al., 1995). Studies have explored a range of models, including primary care psychiatry treatment (Katon, et al., 1995); primary care behavioral health brief treatment (Katon, et al., 1996); problem solving therapy (Mynors-Wallis, et al., 1997; Mynors-Wallis, et al., 2000; Mynors-Wallis, et al., 1995) and cognitive behavioral group therapy (Miranda, et al., 1994; Munoz, et al., 1995). Von Korff and colleagues (1998) pooled information from two randomized controlled trials (Katon, et al., 1995; 1996) to explore the cost effectiveness of collaborative treatment by behavioral health and primary care providers in the primary care setting. These studies employed two models of care: psychiatric consultation and psychological consultation. Both models emphasized co-management with the primary care provider team and patient education concerning self-management strategies. The psychiatric consultation model emphasized pharmacological treatment (involving 1 to 10 hours of evaluation and treatment) while the psychological consultation model emphasized brief instruction in a variety of coping skills, individualized behavior change assignments (involving 2.5 to 3.5 hours of direct contact between the psychologist and patient) and psychologist phone support and primary care team clinic support of a written relapse prevention plan. Both of these models were shown to (a) improve short-term clinical outcomes for major depression, (b) increase patient satisfaction with treatment, and (c) increase the percent of patients receiving antidepressant treatment at or near levels recommended by the Agency for Health Care Policy and Research (AHCPR) (Public Health Service, 1993). For major depression, the extent of improvement in depressive symptoms was comparable to that obtained in randomized controlled trials evaluating the efficacy of pharmacotherapeutic and psychotherapeutic treatments (Katon, et al., 1995; 1996). Care was not significantly improved for primary care patients with sub-threshold levels of depressive symptoms by either model, although the psychologist model did show a positive trend. Both studies involved symptom measures rather than functioning measures as primary outcomes.

Data from the two Katon studies were combined and used to estimate treatment costs and cost-effectiveness of providing integrated treatment services in the primary care clinic to depressed patients during the first year after diagnosis of major depression (Von Korff, et al., 1998). The method of using patients exposed to treatment or usual care conditions on a randomized basis avoids the potential bias of the before-after design employed in some cost-offset studies (Mumford, et al., 1984). For each of the 332 study patients included in the cost analysis, cost data were summed for the one-year period beginning with the date of the initial primary care visit during which depression treatment was initiated. Costs (not charges) were derived from the HMO cost information system. Since mental health services provided by study personnel were not entered into this system, the price of obtaining comparable services in the local community were used to derive estimates. Patients ranged in age from 18 to 80. The costs of specialty mental health services were significantly lower among patients with major depression assigned to integrated care than among those assigned to usual care ($123 versus $317; p = .027). Because of this cost-offset in specialty mental health service use, the added cost of providing integrated behavioral health care for patients with major depression was less than it would have been otherwise. The added cost of mental health treatment in the psychiatric model was $487 and the added cost in the psychologist model was $264. The total costs of providing mental health treatment for major and sub-threshold depression were higher in both studies than the costs of delivering mental health services in the usual care model (see Tables 1 and 2). In the usual care arm of the study, patients could self-refer for out-patient mental health treatment and receive both pharmacological and psychotherapeutic treatment. As can be seen in Table 2, the cost effectiveness ratios did not suggest an offsetting reduction in the utilization of specialty mental health services among patients with minor depression in either model. The additional cost of providing integrated care for patients with minor depression was relatively more expensive (an additional cost of $641 and $520 per patient, respectively), as patients with minor depression who received usual care tended to use less traditional mental health services and to improve without more intensive mental health treatment.

If policy makers used the data from this study and combined medical and mental health dollars for cost-effectiveness analyses, the rank ordering would remain the same, but the magnitude of differences would change. From a policy perspective, this shift in magnitude might make a difference in policies adopted, particularly when factors like patient and provider satisfaction are factored into the decision process. As can be seen in Table 3, patients in the minor depression group had greater

Selection Rank Order	Major Depression		
	% Effectively Treated	Cost	Ratio
Psychologist Model	70.4	1182	1679
Psychiatrist Model	74.4	1337	1797
Usual Care I	43.8	850	1941
Usual Care II	42.3	918	2170

Table 1. Cost effectiveness ratios for treating major depression in primary care: cost of mental health treatment.

Selection Rank Order	Minor Depression		
	% Effectively Treated	Cost	Ratio
Usual Care I	67.9	656	968
Usual Care II	52.8	525	994
Psychologist Model	66.7	1045	1567
Psychiatrist Model	60	1298	2163

Table 2. Cost effectiveness ratios for treating monor depression in primary care: Cost of mental health treatment.

ambulatory medical costs than patients in the major depression group. Table 4 summarizes the cost-effectiveness ratios for major depression when medical and mental health costs are combined. The choice of the psychologist model becomes more convincing, particularly in light of patient and provider preference. Among patients with major depression who participated in the trial evaluating the psychologist model, 88% of the intervention patients rated their treatment for depression as good or excellent, while 56% of the usual care patients rated care for depression as good or excellent. Among patients with minor depression, 97% of the intervention patients, compared with 71% of the usual care patients rated their treatment of depression as good or excellent. One hundred percent of the primary care providers preferred the integrated treatment to usual care. Table 5 summarizes the cost-effectiveness ratios for the psychologist model and usual care treatment for minor depression. Based on the analyses in Table 2 that focused on mental health dollars, a policy of watchful waiting with minor depressives might be selected. Based on Table 5 (where mental health and medical dollars are placed in one pot) and patient and provider satisfaction data, a health care system might elect to treat patients with sub-threshold depression at a lower intensity level. Specifically, the policy might suggest a "watchful waiting" protocol in regards to use of antidepressant medications for patients with subthreshold depression. In lieu of medications, the policy might support primary care provider use of patient education materials to improve patient use of self-management strategies to improve mood. Health care companies adopting such policies would want to evaluate the long-term economic impact, as prevention of episodes of major depression among patients with minor or sub-threshold levels of depression may result in significant cost savings and improved consumer loyalty.

While these two studies make a needed contribution to policy development concerning primary care treatment of depression, they fall short in several important ways. First, they rely on depression symptom measures to estimate cost effectiveness. Patients are more likely to perceive functional measures as more helpful in

Treatment Costs	Major Depression		Minor Depression	
	Usual Care	Integrated Care	Usual Care	Integrated Care
Medical	1249	1349	1734	1844
Depression	918	1182	525	1045
Combined Cost	2167	2531	2259	2889

Table 3. Depression treatment and ambulatory medical treatment costs for depressed primary care patients over 1 year after diagnosis.

Selection Rank Order	Major Depression		
	% Effectively Treated	Combined Medical and Depression Treatment Costs	Ratio
Psychologist Model	70.4	2531	3595
Usual Care	42.3	2167	5123

Table 4. Combined medical and mental health treatment: cost effectiveness ratios treating major depression in primary care.

Selection Rank Order	Minor Depression		
	% Effectively Treated	Cost	Ratio
Psychologist Model	66.7	2889	4331
Usual Care	52.8	2259	4278

Table 5. Combined medical and mental health treatment: cost effectiveness ratios for treating minor depression in primary care.

generating quality of life estimates (Eddy, 1996). Second, the Von Korff group (1998) study failed to attempt any estimates of treatment harms, even though such may exist and may impact both clinical and cost outcomes. For example, both of the Katon studies improved antidepressant medication adherence among patients with minor depression, and there is inadequate evidence for pharmacological treatment of minor depression. Further, many of the patients with minor depression were older adults, and older adults are more vulnerable to experiencing complications with anti-depressant medications.

Policy Suggestions

Table 6 summarizes general guidelines for policies concerning treatment of depression in the primary care setting. They are based on a combination of empirical evidence, cost estimates and expert opinion. They are based on somewhat weak evidence, and they are incomplete without the support of patient preference, cost data, potential harm information, and specific information concerning training requirements for providers charged with implementing these guidelines. These data will need to be collected by individual health care systems and related specifically to the guidelines adopted by the individual system.

By Whom: What Providers Are Prepared to Support a Policy for Treating Depression That Will Yield a Medical Cost-Offset?

Providers want to avoid conflicting responsibilities (Eddy, 1996). They want to take care of their "population" of patients with available resources. Eddy suggests that a team approach can help providers "broaden" their sense of responsibility. He contrasts a "group" approach (where a group of providers goes about his or her own individual responsibilities as he or she sees fit) with a "team" approach (where a group of people work in a coordinated fashion to achieve a common goal). In regards to the primary care setting and treating of depression, the primary care physician is the "coach" for the team that cares for the individual patient, and the nurse, behavioral health consultant, and other members of the primary care team are members of the depression treatment team. At the clinic level, the medical director acts as the "mega-coach" and coordinates the activities of all providers acting to implement a policy concerning depression treatment. Providers vary in their ability to accept aspects of team membership related to suppression of personal objectives in favor of the team's objectives. In part, this is due to a loss of personal autonomy. Other factors include the provider's skill repertoire for implementing specific aspects of a policy. Training, as well as a range of options concerning intensity of treatment implementation, may help providers work successfully within healthcare systems that adopt population-based, empirically validated treatments for depression that are sensitive to limited financial resources.

What Else: What Are the Research Priorities?

Research priorities include dissemination of current knowledge, as well as exploration of questions pertinent to policy formation. Purchasers of research (e.g., funding agencies) and purchasers of primary care (i.e., insurance companies, managed care organizations) need to require investigators to use common outcome measures and to include elements needed for policy formation (e.g., measures of potential harm as well as benefit, measures of cost). Outcome measures need to

Guideline	Objective / Outcome
1. Screen passively for major depression in primary care.	a. Improve detection rate for system (5% for women and 2% for men).
2. Use of same interview approach by all members of team (e.g., SPACE DIGS).	b. Increase rate of accurate diagnosis. c. Increase rate of monitoring in routine appointments.
3. Provide structured antidepressant adherence risk assessments for patients prior to start of antidepressant therapy.	a. Decrease medication adherence failure rates. b. Decrease medication switch rates.
4. Treat all depressed patients in the primary care setting initially and triage those who need specialty services to prevent hospitalization or to manage suicidality.	a. Reduce percentage of depressed patients treated in MH outpatient settings b. Decrease MH clinic costs for treating depression.
5. Provide brief primary care behavioral health services for patients with major depression who prefer behavioral treatment or combination treatment.	a. Improve treatment outcome rates toward 70% (of patients with 50% or more reduction in depression symptoms) at 6 weeks after diagnosis. b. Improve functioning outcomes. c. Decrease work disability days. d. Decrease worker absenteeism.
6. Offer frail elderly patients the option of a group that combines medical and behavioral health care.	a. Shift utilization patterns: Decrease specialty & ER visits; increase primary care group and RN phone visits.
7. Provide a brief, psychoeducational "Quality of Life" class for primary care patients with mild symptoms of depression, particularly patients with chronic medical illnesses.	a. Reduce rates of diagnostic tests. b. Reduce rates of antidepressant prescriptions for patients who do not meet criteria for major depression. c. Increase patient adherence to self-management plans for chronic medical conditions.
8. Screen actively among hospitalized older adults using the Geriatric Depression Inventory.	a. Increase rates of use of primary care behavioral health consultation services by older adults. b. Increase number of patients who have medical advance directives.
9. Offer PC Behavioral Health Consultant visit to older medical inpatients that screen positive for depression.	a. Decrease hospital days.

Table 6. Guidelines and Objectives for Improving
Depression Treatment Outcomes and Value.

include assessment of patient functioning in multiple areas of daily living, as well as symptom severity, as such are most helpful in generating quality of life estimates. Health care systems can enhance the relevance of research studies by employing software that supports linkage between clinical and cost outcomes, such as those offering measurement of an "episode of care" (Lamberts, Wood, & Hofmans-Okkes, 1993).

The North American Primary Care Research Group (NAPCRG) provides a structure for multi-site studies and a list of priorities for investigation (Klickman & Okkes, 1998). Mood disorders, particularly when co-morbid with substance abuse, need to be given priority because they are prevalent and costly in both the medical and mental health budget. Replication studies are necessary for confident development of radically different models of care, such as the Primary Care Behavioral Health model (Strosahl, 1998), and depression disease management programs designed for primary care, such as the Integrated Care Program (Robinson, Wischman & Del Vento, 1996; Robinson, 1996). In addition to further evaluation of empirically validated treatments for depressed primary care patients in diverse settings (including public health care clinics), researchers need to further explore the relationship between physician and patient interactions and the prevention, detection and management of psychosocial and mental health problems (Klickman & Okkes, 1998). Provider autonomy, job satisfaction, and training need further study because policies are effective only when implemented with fidelity by providers. Issues related to consumer participation in policy development constitute another area for exploration. Cost studies, while complex, are critical. Issues related to where to draw the line on cost (i.e., people vs. treatment intensity) need attention, and cost studies need to be conducted over longer time periods. While private funding for basic descriptive research and methodologic development in the area of primary care behavioral health has been minimal, the MacArthur Foundation Depression in Primary Care Initiative is now providing more substantial support for investigation. While the quality of evidence concerning behavioral health treatments in primary care is limited, there is a consistent trend toward better data. Researchers are challenged to continue to build a strong foundation for innovative policy development in this area. They have a huge opportunity to alleviate suffering among the large group depressed primary care patients, the providers who care for them and the payors and purchasers who sponsor the care.

References

Barefoot, J. C., & Schroll, M. (1996). Symptoms of depression, acute myocardial infarction, and total mortality in a community sample. *Circulation, 93,* 1976-1980.

Barefoot, J. C., Helms, J. C., Mark, D. B., Blumenthal, J. A., Califf, R. M., Haney, T. L., O'Connor, C. M., Siegler, I. C., & Williams, R. B. (1996). Depression and long-term mortality risk in patients with coronary artery disease. *American Journal of Cardiology, 78*, 613-617.

Bennett, K. J., Torrance, G. W., Boyle, M. H., & Guscott, R. (2000). Cost utility analysis in depression: The McSad Utility Measure for Depression Health States, *Psychiatric Services, 51* (9), 1171-1176.

Birnbaum, H. G., Greenberg, P. E., Barton, M., Kessler, R. C., Rowland, C. R., & Williamson, T. E. (1999). Workplace burden of depression: A case study in social functioning using employer claims data. *Drug Benefit Trends, 11* (8), 6BH-12BH).

Buchanan, G. M., Rubenstein, C. A., & Seligman, M. E. P. (1999). Physical health following a cognitive-behavioral intervention. *Prevention and Treatment, 2,* Article 10. Available on the World Wide Web: http://journals.apa.org/prevention/volume2/pre0010010a.html.

Callahan, C. M., Hui, S. L., Nienaber, N. A., Musick, B. S., & Tierney, W. M. (1994). Longitudinal study of depression and health services use among elderly primary care patients. *Journal of the American Geriatrics Society, 42,* 833–838.

Callahan, C. M., Kesterson, J. G., & Tierney, W. M. (1997). Association of symptoms of depression with diagnostic test charges among older adults. *Annals of Internal Medicine, 126,* 417-425.

Callahan, C. M., & Wolinsky, F. D. (1995). Hospitalization for major depression among older Americans. *Journals of Gerontology. Series A, Biological Sciences and Medical Sciences, 50,* M196–M202.

Cassem, E. H. (1995). Depressive disorders in the medically ill: An overview. *Psychosomatics, 36,* S2-S10.

Cooper-Patrick, L., Crum, R. M., & Ford, D. E. (1994). Characteristics of patients with major depression who received care in general medical and specialty mental health settings. *Medical Care, 32,* 15–24.

Croghan, T. W., Obenchain, R. L., & Crown, W. E. (1998). What does treatment of depression really cost? *Health Affairs, 17,* 198-208.

Cummings, N. (1993). Somatization: When physical symptoms have no medical cause. In Goleman, D., & Gurin, J. (Eds.), *Mind Body Medicine.* New York: Consumers Union.

Cummings, N., & VandenBos, G. (1981). The twenty years Kaiser-Permanente experience with psychotherapy and medical utilization: Implications for national health policy and national health insurance. *Health Policy Quarterly, 1,* 159-175.

Depression Guideline Panel. *Depression in primary care. Clinical practice guideline, No. 5.* Rockville, MD: U.S. Department of Health Human Services, Public Health Service, Agency for Health Care Policy and Research; April, 1993. AHCPR publication no. 93-0551.

Diagnostic and Statistical Manual of Mental Disorders. (1994). 4th Ed., Washington: American Psychiatric Association.

Eddy, D. M. (1996). *Clinical decision making from theory to practice: A collection of essays from the Journal of the American Medical Association.* Sudbury, MA: Jones and Bartlett.

Finkelstein, S. N., Berndt, E. R., & Greenberg, P. E. (1996). Economics of Depression: A Summary and Review. *NDMDA Paper,* January, 1996.

Frasure-Smith, N., Lesperance, F., Juneau, M., Talajic, M., & Bourassa, M. G. (1999). Gender, depression, and one-year prognosis after myocardial infarction. *Psychosomatic Medicine, 61*, 26-37.

Frasure-Smith, M., Lesperance, F., & Talajic, M. (1993). Depression following myocardial infarction. Impact on 6-month survival. *Journal of the American Medical Association, 270*, 1819-1825.

Gruen, W. (1975). Effects of brief psychotherapy during the hospitalization period on the recovery process in heart attacks. *Journal of Consulting and Clinical Psychology, 2*, 223-232.

Herman, C., Brand-Driehorst, S., Kaminsky, B., Leibing, E., Staats, H., & Ruger, U. (1998). Diagnostic groups and depressed mood as predictors of 22-month mortality in medical inpatients. *Psychosomatic Medicine, 60*, 570-577.

Hirschfeld, R. M., Keller, M. B., Panico, S., Arons, B. S., Barlow, D., Davidoff, F., Endicott, J., Froom, J., Goldstein, M., Gorman, J. M., Marek, R. G., Maurer, T. A., Meyer, R., Phillips, K., Ross, J., Schwenk, T. L., Sharfstein, S. S., Thase, M. E., & Wyatt, R. J. (1997). The National Depressive and Manic-Depressive Association consensus statement on the undertreatment of depression. *Journal of the American Medical Association, 277*, 333-340.

Hayami, D. E., & Freeborn, K. K. (1981). Effect of coverage on use of an HMO alcoholism treatment program, outcomes, and medical care utilization. *American Journal of Public Health, 71*, 1133-1143.

Hays, R. D., Wells, K. B., Sherbourne, C. D., Rogers, W., & Spritzer, K. (1995). Functioning and well-being outcomes of patients with depression compared with chronic general medical illnesses. *Archives of General Psychiatry, 52*, 11-9.

Hoffman, C., Rice, D., & Sung, H. Y. P. (1996). Persons with chronic conditions. *Journal of the American Medical Association, 276*, 1473-1479.

Holder, H. D., & Blose, J. O. (1986). Alcoholism treatment and total health care utilization and costs: A four-year longitudinal analysis of federal employees. *Journal of the American Medical Association, 256*, 1456-1460.

Humphry, D. (1991). *Final exit.* Secaucus, NJ: Carol Publishing Group.

Kathol, R. G., & Wenzel, R. P. (1992). Natural history of symptoms of depression and anxiety during inpatient treatment on general medicine wards. *Journal of General Internal Medicine, 7*, 287-293.

Katon, W., Von Korff, M., Lin, E., Walker, E., Simon, G., Bush, T., Robinson, P., & Russo, J. (1995). Collaborative management to achieve treatment guidelines: Impact on depression in primary care. *Journal of the American Medical Association, 273*, 1026-1031.

Katon, W., Robinson, P., Von Korff, M., Lin, E., Bush, T., Ludman, E., Simon, G., & Walker, E. (1996). A multifaceted intervention to improve treatment of depression in primary care. *Archives of General Psychiatry, 53*, 924-932.

Kessler, R. C., McGonagle, K. A., Zhao, S., Nelson, C. B., Hughes, M., Eshleman, S., Wittchen, H. U., & Kendler, K. S. (1994). Lifetime and 12-month prevalence of DSM-III-R psychiatric disorders in the United States. Results from the National Comorbidity Survey. *Archives of General Psychiatry, 51*, 8-19.

Klickman, M. S., & Okkes, I. (1998). Mental health problems in primary care: A research agenda. *Journal of Family Practice, 47* (5), 379-384.

Kroenke, K. (1997). Discovering depression in medical patients: Reasonable expectations. *Annals of Internal Medicine, 126,* 463-465.

Lamberts, H., Wood, M., & Hofmans-Okkes, I. (Eds.) *The international classification of primary care in the European Community, with a multi-language layer.* Oxford, England: Oxford University Press, 1993.

Levenson, J. L., Hamer, R. M., & Rossiter, L. F. (1992). A randomized controlled study of psychiatric consultation guided by screening in general medical inpatients. *American Journal of Psychiatry, 149,* 631-7.

Miranda, J., Hohmann, A. A., Attkisson, C. C., & Larson, D. B., (Eds.). (1994). *Mental disorders in primary care.* San Francisco: Jossey-Bass.

Mumford, E., Schlesinger, H., Glass, G., Patrick, C., & Cuerdon, T. (1984). A new look at evidence about reduced cost of medical utilization following mental health treatment. *American Journal of Psychiatry, 141,* 1145-1149.

Munoz, R. F., Ying, Y. W., Bernal, G., Perez-Stable, E. J., Sorensen, J. L., Hargreaves, W. A., Miranda, J., & Miller, L. S. (1995). Prevention of depression with primary care patients: A randomized controlled trial. *American Journal of Community Psychology, 23,* 199–222.

Mynors-Wallis, L. M., Davies, I., Gray, A., Gath, D. H., & Barbour, F. (1997). Randomised controlled trial and cost analysis of problem-solving treatment for emotional disorders by community nurses in primary care. *British Medical Journal, 170,* 113-119.

Mynors-Wallis, L. M., Gath, D. H., Day, A., & Baker, F. (2000). Randomised controlled trial of problem solving treatment, antidepressant medication, and combined treatment for major depression in primary care. *British Medical Journal, 320,* 26-30.

Mynors-Wallis L. M., Gath, D. H., Lloyd-Thomas, A., & Tomlinson, D. (1995). Randomised controlled trial comparing problem solving treatment with amitriptyline and placebo for major depression in primary care. *British Medical Journal, 310,* 441-445.

National Institutes of Health. (1995). *Disease-specific estimates of direct and indirect costs of illness and NIH support.* Bethesda, MD: Office of the Director.

Olfson, M., Sing, M., & Schlesinger, K. (2001). Mental health / medical care cost offsets: Opportunities for managed care. http://www.projhope.org/HA/bonus/180209.htm; 12/30/00, 1-9.

Ornstein, R., & Sobel, D. (1988). *The Healing Brain.* New York: Simon & Schuster.

Ornstein, R., & Sobel, D. (1990). *Healthy Pleasures.* Reading, Mass: Addison-Wesley.

Pautler, T. (1991). A Cost-effective mind-body approach to psychosomatic disorders. In Anchor. K. N. (Ed.), *Handbook of medical psychotherapy: Cost-effective strategies in mental health.* New York: Hogrefe & Huber.

Perez-Stable, E. J., Miranda, J., Bunoz, R. J., & Ying, Y. W. (1990) Depression in medical outpatients: Underrecognition and misdiagnosis. *Archives of Internal Medicine, 150,* 1083-1088.

Public Health Service Agency for Health Care Policy and Research (1993). *Depression in primary care: Volume 2. Treatment of major depression.* Rockville, MD: U.S. Department of Health and Human Services (AHCPR Publication No. 93-051).

Regier, D. A., Narrow, W. E., Rae, D. S., Manderscheid, R. W., Locke, B. Z., & Goodwin, F. K. (1993). The de facto US mental and addictive disorder service system: Epidemiologic Catchment Area prospective 1-year prevalence rates of disorders and services. *Archives of General Psychiatry, 50,* 85-94.

Robins, L. N., & Regier, D. A. (1991). *Psychiatric disorders in America: The epidemiologic catchment area study*, New York: Free Press, 1991.

Robinson, P. (1996). *Living life well: New strategies for hard times.* Reno, Nevada: Context Press.

Robinson, P., Bush, T., Von Korff, M., Katon, W., Lin, E., Simon, G. E., & Walker, E. (1997). The education of depressed primary care patients: What do patients think of interactive booklets and a video? *Journal of Family Practice, 44*, 562-571.

Robinson, P., Del Vento, A., & Wischman, C. (1998). Integrated treatment of the frail elderly: The group care clinic. In Blount, S. (Ed.), *Integrated Care: The Future of Medical and Mental Health Collaboration,* (pp.), New York: Norton.

Robinson, P., Wischman, C., & Del Vento, A. (1996). *Treating depression in primary care: A manual for primary care and mental health providers.* Reno, Nevada: Context Press.

Schappert, S. M. (1993). Office visits to psychiatrists: United States, 1989-90. *Advance data from vital and health statistics, No. 237.* Hyattsville, MD: National Center for Health Statistics.

Simon, G. E., & Von Korff, M. (1995). Recognition, management, and outcomes of depression in primary care. *Archives of Family Medicine, 4*, 99-105.

Smith, G. R., Rost, K., & Kashner, T. M. (1995). A trial of the effect of a standardized psychiatric consultation on health outcomes and costs in somatizing patients. *Archives of General Psychiatry, 52*, 238-243.

Spitzer, R. L., Kroenke, K., Linzer, M., Hahn, S. R., Williams, J. B., & deGruy, F. V. (1995). Health-related quality of life in primary care patients with mental disorders. Results from the PRIME-MD 1000 Study. *Journal of the American Medical Association, 274*, 1511-7.

Strosahl, K. (1998). Integration of primary care and behavioral health services: The Primary Mental Health Care Model. In A. Blount (Ed.), *Integrative primary care: The future of medical and mental health collaboration* (pp. 43-56). New York: Norton, Inc.

Sturm, R., & Wells, K. B. (1995). How can care for depression become more cost-effective? *Journal of the American Medical Association, 273*, 51-58.

Torrance, G. W., Boyle, M. H., & Horwood, S. P. (1982). Application of multi-attribute utility theory to measure social preferences for health states. *Operations Research, 30*, 1043-1069

Unutzer, J., Katon, W. J., Simon, G., Walker, E. A., Grembowski, D., & Patrick, D. (1996). Depression, quality of life, and use of health services in primary care patients over 65: A 4-year prospective study. *Psychosomatics, 37*, 35.

Von Korff, M., Katon, W., Simon, G., Lin, E., Bush, T., & Ludman, E. (1998). "Treatment Costs, Cost Offset, and Cost-Effectiveness of Collaborative Management of Depression." *Psychosomatic Medicine, 60*, 143-149.

Wells, K. B., Stewart, A., Hays, R. D., Burnam, M. A., Rogers, W., Daniels, M., Berry, S., Greenfield, S., & Ware, J. (1989). The functioning and well-being of depressed patients. Results from the Medical Outcomes Study. *Journal of the American Medical Association, 262*, 914–919.

Whooley, M. A., & Browner, W. S. (1998). Association between depressive symptoms and mortality in older women. *Archives of Internal Medicine, 158*, 2129-2135.

Zimmerman, M., & Mattia, J. I. (2000). Principal and additional DSM-IV disorders for which outpatients seek treatment. *Psychiatric Services, 51* (10), 1299- 1304.

Treatment of Anxiety Disorders: Implications for Medical Cost Offset

Michael J Telch
Jasper A. J. Smits
Matt Brown
Victoria Beckner
The University of Texas at Austin

Identification and amelioration of psychological factors that contribute to unnecessary medical service utilization and excessive diagnostic procedures is of the utmost importance in developing a more cost-effective health care system. Anxiety and its pathological expression represent one of the most crucial challenges facing our health care system.

The overall aim of this chapter is to acquaint the reader with an overview of anxiety disorders and their treatment. In so doing we will focus our review on addressing the following questions: (a) what are the direct and indirect costs of anxiety disorders?; (b) what are the fundamental features of anxiety that lead sufferers to seek medical services with such fervor?; (c) what is the available scientific evidence supporting the efficacy of existing empirically-supported treatments for anxiety disorders?; (d) what is the evidence that these treatments are effective when delivered in the real world as opposed to a research center?; (e) are there factors that predict treatment response?; and (f) what are the priorities for future research on treating anxiety disorders medical cost offset?

Costs of Anxiety Disorders

The costs of anxiety disorders are considerable. The high costs are due to several factors including their extremely high prevalence (Kessler, et al., 1994), their debilitating nature, and their chronicity when left untreated. Some costs of anxiety disorders cannot be quantified monetarily. These include the emotional suffering of the afflicted person and their loved ones as well as the overall lowering of one's quality of life. Specific data illustrating these non-monetary costs will be presented in the context of our discussion of specific anxiety disorders and their consequences. Several attempts have been made to estimate the monetary costs of anxiety disorders (Dupont, Rice, Shiraki, & Rowland, 1996; Greenberg, et al., 1999). Cost of illness studies typically divide the costs of an illness into direct costs such as those associated with providing both psychiatric and nonpsychiatric treatments, and indirect costs associated with loss of productivity among those suffering from the illness.

The most comprehensive study of the monetary costs of anxiety disorders was conducted by Greenberg et al. (1999) using data from both the National Comorbidity Study and supplemental data on nonpsychiatric medical costs from a large health maintenance organization (HMO). Like other cost-of-illness studies, costs were calculated using a prevalence-based human capital approach which estimates the annual costs of all individuals suffering from the illness within a given year regardless of when the condition was diagnosed. One of the more significant strengths of the study was the effort made to statistically control for extraneous demographic factors (e.g., age, education, number of children) that have been shown to relate to cost variables. Based on 1990 dollars, the total costs of anxiety disorders were estimated at 42.3 billion which translates into 63.1 billion in 1998 dollars. This translates into a per sufferer 1990 annual cost of $1542. The breakdown of the major cost categories are presented in Figure 1.

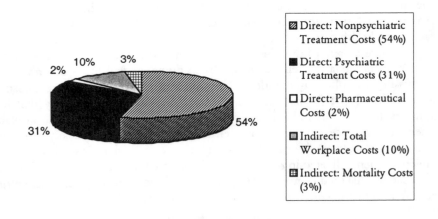

Figure 1. Breakdown of direct and indirect costs of anxiety disorders.

There are several compelling reasons to suggest that the 42.3 billion dollar cost estimate represents a significantly underestimate of the true financial burden of anxiety disorders. First, obsessive-compulsive disorder (OCD) - the most disabling of all the anxiety disorders - was not assessed in the National Comorbidity Study. Consequently, the Greenberg et al.cost estimates do not take into account the added costs associated with those suffering from OCD. Second, the NCS did not include people younger than 15 or older than 54. Third, legitimate cost categories such as the use of alternative medical practitioners, costs associated with secondary consequences of anxiety disorders (e.g., substance abuse), and other societal costs resulting from early onset anxiety disorders such as early school drop-outs, marital discord, etc. were not included in the Greenberg et al. cost estimates.

As seen in Figure 1, over half of the total estimated costs of anxiety disorders results from nonpsychiatric medical services. This fact has significant implications for medical cost offset. Early identification of anxiety disorders and delivery of effective treatments are likely to result in a sizeable reduction of nonpsychiatric treatment costs.

Nature of Anxiety and Its Relationship to Medical Treatment Seeking

Anxiety has been conceptualized as an emotional response to anticipated threat consisting of physiologic, behavioral, and cognitive/subjective components. As a class, anxiety disorders share several common factors. These include: (a) activation of the sympathetic nervous system; (b) faulty threat perception; (c) attentional hypervigilance; (d) ruminative worry; and (e) safety-seeking behavior.

Sympathetic Activation

Most anxiety states produce an activation of the sympathetic nervous system. With this activation come numerous physiologic changes including increases in muscle tension, cardiac output, respiration, sweating, and vascular changes resulting in reduced blood flow. These physiologic effects of sympathetic activation have considerable adaptive significance from an evolutionary perspective (facilitating successful defensive response to potential threat). However, in the case of anxiety disorders, one's innate alarm mechanism is triggered in the absence of any objective threat. Consequently, the salient somatic perturbations associated with anxiety arousal are more likely to be experienced as highly aversive and sometimes even harmful, thus prompting anxiety sufferers to seek out medical evaluation and treatment.

Faulty Threat Perception

Faulty threat perception appears to be present in all the anxiety disorders. Cognitively-oriented theorists go one step further in asserting that faulty threat perception is the central cause of anxiety disorders; whereas biologically-oriented theorists argue instead that anxiety disorders are the result of abnormalities in one's neurobiology. A more lengthy discussion of this debate takes us too far a field from our major focus. Suffice it to say that regardless of its causal status, faulty threat perception is present in all the anxiety disorders. This has considerable implications for medical treatment seeking, since erroneous perceptions of threat are common among anxiety disorder sufferers.

It is likely that cognitive appraisal interacts significantly with physiologic activation to determine which features become the primary sources of medical concerns. For instance, the patient who perceives increased cardiac output as a sign of a potential heart problem is likely to seek out medical services; whereas one who perceives increased cardiac output as a benign consequence of anxiety will likely not. Similarly, one who interprets breathlessness associated with anxiety-induced hyperventilation as a sign of breathing difficulties is more likely to seek out medical service than someone who is aware that their breathlessness is a harmless consequence of over breathing in response to anxiety or stress.

Attentional Hypervigilance and Worry

The shift in focus of attention to threat cues is a well established feature of anxiety. Undoubtedly, this feature accomplishes an important function when faced with real danger - namely providing much needed information to facilitate preparatory action. In the case of anxiety disorders, attentional hypervigilance contributes to the maintenance of pathological anxiety by limiting available attentional resources for the cognitive processing of corrective threat disconfirming information. In many cases, attentional hypervigilance may exacerbate anxiety by serving as a perceptual amplifier thus resulting in heightened threat perception and ruminative worry. Even when the original threat focus is unrelated to one's physical health (e.g., work or relationship concerns), the resulting anxiety arousal may lead to secondary concerns related to the adverse medical consequences of anxiety, thus prompting the individual to seek out medical services.

Avoidance and Other Safety-Seeking Behavior

The previously mentioned physiologic and cognitive features of anxiety would be of little import if they were not of assistance in mobilizing escape or avoidance from potential threats. Defensive actions figure prominently in anxiety. More recently, attention has focused on other forms of safety-seeking behavior such as checking behaviors, reassurance seeking, use of companions, and use of physical aids (Kamphuis & Telch, 1998). Although some evidence suggests that safety-seeking behaviors may have short-term anxiety-reducing effects, several lines of evidence across multiple anxiety disorders now suggest that safety-seeking behaviors may play an important role in the maintenance of pathological fear reactions. This central feature of anxiety disorders has particular relevance for health care utilization and medical cost offset. Patients with anxiety disorders often use repeated visits to the emergency room or primary care physician as a safety behavior to cope with their anxiety. In the process, some patients will undergo multiple diagnostic work-ups that are both costly and often unnecessary. Several years ago we treated a panic disorder patient who experienced esophageal distress in response to his anxiety. At intake the patient had resorted to the safety behavior of pureeing all his food in a blender in order to cope with his fear that he would choke if he ate "regular" food. He had also undergone an amazing number of costly diagnostic work-ups over a span of about 18 months. Although treatment with benzodiazepines provided him some relief, his symptoms persisted and his functioning was significantly impaired. Exposure to interoceptive fear cues combined with graduated safety behavior fading resulted in a complete resolution of his symptoms and a return to normal functioning.

Let us now turn to a brief examination of several specific anxiety disorders. Note that due to space limitations, we have chosen to focus only on generalized anxiety disorder, obsessive-compulsive disorder, and panic disorder. These were selected for two major reasons. First, each of these disorders has been associated with significant non-psychiatric health care utilization; second, each has been the focus of significant pharmacological and psychological treatment research. For readers who may be unfamiliar with these disorders, we provide a brief description of the nature and epidemiology, along with relevant data (when available) pertaining to health care utilization, short and long-term treatment efficacy, moderators of treatment outcome, and treatment effectiveness.

Generalized Anxiety Disorder

Defining Features and Epidemiology of GAD

Since its introduction as a diagnostic entity in DSM-III (American Psychiatric Association, 1980), generalized anxiety disorder (GAD) has undergone considerable transformation in terms of both its conceptualization and diagnostic criteria. GAD was first described as a residual diagnosis for those presenting with significant chronic anxiety that could not be better accounted for by a mood disorder or another anxiety disorder. As research on GAD progressed, recognition for the role of uncontrollable worry as a central feature of GAD increased. This led to a major shift in the conceptualization of GAD from a residual anxiety disorder category in DSM-III, to a bona fide anxiety disorder characterized by uncontrollable worry. GAD is currently diagnosed when the individual presents with excessive and uncontrollable anxiety and worry in multiple life spheres (e.g., relationships, finances, health, work performance, etc.) for a period of at least six months. The anxiety must be accompanied by at least three of the following symptoms: restlessness or feeling on edge, becoming easily fatigued, difficulty concentrating or mind going blank, irritability, muscle tension, or sleep disturbance, and must result in significant impairment or distress (APA, 1994).

Approximately 5.1% of the general population will have GAD at some point during their lifetime, and women (6.6%) are twice as likely as men (3.6%) to suffer its effects (Kessler, McGonagle, Zhao, et al., 1994). Interestingly, GAD has the highest rate of comorbidity with any Axis I anxiety disorder or depression (23%), and ranks first as the principal anxiety disorder most likely to have a comorbid condition associated with it (82%; Moras & Barlow, 1992). The onset of GAD usually occurs early in life and it tends to run a fluctuating but chronic course in which symptoms become exacerbated during times of stress. It is unlikely to remit without treatment (Wittchen, Carter, Pfister, Montgomery, & Kessler, 2000; Yonkers, Dyck, Warshaw, & Keller, 2000).

Social and Economic Costs of GAD

GAD is associated with significant impairment in social and occupational functioning as well as increased health concerns (Wittchen, et al., 2000; Kessler, et al., 1994; Wittchen, Zhao, Kessler, & Eaton, 1994). While little is known about the monetary impact of GAD, the National Comorbidity Survey revealed that approximately half of those with GAD seek services in the primary care setting (Kessler, et al., 1994; Wittchen, et al., 1994). Moreover, patients with GAD often remain undiagnosed and untreated in these settings (Ormel, Koeter, van den Grink, & van de Willige, 1991; Fifer, et al., 1994; Roy-Byrne, 1996; Zajecka, 1997). Due to its unremitting nature, the failure to identify and treat GAD in primary care may contribute to a markedly higher rate of health care utilization among this population.

Following depression, GAD is the most prevalent mental disorder found in the primary care setting (Barrett, Barrett, Oxman, & Gerber, 1988). Among patients high in health care utilization, 40% have a lifetime history of GAD, and 22% meet for a current GAD diagnosis (Katon, Von Korff, & Lin, 1990). Given the physical symptoms associated with GAD, these findings are not surprising. Moreover, physical complaints associated with chronic anxiety, may also drive up medical service seeking (Roy-Byrne, 1996). In a study by Wulsin, Arnold, and Hillard (1991), 23% of emergency room patients presenting with atypical chest pain met criteria for a current GAD diagnosis. In a study of 216 chest pain patients with normal coronary angiograms, 56% met diagnostic criteria for GAD (Kane, Harper, & Wittels, 1988). In addition to chest pain symptoms, individuals suffering from GAD often report symptoms of gastrointestinal discomfort. For example, among patients diagnosed with irritable bowel syndrome, 34-54% will suffer from GAD sometime in their lifetime; and 11 - 26% will meet for a current GAD diagnosis. Interestingly, among IBS patients with comorbid GAD, 80% report that their GAD symptoms preceded the onset of their irritable bowel symptoms (Lydiard, Fossey, Marsh, & Ballenger, 1993). Taken together, these findings indicate that GAD is associated with a variety of physical complaints likely to be presented in the primary care setting.

Efficacy of Current Treatments for GAD

Treatment research for GAD can be broadly divided into research investigating the efficacy of pharmacotherapy and psychotherapy. Among pharmacological treatments for GAD, benzodiazepines have been the most extensively investigated. However, buspirone and antidepressants have more recently become a focus of GAD treatment research (Ballenger, 1999).

Among psychosocial interventions, behavioral and cognitive-behavioral therapies (CBT) have been the most extensively investigated. However, a significant body of this research has focused on dismantling studies aimed at investigating the efficacy of the individual procedural components of CBT (Butler, Fennell, Robson, & Gelder, 1991; Barlow, Rapee, & Brown, 1992; Borkovec & Costello, 1993). Cognitive-behavioral treatments for GAD share much in common with CBT for other anxiety disorders. The major treatment procedures commonly used in CBT treatments for GAD include: (a) self-monitoring of anxiety-provoking situations; (b) applied relaxation; (c) coping desensitization; (d) cognitive-restructuring of anxiety-provoking cognitions; and (e) worry exposure. The overarching strategy with these treatments is to increase the patient's mastery to cope with stressful life situations.

A comprehensive meta-analysis of pharmacological and psychosocial treatments for GAD was conducted by Gould, Otto, Pollack, and Yap (1997). They included 35 controlled studies published from 1974 to 1996. Of these, 22 investigated pharmacological treatments, 11 investigated psychosocial treatments, and two investigated combined pharmacological plus psychosocial treatments. Interestingly, only one of these studies directly compared pharmacotherapy to psychosocial interventions. Employing the same search procedures as Gould et al., a total of 18 additional controlled studies were identified from 1996 to the present. However, only two of these investigated psychosocial interventions.

Under the classification criteria used by Gould et al. (1997), five studies classified as CBT employed relaxation training alone or relaxation training in combination with biofeedback as the sole treatment. Because treatments that target anxiety reduction through relaxation strategies as their sole focus may lack therapeutic potency relative to a more comprehensive CBT approach, we have provided a further subdivision of the effects size analyses for psychosocial interventions. Effect sizes reported for CBT under the criteria used by Gould et al. will be referred to as *CBT – All Inclusive*. For purposes of this chapter, we have added an additional category that we will refer to as *CBT- Contemporary*. This includes only those studies in which the treatment included additional strategies (in addition to relaxation or biofeedback) targeting other facets of GAD (i.e., dysfunctional cognitions or pathological worry). Table 1 provides a breakdown of the number of studies in each category, the number of patients included in the studies, the average duration of treatment, and the average duration at follow-up assessment.

Treatment	Number of Studies	Total Number of Patients	Average Treatment Duration	Average Follow-up Duration
RX	22	3280	4.4 wks	N/A
CBT	11	590	8.1 wks	6 mo.
RX + CBT	2	132	8 wks	6 mo. (1 study)

Table 1. Specifications of treatment efficacy research for GAD.

Short-term Efficacy

As reported by Gould et al. (1997), both CBT and pharmacotherapy led to significant improvement in GAD symptoms; but neither treatment showed a clear advantage over the other. However, when effect size estimates were based on the subset of studies in which a more multifaceted CBT approach was used (CBT-Contemporary), effect sizes were slightly higher for CBT relative to pharmacotherapy (See Figure 2).

Gould et al. (1997) also examined treatment effects on depression and found that compared to pharmacotherapy, CBT yielded a significantly greater treatment effect (ES = 0.77 vs. .46). Among the pharmacological interventions, the greatest treatment effects were associated with benzodiazepines, followed by antidepressants, and buspirone (See Figure 2). Comparisons of attrition across the major treatment modalities revealed no significant difference in attrition between CBT (M = 10.6%) and pharmacotherapy (M = 15.2%); however, antidepressants were associated with the largest attrition rate (33.5%), which is likely attributable to medication side effects.

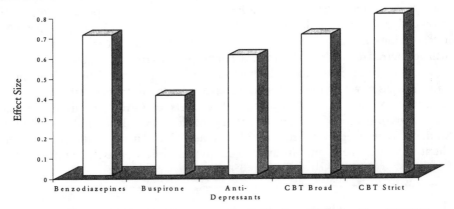

Figure 2. Short-term efficacy of treatments for GAD. Data from Gould et al. (1997).

Long-term Efficacy

Of the 35 studies included in the meta-analysis of Gould et al. (1997), only 7 studies included follow-up assessments of six months or longer. The results indicate that treatment gains for CBT (all inclusive) were generally maintained at follow-up. When only contemporary CBT treatments are examined, the follow-up results are more encouraging with a trend toward continued improvement beyond posttreatment (See Figure 3). This is in sharp contrast to the one study that examined the long-term effects of a pharmacological treatment following medication discontinuation; not surprisingly, patients treated with diazepam alone lost much of their improvement at the treatment-free follow-up (Power, et al., 1990).

Clinical Significance of Treatment Effects

Do GAD patients receiving treatment show a level of improvement that is clinically significant? The best data available for addressing this question comes from a report by Fisher and Durham, (1999). Using clinical significance criteria established by Jacobson and Truax (1991), the authors examined end state recovery status for 20 psychosocial treatment comparisons groups across 6 studies. Across all 20 comparisons, including 17 different psychosocial interventions and CBT variants, they identified a 40% recovery rate, and when examining recovery rates atthe 6-month follow-up, they found that 50-60% of patients who received either CBT or applied relaxation achieved high endstate functioning (recovery status).

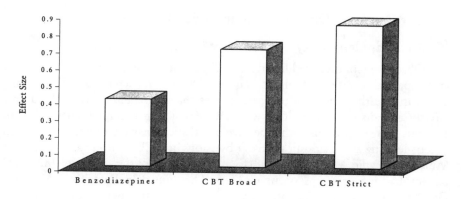

Figure 3. Long-term efficacy of treatments for GAD. Data from Gould et al. (1997).

Predictors of Clinical Response to Treatment in GAD

Data on predictors of clinical response among GAD patients are limited. In a five year, prospective, naturalistic follow-up study 167 GAD patients were assessed at intake and every 6-12 months for five years (Yonkers et al., 2000). Analysis of the cross-sectional data revealed that remission was less likely to occur in the presence of low overall life satisfaction, a cluster B or C comorbid personality disorder, and poor spousal or family relationships. Consistent with the Yonkers et al. report, the presence of comorbid personality disorders was also predictive of a poorer clinical response among 50% of GAD patients treated with pharmacotherapy (Mancuso, Townsend, & Mercante, 1994). Specifically, cluster B and C personality disorders as well as significant life dissatisfaction was associated with poorer outcome at the 16-week follow-up. In a study examining predictors of clinical response to cognitive therapy, Sanderson, Beck, and McGinn (1994) found patients diagnosed with a comorbid personality disorder were more likely to drop out of treatment.

Cost Effectiveness

We were unable to locate any data pertaining to the cost-effectiveness of the treatments for GAD. Given that the treatments for GAD resemble those for panic disorder, it could be argued that the findings on the cost-effectiveness of treatments for panic disorder described later in this chapter suggest that both medication and CBT are reasonably cost-effective in the short-term and that CBT is a more cost-effective treatment in the long-term. Of course, this conclusion is highly speculative and awaits research that directly examines the cost-effectiveness of treatments for GAD.

Treatment Effectiveness

No research was identified that investigates the transportability of GAD treatments from the research setting to the primary care or community mental health arena.

Obsessive-Compulsive Disorder

Nature & Epidemiology of Obsessive-Compulsive Disorder

Obsessive-Compulsive Disorder (OCD) is one of the most intense, chronic, and impairing forms of pathological anxiety. OCD is characterized by threatening and intrusive thoughts, images, or impulses that cause the individual extreme anxiety and distress. Individuals with OCD typically attempt to neutralize or suppress these obsessions with repetitive, ritualistic behaviors or compulsions. In a study looking at the classification of obsessions in OCD, Antony and colleagues (Antony, Downie, & Swinson, 1998) found that 68.7% of the sample of 182 OCD patients had aggressive obsessions (e.g., fear of harming oneself or another), 57% of OCD patients had contamination obsessions, 53.2% symmetry / exactness concerns, 30% had hoarding or saving obsessions, and 24% had religious (blasphemous) obsessions. Significantly, 34.1% had somatic concerns, which often involve fear of having contracted an infection or disease, or hypochondriacal conviction of being ill.

The compulsions are often linked logically to the obsession, as is the case with washing rituals triggered by contamination fears or checking behavior in response to obsessive fears of having left doors unlocked or stoves on. Other compulsions seem to have a more superstitious or "magical" link to an obsession, such as counting, repeating words, or ordering objects to avert some vague, dreaded outcome. OCD patients are often painfully aware that their obsessions and compulsions are "senseless," and often hide their symptoms for years before seeking treatment. They also commonly suffer depression, panic attacks, generalized anxiety and worry, and debilitating avoidance.

OCD was once considered rare. The Epidemiology Catchment Area (ECA) survey in 1984, however, found a 2.5% lifetime prevalence for the disorder in the U.S., with a slightly higher rate in women (Robins, Helzer, Weissman, & Orvaschel, 1984).. Mean age of onset is 17.5 years in males, and 20.8 in females (Rasmussen & Eisen, 1990). Notably, one third to one half of OCD patients first experience OCD symptoms in childhood, and the phenomenology of the disorder is nearly identical in children and adults (Rapoport, 1989). The disorder tends to be chronic without treatment, with a waxing and waning of symptoms throughout the lifespan (Antony et al., 1998).

Individuals with OCD often have psychiatric comorbidity. Nearly a third of OCD patients meet criteria for major depression upon diagnosis, while two-thirds report a history of depression (Rasmussen & Eisen, 1992). Comorbid anxiety disorders is also high: 30% of OCD patients have a simple phobia, 20% have social phobia, 15% are diagnosable with panic disorder (Rasmussen & Tsuang, 1986). Ten percent of women with OCD have a history of anorexia (Kasvikis, Tsakiris, Marks, & Basoglu, 1986), while 33% of bulimic women have a history of OCD (Hudson & Pope, 1987). There is also a strong association between OCD and tic disorders. The OCD prevalence among Tourette's patients is high: 30-60% (Leckman,

Peterson, Pauls, & Cohen, 1997). Approximately 5% of OCD patients have comorbid Tourette's syndrome (Rasmussen & Eisen, 1992), while many more report a history of tics (Leckman et al., 1997). Perhaps most relevant to medical utilization is the 8% rate of hypochondriasis among OCD patients, likely related to the previously noted somatic obsessions.

Non-Financial Costs of OCD

OCD sufferers often pay a large price tag with respect to emotional distress and impairment in social and occupational functioning. Given the large amount of time OCD sufferers spend on performing rituals and the often bizarre nature of the rituals (which motivates secrecy), it is not surprising that OCD patients find themselves socially isolated. A 1990 Gallup poll examining quality of life of OCD sufferers, found that 20% spent 5-8 hours a day engaged in rituals, and 13% spent over 17 hours a day during the most severe period of their disorder (Gallup Organization, 1990). Moreover, 48% had lost friends, 26% reported that their symptoms caused the end of their intimate relationship, and 57% reported difficulty making new friends. This is consistent with other studies reporting that 62% of OCD patients have difficulty maintaining a relationship (Calvocoressi, Lewis, Harris, Trufan, Goodman, McDougle, & Price, 1995), and that celibacy rates are high relative to other anxiety disorders (Steketee, Grayson, & Foa, 1987). Koran and colleagues compared quality of life issues in OCD patients to the general U.S. population and depressive or diabetic patients, and found social functioning and instrumental role performance to be significantly more impaired in the OCD sample (Koran, Thienemann, & Davenport, 1996).

Financial Costs of OCD

The financial costs of OCD are considerable. Morbidity costs due to reduced work productivity are staggering. Steketee and colleagues found a 40% unemployment rate for OCD patients, and reduced income due to impairment (Steketee, et al., 1987). A survey of patient members of the OC foundation found that patients lost an average of two years wages due to their illness (Hollander, et al., 1996). In the most extensive cost analysis of OCD, Dupont and colleagues estimated the 1990 costs of OCD to be 8.4 billion. Approximately 70% or 6.2 billion of which was due to morbidity costs associated with lost productivity; whereas 25% or 2.1 billion was the estimated direct costs associated with providing treatment services. Mortality costs due to lost wages were estimated at 3% and were based on the assumption that 2% of all suicides are OCD-related. A final 1% included expenses for legal, and social services (DuPont, Rice, Shiraki, & Rowland, 1996). Frost and Steketee (1997) note that the DuPont et al. figures likely underestimate the overall costs of OCD since they are based on the percentage of anxiety disorder patients with OCD. However, it has been noted that certain costs of OCD may be higher than those for other anxiety disorders (Turner, Beidel, Spaulding, & Brown, 1995).

Health Care Utilization in OCD

There are several reasons why individuals with OCD might be expected to over-utilize medical services. Because OCD patients commonly have somatic obsessions, the disorder has similarities to hypochondriasis: both involve a fear of illness or contamination which is not delusional, but the belief resists explanation or reassurance (Barsky, 1992). This makes it likely that individuals with OCD will seek out medical services to alleviate their fears.

Based on data from the ECA 80% of OCD sufferers are treated as outpatients (80%), and of these, 40.4% saw a general physician an average of 4.6 times a year (Narrows, Regier, Rae, Manderscheid, & Locke, 1993). There is evidence that patients with OCD may present more often to medical *specialists*– particularly dermatologists for skin conditions related to excessive washing and infectious disease specialists (Rapoport, 1988). Rasmussen (1985) argues that individuals with undiagnosed OCD are likely to present themselves first to primary care physicians or dermatologists–and that the latter should be trained to diagnose the disorder. A study looking at the incidence of OCD in African Americans presenting for treatment of chronic pruritic conditions in an urban dermatology clinic found that 15% met criteria for OCD (Friedman, Hatch, & Paradis, 1993). Kennedy & Schwab (1997) conducted a survey of anxiety patients participating in drug trials in a university outpatient clinic to determine the number of primary care physicians and specialists seen in the last year. They found that of the 32 OCD patients, 28% had seen a physician in primary care, 28% in dermatology, 22% in internal medicine, 25% in cardiology, and 19% had seen an ear-nose-throat physician. The OCD patients saw significantly more dermatologists and cardiologists than individuals with panic disorder or GAD, or the general public. Surprisingly, only 3% of the OCD patients had seen a psychiatrist in the past year.

Treatment Efficacy Studies for OCD

As in the case for other anxiety disorders, both antidepressant medication and specific forms of psychosocial treatments have well-established clinical efficacy in the treatment of OCD. Given that one of the important brain regions affected in OCD–the basal ganglia–is served by seratonergic pathways, it is no surprise that the most widely studied and most effective drug treatment for OCD involve medications which inhibit the reuptake of serotonin. Clomipramine was the first medication to demonstrate clinical efficacy in the treatment of OCD. More recently, several SSRIs including fluoxetine, fluvoxamine, sertraline and paroxetine have all demonstrated clinical efficacy in placebo controlled clinical trials.

Based on a recent review (Greist, Jefferson, Kobak, Katzelnick, & Serlin, 1995) and literature search of journal publications from 1996-present using Psych-Info and MEDLINE, we found 34 controlled studies investigating treatment efficacy of seratonergic-acting medications, with 3,060 patients treated, an average treatment length of 9.2 weeks, and an average follow-up period of 18 months.

Among psychosocial treatments for OCD, the most widely investigated is a structured learning based treatment known as exposure and response prevention or ERP for short. The basic components of ERP are similar to those used in the behavioral treatment of other anxiety disorders. They include (a) thorough *assessment* of the nature, course, and prior treatment of the patient's OCD symptoms, specific information on the internal and external fear cues that trigger compulsions and avoidance behavior; (b) *education* about the disorder and anxiety reduction principles; (c) in-session imaginal and *in vivo exposure* to fear-provoking cues; (d) response prevention in which the patient is encouraged to refrain from engaging in the compulsion; and (e) daily *home practice of exposure and response prevention exercises.* Based on a recent review of studies through 1995 (Abramowitz, 1997) and a subsequent literature search, we found 16 controlled studies investigating the efficacy of ERP, with 376 participants treated, an average treatment length of 9.4 weeks, and an average follow-up period of 29 months.

Evidence for Short-term Efficacy

Research on effective pharmacological treatments for OCD has focused on the seratonin reuptake inhibitors clomipramine (CMI), fluoxetine, fluvoxamine, and sertraline. Greist and colleagues (1995) reported on the short-term efficacy of the four most widely studied medications (i.e., clomipramine, fluoxetine, fluvoxamine, and sertraline) using data from four, large, industry-sponsored randomized clinical trials conducted at 48 sites. The treatments were 10-13 weeks in length, and the results are based on intent-to-treat samples (Total $N = 1,520$). All four medications were significantly more effective than placebo. The effect sizes for the three medications are presented in Figure 4.

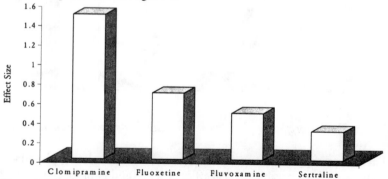

Figure 4. Effect sizes from 4 large industry sponsored randomized clinical trials. Data from Greist et al. (1995).

As seen in Figure 4, the effect size for clomipramine was significantly greater than those for the three SSRIs, which did not differ significantly from each other. The response rates based on clinician ratings of "improved" or "very much improved" was 60% for clomipramine, 38% for fluoxetine, 43% for fluvoxamine, and 39% for sertraline. The authors suggested that the apparent superiority of clomipramine in these studies may be a subject selection artifact in which non-responders from the earlier clomipramine study were entered as subjects in the latter SSRI studies. The fact that they were previously non-responsive to clomipramine may have decreased the likelihood that they would be responsive to another SRI medication. Regardless, all four medications provide significant short-term benefit for OCD sufferers. Several other SSRI medications under investigation are paroxetine and citalopram (Mundo, Bianchi, & Bellodi, 1997). Several controlled studies have tested the efficacy of adding seratonin-enhancing drugs (such as buspirone and clonazepam), and dopamine antagonists (such as haloperidol and risperidone), to SRI regimens with some promising results (McDougle, Epperson, Pelton, Wasylink, & Price, 2000).

Evidence for the short-term efficacy of psychosocial treatment for OCD comes mostly from randomized clinical trials of exposure and response prevention (ERP). In a review of 12 ERP treatment outcome studies (N=330), 83% of treatment completers were classified as responders at posttreatment based on clinician ratings (Foa & Kozak, 1996). Depicted in Figure 5 are data examining the short-term efficacy of clomipramine, SRI medications combined, and ERP come from a meta-analysis of 32 clinical trials in OCD published between 1975 and 1995 (Abramowitz, 1997).

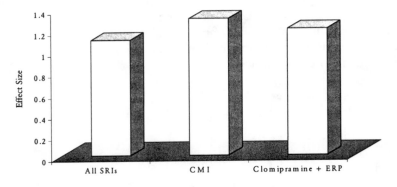

Figure 5. Short-term efficacy of treatments for OCD. Data from Abramowitz (1997).

These data suggest that in the short-term, behavioral and pharmacological treatments are of comparable clinical efficacy. The validity of meta-analytic results, however, rests upon the individual studies used in the analyses—some of which have significant methodological limitations. To address this problem, Foa and colleagues began a large, multisite, randomized control trial in 1990 at a cognitive-behavioral-oriented site and a pharmacologically-oriented site. They are comparing the short- and long-term efficacy of four treatments: clomipramine (CMI) alone, ERP alone, CMI plus ERP, and pill placebo. The treatment phase was 12 weeks, with a 6-month, no-treatment follow-up. Preliminary results suggest an acute response rate for ERP which is similar to the meta-analysis: 84.6% for the 61 completers, and 61.1% for the 83 intent-to-treat sample (Kozak, Liebowitz, & Foa, 2000).

Long-term Efficacy

Although the SSRIs provide effective short-term treatment for OCD, few studies have examined the long-term efficacy of pharmacological treatments. One study by Ravizza and colleagues followed 130 subjects for 2 years following a 6-month treatment with clomipramine, fluoxetine, or fluvoxamine (Ravizza, Barzega, Bellino, Bogetto, & Maina, 1996). During the follow-up, subjects continued with the same dosage, continued with half the dose, or discontinued the medication. No differences were found in outcome between full and half dosages, and continuation of medication was significantly more effective than discontinuation. The relapse rates were equally high for all three pharmacological treatments when the patients discontinued medication altogether: 76.9% for clomipramine, 80.0% for fluoxetine, and 84.6% for fluvoxamine. A more recent review of the effects of discontinuation of SSRI medications indicates that approximately 80% of successfully-treated OCD patients relapse once medication is discontinued (Ravizza, Maina, Bogetto, Albert, Barzega, & Bellino, 1998).

In contrast to pharmacotherapy, treatment gains for ERP are largely maintained after treatment completion. In a review of 16 ERP studies with 376 participants and a mean follow-up period of 29 months, 76% continued to be much improved or very much improved on the CGI at follow-up (Foa & Kozac, 1996). The multi-site study by Kozac and colleagues (Kozac, Liebowitz, & Foa, 2000) provides additional evidence of the superior long-term durability of ERP to pharmacotherapy. Preliminary results of relapse rates at the 3-month follow-up are presented below. As seen in Figure 6, ERP whether given alone or in combination with medication is associated with a low rate of relapse, whereas most patients treated with clomipramine alone relapse following discontinuation of medication.

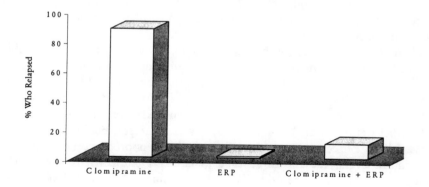

Figure 6. Relapse following discontinuation of treatment. Data from Kozak et al. (2000).

Are the Symptom Changes Clinically Meaningful?

The effect sizes for pharmacological and psychological interventions for OCD clearly indicate significant gains with these treatments. The improvements in symptoms and global functioning ratings at posttest are at least one standard deviation better in the treated groups than in the control groups. It is difficult to tell from the efficacy data, however, whether such a difference *is clinically significant*: does the treatment meet improvement standards desired by the patients and their clinicians? To answer this question with regards to ERP, Abramowitz (1998) compared the posttreatment functioning of OCD patients from 16 outcome studies with 9 samples from the general public (mostly university students not screened for OCD) who were administered OCD symptom measures in 6 studies. The author found that at posttest, although treated patients were not symptom-free, they were functioning at a level more similar to the normative sample than to untreated OCD patients up to 5 months after treatment.

Predictors of Treatment Outcome

A number of factors have been investigated as predictors of outcome in the treatment of OCD, including comorbid Axis I and II disorders, pre-treatment OCD severity, and treatment adherence to ERP homework. Although early studies suggested that Axis I comorbidity predicted poor outcome, the evidence to date is equivocal. Many studies have looked at depressed *mood* as a treatment predictor with mixed results (see Steketee, Henninger, & Pollard, 2000, for review). Steketee and colleagues found that pre-treatment major depression predicted poor outcome following 16 weeks of ERP (Steketee, Henninger, & Pollard, 2000), but comorbid depression was not found to affect treatment outcome in several medication trials (Goodman, et al., 1989). Steketee and colleagues also examined comorbid anxiety disorders and found that GAD was related to drop-out rates and poorer outcome at follow-up, while social phobia was not (Steketee, Henninger, & Pollard, 2000). Other studies have not found comorbid anxiety to moderate the effects of behavioral treatments for OCD (Stekeetee & Shapiro, 1995) or pharmacotherapy (Orloff, Battle, Baer, & Ivanjack, 1994).

There is stronger evidence that Axis II comorbidity predicts a less favorable outcome for both ERP and pharmacotherapy. Borderline and avoidant personality disorder were found to predict poor outcome in the treatment of OCD with CMI (Baer & Jenike, 1992) and fluvoxamine (Cottraux, Mollard, Bouvard, & Marks, 1993), while schizotypal personality disorder predicted poor outcome in several SSRI studies (Jenike, Baer, & Carey, 1986; Ravizza, Barzega, Bellino, Bogetto, & Maina, 1995). Personality disorders also predicted poor outcome with ERP treatments in several studies (AuBuchon & Malatesta, 1994; Cottraux et al., 1993), although they did not in one study (Steketee, Henninger, & Pollard, 2000).).

Although overall pre-treatment OCD severity has not been found to predict treatment outcome in either the psychosocial or pharmacological treatments (O'Sullivan, Noshirvani, Marks, Monteiro, & Lelliott, 1991; Steketee, 1993), the data is mixed regarding the predictive value of specific symptoms (see Kozac, et al., 2000). A positive predictor of outcome in the behavioral treatment of OCD is treatment compliance, particularly with homework assignments (Araujo, Ito, & Marks, 1996; Keijsers, Hoogduin, & Schaap, 1994; O'Sullivan, et al., 1991).

Do Treatment Effects Generalize to the Real World?

Some argue that efficacy data gathered through RCT studies may exaggerate the true effectiveness of treatments. The therapists in RCTs are often highly trained in the treatment approach, while private clinicians may have difficulty effectively using the treatment manual. Researchers also commonly exclude the more severe patients with comorbid diagnoses in order to obtain a homogenous experimental group, while many of the eligible patients may refuse randomization to placebo conditions (creating a "self-selected" group). Thus the treated patients in RCT studies may not be representative of the typical outpatient seen in private practice. To determine whether ERP efficacy data generalizes to the real world of clinical practice, Franklin and colleagues compared outcome data from 4 RCTs with data from 110 outpatients with OCD seen at a university-based anxiety research clinic on a fee-for-service basis (Franklin, Abramowitz, Kozak, Levitt, & Foa, 2000). No outpatients were excluded for comorbidity, concomitant or past treatment, age, or OCD severity. The results provided strong support for the effectiveness of ERP. Pre-post change in symptom scores yielded comparable, clinically significant improvement in both the RCT and clinic groups. The pre- to posttreatment size was 3.26 for the clinic sample, in comparison to 3.88 and 2.31 from two of the RCT studies. The effect sizes for the other RCT outcome studies were significantly lower, possibly related to the less-intensive approach used in these two studies. Thus, the limited available data support the efficacy of ERP when delivered in a non-research setting.

Cost effectiveness

Although the benefits of effectively treating OCD are clear, only one study has examined the costs associated with providing behavioral therapy to OCD patients. Turner and colleagues found in their survey of behavior therapists that OCD cost significantly more to treat than other anxiety disorders: the mean cost per OCD case was $4,370, compared to $2,695 for social phobia, for example (Turner, Beidel, Spauling, & Brown, 1995). This was due to the increased number of sessions typically required for treating OCD: 46.4 hours, compared with a mean of 20.7 hours for the other anxiety disorders. Given the substantial impairment, healthcare utilization, and other economic costs associated with obsessive-compulsive disorder, such a price for effective treatment may well be cost-effective in the long term.

Panic Disorder

Defining Features and Epidemiology

Panic disorder is a debilitating anxiety disorder characterized by recurring unexpected episodes of intense fear (panic attacks) coupled with persistent apprehension surrounding the attacks. The panic-related apprehension manifests in one or more of the following ways: (a) persistent worry about future attacks; (b) unrealistic concern about the consequences of having a panic attack (e.g., heart attack, insanity, social humiliation); or (c) changes in behavior to cope with the fear of panic e.g., avoidance of situations that might trigger an attack (American Psychiatric Association, 1994).

Panic disorder affects approximately 3% of the general population and is about twice as prevalent among women(Kessler, et al., 1994).

Social and economic costs of panic disorder

Panic disorder is associated with significant impairment. A recent study showed that the quality of life of individuals suffering from panic disorder is comparable to those suffering from major depression (Candilis, et al., 1999). Compared to the general population, patients with panic disorder show higher prevalence rates of chronic medical conditions (e.g., hypertension, migraine headaches, thyroid disease) (Rogers, et al., 1994). Other medical conditions that are more frequently observed in patients suffering from panic disorder include mitral valve prolapse and cardiorespiratory disorders, such as asthma and chronic obstructive pulmonary disease (Gorman, et al., 1988; Karajgi, Rifkin, Doddi, & Kolli, 1990; Weissman, Markowitz, Ouellette, Greenwald, & Kahn, 1990; Zandbergen, et al., 1991).

Panic disorder is frequently associated with comorbid psychiatric problems such as alcohol abuse, drug abuse, and suicide (Markowitz, Weissman, Ouellette, Lish, & et al., 1989). It has been demonstrated that approximately 70% of patients with panic disorder have at least one comorbid Axis I or Axis II disorder (Brown & Barlow, 1992; Sanderson, Di Nardo, Rapee, & Barlow, 1990). Emotional and physical health ratings of patients with panic disorder are presented in Table 2.

Domain	%
Health	
Poor Physical Health	35
Poor Emotional Health	38
Psychiatric Problems	
Alcohol Abuse	27
Other Drug Abuse	18
Attempted Suicides	20
Work Impairment	
Full-Time Employed	55
Unemployed	25
Financially Dependent	27

Table 2. Impared quality of life in panic disorder.
Data from Markowitz et al. (1989) and Massion et al. (1993).

In addition to health and emotional impairment, panic disorder often contributes to significant impairment in occupational functioning. Massion, Warshaw, and Keller (1993) reported a fourfold rate of unemployment (relative to the national average) among patients with panic disorder. Not surprisingly, their results also revealed increased financial dependency (e.g., receiving disability or welfare) among patients with panic disorder relative to the general population.

Healthcare Utilization

Given the adverse effects of panic disorder on health and quality of life, it is not surprising that the disorder is associated with increased use of medical services. Data from the Cross National Collaborative Study indicated high utilization rates of specialists such as cardiologists, neurologists, and primary care physicians, as well as outpatient mental health clinics and psychotherapists (Leon, Olfson, & Portera, 1997). The results further showed that 48% of patients with panic disorder were seen by a non-mental health care provider. The estimated mean expenditure for a panic episode was $3,393 (Leon, et al., 1997). Table 3 presents data on the utilization of medical services among those afflicted with panic disorder.

	% Using Service	Median Number of Visits
General Medical Sector		
Cardiologist	20.6	2.0
Neurologist	13.4	2.0
Other specialists	31.2	3.5
Any of the above	47.2	9.5
Primary Care Physicians	70.4	7.0
General practitioner	67.8	4.5
Outpatient clinic	13.9	14.0
Mental Health Sector		
Outpatient	47.9	26.0
Community mental health	12.9	12.0
Psychotherapist or counselor	44.3	24.0

Table 3. Utilization of medical services in panic disorder.
Data from Leon et al. (1997).

Treatment Efficacy

The most extensively researched approaches to the treatment of panic disorder are pharmacotherapy and cognitive-behavioral therapy (CBT). Several classes of pharmacological agents have been extensively investigated and proven beneficial in the treatment of panic disorder. These consist of several classes of antidepressants including TCAs such as Imipramine, MAOIs such as Phenelzine, and the SSRIs such as Paroxetine; as well as several classes of anxiolytics such as the high potency BZs such as Alprazolam and the non-BZ anxiolytic Buspirone.

Most research on psychosocial treatments for panic disorder has focused on cognitive-behavioral interventions. These treatments focus on providing patients specific training in identifying internal and external cues that trigger panic and assisting the patient in learning techniques to eliminate their faulty emotional responding to these cues. Specific procedural components included in contemporary cognitive-behavior therapy for panic disorder include: (a) education about the nature and physiology of panic and anxiety; (b) breathing retraining designed to assist patients in learning to control hyperventilation; (c) cognitive restructuring aimed at teaching patients to identify and correct faulty threat perceptions that contribute to their panic and anxiety; (d) interoceptive exposure aimed at reducing patients' fear of harmless bodily sensations associated with physiological activation; and (e) fading of maladaptive defensive behaviors such as avoidance of external situations (Barlow, Craske, Cerny, & Klosko, 1989; Clark, et al., 1994; Margraf, Barlow, Clark, & Telch, 1993; Telch, et al., 1993).

Since 1974, approximately 44 controlled clinical trials have been published investigating the efficacy of pharmacotherapy in the treatment of panic disorder, and an additional 24 controlled studies have examined the efficacy of CBT for panic disorder. Moreover, we found 12 controlled trials that investigated combined medication plus psychological treatment. Table 4 presents a summary of these studies.

Treatment	Number of Studies	Number of Patients	Duration of Treatment, Weeks	Length of Follow-Up, Weeks
TCAs	17	25-1168	6-28	0-24
BZs	13	25-1168	5-32	
SSRIs	14	55- 367	8-16	
CBT	24	18- 312	1-16	0-48
RX + CBT	12	21- 312	12-28	0-72

Table 4. Summary of treatment efficacy research in panic disorder.

Short-term Efficacy

In the last decade, the efficacy of treatments for panic disorder has been systematically reviewed in several meta-analytic studies (Gould, Otto, & Pollack, 1995; Clum, Clum, & Surls, 1993). Gould, Otto, and Pollack compared the efficacy of pharmacological, cognitive-behavioral, and combined pharmacological and cognitive-behavioral treatments in a meta-analysis of 43 controlled studies that included 76 treatment conditions. The clinical trials included in this study were conducted between 1974 and 1994. The short-term efficacy data are depicted in Figure 7. The results showed that all three modalities were effective in reducing the prominent features of the disorder as evidenced by the large average effect size. A comparison of the treatment modalities revealed an advantage of CBT alone over medication and the combination treatment (effects sizes (ES), 0.88, 0.47, and 0.56 respectively). CBT also yielded the smallest attrition rates (5.68%), indicating that is it is better tolerated than pharmacotherapy alone (average attrition rate of 19.8%) or combined medication plus CBT (average attrition rate of 22%).

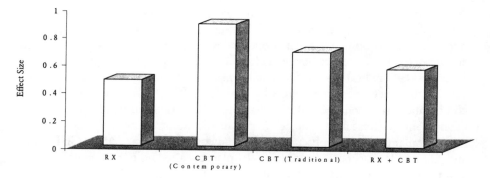

Figure 7. Short-term efficacy for CBT, medication, and their combination. Data from Gould et al. (1995).

In the most ambitious clinical trial to date, Barlow, Gorman, Shear, and Woods (2000) compared the efficacy of CBT, Imipramine, and their combination in a large sample (N=312) of carefully diagnosed panic disorder patients at four sites. A noteworthy aspect of this trial was the teaming up of investigators with different therapeutic expertise, thus controlling for allegiance effects. Patients (N = 312) were randomly assigned to one of five treatment conditions: (a) CBT; (b) Imipramine; (c) Imipramine plus CBT; (d) CBT plus placebo; or (e) pill placebo. Treatment efficacy was evaluated at three different stages: 12 weeks of acute treatment, six-month treatment continuation phase, and 6 month treatment-free follow-up. The acute response rates are shown in Figure 8. After acute treatment all four active treatments showed marked improvements that were significantly greater than those observed for the pill placebo condition. Results at the six-month treatment-free follow-up are reported below.

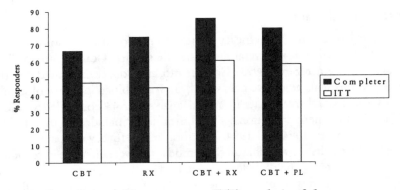

Figure 8. Completer and intent-to-treat (ITT) analysis of short-term response rates from most definitive randomized clinical trial.
Data from Barlow et al. (2000).

Long-term Efficacy

In order to evaluate the long-term treatment efficacy, Gould et al. (1995) calculated mean posttreatment to follow-up effects sizes of studies using a minimum follow-up period of six months. Posttreatment to follow-up effect sizes are presented in Figure 9. The mean effect size among pharmacological interventions was 0.46, indicating considerable relapse after discontinuation of treatment. The small effect sizes that were observed for CBT (ES = 0.06) and for the combination treatment (ES = 0.07) suggest that CBT results in significantly greater maintenance of treatment gains relative to medication treatments.

A similar pattern was observed in the study by Barlow et al. (2000). CBT alone and CBT plus placebo were superior to placebo after no-treatment follow-up. Contrary to expectation, the combination of Imipramine plus CBT was significantly less effective than CBT alone or CBT plus pill placebo. Response rates at no-treatment follow up are presented in Figure 10.

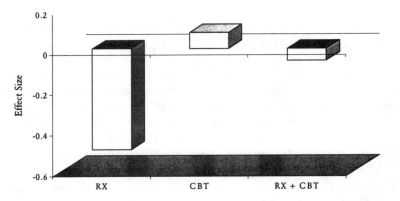

Figure 9. Long-term efficacy for CBT, medication, and their combination.
Data from Gould et al. (1995).

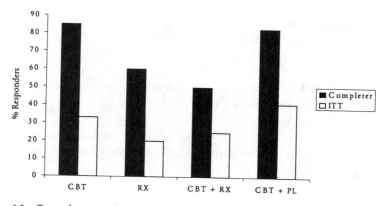

Figure 10. Completer and intent-to-treat (ITT) analysis of long-term response rates from most definitive randomized clinical trial. Data from Barlow et al. (2000).

Quality of Life

Few studies have directly evaluated the impact of interventions for panic disorder on patients' quality of life. Telch, Schmidt, Jaimez, Jacquin, and Harrigton, (1995) examined changes in quality of life following eight weeks of CBT administered in a group format. Participants who had received CBT showed more improvement in the domains of work functioning, social functioning, and family functioning compared to wait-list controls. These gains were maintained at a 6-month follow-up.

Improvement in quality of life is not restricted to CBT treatments. Jacobs, Davidson, Gupta, and Meyerhoff (1997) found that panic patients treated with clonazepam showed significant gains in quality of life relative to placebo-treated patients. Moreover, they showed that improvement in quality of life was directly related to improvement in panic symptoms.

Predictors of Clinical Response

Incidence of treatment non-response and relapse suggests that there are factors that moderate the efficacy of existing interventions. Cowley, Flick, and Roy-Byrne (1996) conducted follow-up interviews with panic disorder patients up to 60 months after completion of treatment. Consistent with previous findings (e.g., Warshaw, Massion, Shea, Allsworth, & Keller, 1997), level of agoraphobia proved to be the strongest predictor of overall improvement. In addition, the presence of major depression or Axis-II comorbidity at pre-treatment predicted a less favorable clinical response.

Several other studies have demonstrated an association between Axis-II comorbidity and poorer treatment outcome (e.g., Pollack, Otto, Rosenbaum, & Sachs, 1992). However, results of a recent study by Telch, Kamphuis, & Schmidt (2001) showed that Axis-II comorbidity no longer predicted level of improvement after controlling for baseline differences in panic disorder symptom severity.

Schmidt and Telch (1997) observed a relationship between panic patients perceived physical health and clinical response to CBT. Immediately following treatment, 71% of patients who perceived their physical health at intake as good met recovery criteria, compared to only 35% of those who perceived their health as poor. At a six-month no-treatment follow-up, 67% of those who perceived their physical health as good met composite recovery criteria compared to only 33% of those who perceived their health as poor.

Finally, Schmidt and Woolaway-Bickel (2000) found that patients' adherence to CBT as measured by therapist ratings predicted a more favorable response to CBT.

Treatment Effectiveness

Efficacy research is conducted under controlled circumstances. This has led to reservations regarding the generalizability of findings from randomized clinical trials. For example, it has been argued that the study samples might not be representative of the clinical population encountered in the community. Also, the utilization of treatment manuals in clinical trails is not as frequently observed in clinical practice.

To date, little attention has been given to the question of whether efficacy data from panic treatments delivered in the context of randomized clinical trials can be generalized to "real world" clinical practice. Fortunately, preliminary findings are promising. Wade, Treat, and Stuart (1998) compared the results of a 15-session CBT protocol in a community mental heath center (CMHC) to the results of two CBT efficacy studies. Pre-to post treatment changes as well as longer term follow-up findings observed in the CMCH sample were comparable to those observed in the two controlled efficacy studies (Stuart, Treat, & Wade, 2000).

Cost-Effectiveness

In addition to treatment efficacy and tolerability, treatment costs should be considered in the overall evaluation of the utility of a treatment. Margraf and Schneider (1995) reported an 81% decrease in healthcare costs associated with anxiety symptoms over 3 years following a 15-session cognitive behavioral treatment for individuals with panic disorder. They concluded that for every dollar spent on the treatment, 5.6 dollars were saved in healthcare costs. In their meta-analyses of interventions for panic disorder, Gould, Otto, and Pollack, (1995) compared the expenses for CBT to those for pharmacological treatment. Their findings indicated that Imipramine and group-administered CBT were the most cost-effective interventions. The total cost over a 12-month period was approximately $600 for Imipramine and group CBT, compared to a total yearly cost of approximately $1400 for individual CBT.

Otto, Pollack, and Maki (2000) examined whether the cost estimates provided by Gould et al. (1995) were representative of treatments as they are delivered in the community. Otto et al. argued that previous estimates might have been colored by the controlled conditions evident in clinical trials (e.g., sample characteristics, manualized treatment). Using an outpatient clinic sample, the authors calculated the average visit costs, medication costs, and alternative treatment costs per patient for both the acute treatment phase as well as for a one-year interval. As shown in Figure 11, CBT was the most cost-effective intervention for the acute phase ($518) as well as for a one-year interval ($523). Pharmacological treatment was shown to be more cost-effective than individual CBT during the acute phase (Costs $839, $1357, respectively). However, the cost for individual CBT was 59% of the cost for pharmacological treatment for a one-year interval.

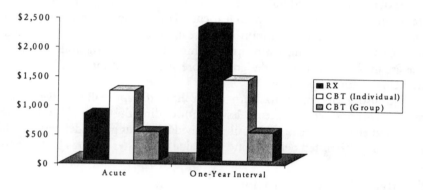

Figure 11. Cost of treatment. Data from Otto et al. (2000).

Otto et al. (2000) also estimated cost-benefit ratios for each treatment modality. The cost-benefit ratio was calculated by dividing the total cost of the intervention by the change in clinical status as measured by clinicians' ratings of global improvement. The findings matched the pattern observed for cost estimates, indicating superiority for group CBT for both the acute phase and one-year interval. Figure 12 presents the cost-effectiveness ratios for each treatment modality.

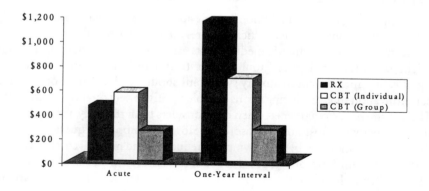

Figure 12. Cost-benefit ratios for each treatment modality. Data from Otto et al. (2000).

Comments: Future Directions

Despite the extensive treatment literature with respect to anxiety disorders, there is a striking paucity of research addressing various issues relevant to medical cost offset. In this next section, we discuss potential areas for future research.

Improving on Existing Treatments

The empirically-supported treatments currently available for anxiety disorders consist of multiple procedural elements such as education, cognitive restructuring, relaxation training, and exposure to fear cues. For the most part, there is a lack of data on the relative contribution of these procedural elements on treatment outcome. Can our existing treatments be trimmed? Dismantling studies are needed to assist in the challenge of designing more streamlined interventions without sacrificing treatment potency.

We also have much to learn about how to optimally deliver existing empirically-supported treatments. Issues surrounding the optimal sequencing of procedural elements, treatment dosing, individual versus group delivery, self-help versus therapist-assisted delivery, and the value of booster sessions have yet to be delineated.

Identifying Predictors of Clinical Response

Our review revealed that progress has been made in the identification of variables that predict patients' clinical response to existing treatments. For instance, we know that panic disorder patients with accompanying agoraphobia respond less favorably to either pharmacotherapy or CBT. Unfortunately, the treatment moderator analyses to date have yet to identify moderators of *differential* treatment response. In other words, little progress has been made in our ability to match patients to different treatments as a way of optimizing clinical response. Developing effective treatment matching algorithms hold much promise for medical cost offset.

Expanding the Range of Outcome Measures

In preparing this chapter it soon became apparent that we have virtually no data yet available on how treatment efficacy relates directly to medical cost offset. Given the staggering non-psychiatric medical costs associated with anxiety disorders, we might conclude on logical grounds that treatments that results in clinically significant improvement in anxiety symptoms should lead to reductions in health care utilization thus producing a considerable positive effect on medical cost offset. This argument is strengthened when one considers both the early age of onset and the chronicity of most anxiety disorders. However important questions remain. What is the relationship between symptom reduction and medical cost offset? What is the minimum level of symptom reduction necessary to produce medical cost offset? What is the relative effect of different treatment modalities (e.g., pharmacotherapy versus CBT) on medical cost offset? These and other questions can only be answered by clinical investigators incorporating a broader range of outcome indices in their analyses. These include both direct and indirect treatment costs, psychiatric and non-psychiatric comorbidity, earnings data, work absenteeism, work productivity, and quality of life indices including family outcome indices.

Developing Empirically-Supported Interventions for Managed Care

The availability of empirically-supported treatments for anxiety disorders does not insure that patients will seek them out. Indeed, evidence suggests that only about 27% of adults with a diagnosed anxiety disorder will receive treatment for it (Kessler et al., 1994). Consequently, more effective screening strategies need to be developed in primary care settings so that anxiety disorders can be identified and appropriately treated. Managed care organizations have great potential to offer integrated physical and mental health services to their members. However, these organizations are unlikely to provide more effective screening and treatment for anxiety disorders in the absence of incentives to do so. When one considers that membership in any one managed care organization is often short-lived, there exists little incentive for the organization to offer science-based integrated health care that is cost-effective for the organization and society in the long-term. Mechanisms for overcoming this structural impediment need to be developed and implemented.

Concluding Remarks

Anxiety disorders are debilitating and chronic conditions that represent a major challenge to our health care system. The costs of anxiety disorders– both monetary and non-monetary – to the patient, family, and society are staggering. Two decades of research have demonstrated that pharmacotherapy, CBT, and their combination are all markedly effective in the short-term, but cognitive-behavioral treatments have demonstrated a clear advantage with respect to durability of treatment gains. Contrary to expectation, there appears to be growing evidence that combining medication and psychosocial interventions does not lead to greater improvements than psychosocial treatment alone. Findings from effectiveness studies – although limited in number – provide preliminary support that the treatment gains observed in controlled randomized clinical trials seem to also hold when these treatments are delivered in the "real-world." Although some progress has been made in the identification of factors that predict clinical response to treatment, there has been little progress in developing strategies for matching treatments to patient characteristics. Finally, there is a shocking absence of data on the effects of treating anxiety disorders on subsequent health care utilization and medical cost offset. This state of affairs requires creative new research directions integrating methods from psychology, psychiatry, primary care medicine, economics, epidemiology, and health policy research.

References

Abramowitz, J. S. (1997). Effectiveness of psychological and pharmacological treatments for obsessive-compulsive disorder: A quantitative review. *Journal of Consulting and Clincial Psychology, 65 (1)*, 44-52.

Abramowitz, J. S. (1998). Does cognitive-behavioral therapy cure obsessive-compulsive disorder? A meta-analytic evaluation of clinical significance. *Behavior therapy, 29*, 339-355.

American Psychiatric Association. (1994). *Diagnostic and statistical manual of mental disorders* (4th ed.). Washington, DC: Author

Antony, M. M., Downie, F., & Swinson, R. P. (1998). Diagnostic issues and epidemiology in obsessive-compulsive disorder. In R. P. Swinson (Ed.), *Obsessive-compulsive disorder: Theory, research, and treatment* (pp. 3-32). New York, NY: The Guildford Press, 3-32.

Araujo, L. A., Ito, L. M., & Marks, I. M. (1996). Early compliance and other factors predicting outcome of exposure for obsessive-compulsive disorder: results from a controlled study. *British Journal of Psychiatry, 169*, 747-52.

AuBuchon, P. G., & Malatesta, V. J. (1994). Obsessive compulsive patients wit comorbid personality disorder: Associated problems and response to a comprehensive behavior therapy. *Journal of Clinical Psychiatry, 55*, 448-453.

Baer, L., & Jenike, M. A. (1992). Personality disorders in obsessive compulsive disorder. *Psychiatric Clinics of North America, 55*, 803-812.

Ballenger, J. (1999). Current treatments of anxiety disorders in adults. *Biological Psychiatry, 46 (11)*, 1579-1594.

Barlow, D. H., Craske, M. G., Cerny, J. A., & Klosko, J. S. (1989). Behavioral treatment of panic disorder. *Behavior Therapy, 20*, 261-282.

Barlow, D. H., Gorman, J. M., Shear, M. K., & Woods, S. W. (2000). Cognitive-behavioral therapy, imipramine, or their combination for panic disorder: A randomized controlled trial. *JAMA, 283*, 2529-36.

Barlow, D. H., Rapee, R. M., & Brown, T. A. (1992). Behavioral treatment of generalized anxiety disorder. *Behavior Therapy, 23*, 551-570.

Barrett, J. E., Barrett, J. A., Oxman, T. E., & Gerber P. D. (1988). The prevalence of psychiatric disorders in a primary care practice. *Archives of General Psychiatry, 45*, 1100-1106.

Barsky, A J. (1992). Hypochondriasis and obsessive compulsive disorder. *Psychiatric Clinics of North American, 15 (4)*, 791-801.

Borkovec, T. D., & Costello, E. (1993). Efficacy of applied relaxation and cognitive-behavioral therapy in the treatment of generalized anxiety disorder. *Journal of Clinical and Consulting Psychology, 61 (4)*, 611-619.

Brown, T. A., & Barlow, D. H. (1992). Comorbidity among anxiety disorders: Implications for treatment and DSM-IV. *Journal of Consulting and Clinical Psychology, 60*, 835-844.

Butler, G., Fennell, M., Robson, P., & Gelder, M. (1991). Comparison of behavior therapy and cognitive behavior therapy in the treatment of generalized anxiety disorder. *Journal of Consulting and Clinical Psychology, 59*, 167-175.

Calvocoressi, L., Lewis, B., Harris, M., Trufan, S. J., Goodman, W. K., McDougle, C J., & Price, L. H. (1995). Family accommodation in obsessive-compulsive disorder. *American Journal of Psychiatry, 152 (3)*, 441-443.

Candilis, P.J., McLean, R.Y.S, Otto, M.W., Manfro, G.G., Worthington, J.J. III, Penava, J., Marzol, P.C., & Pollack, M.H. (1999) Quality of life in patients with panic disorder. *Journal of Nervous & Mental Disease, 187*, 429-434.

Clark, D. M., Salkovskis, P. M., Hackmann, A., Middleton, H., & et al. (1994). A comparison of cognitive therapy, applied relaxation and imipramine in the treatment of panic disorder. *British Journal of Psychiatry, 164*, 759-769.

Clum, G.A., Clum, G.A., & Surls, R. (1993). A meta-analysis for panic disorder. *Journal of Consulting and Clinical Psychology, 61*, 317-326.

Cottraux, J., Mollard, E., Bouvard, M., & Marks, I. (1993). Exposure therapy, fluvoxamine, or combination treatment in obsessive-compulsive disorder: One-year follow-up. *Psychiatry Research, 49*, 63-75.

Cowley, D. S., Flick, S. N., & Roy-Byrne, P. P. (1996). Long-term course and outcome in panic disorder: a naturalistic follow- up study. *Anxiety, 2*, 13-21.

DuPont, R. L., Rice, D. P., Shiraki, S., & Rowland, C. R. (1996). Economic costs of obsessive-compulsive disorder. *Medical Interface, 8*, 102-109.

Fifer, S. K., Mathias, S. D., Patrick, D. L., Mazonson, P. D., Lubeck, D. P., & Buesching, D. P. (1994). Untreated anxiety among adult primary care patients in a health maintenance organization. *Archives of General Psychiatry, 51*, 740-750.

Fisher, P. L., & Durham, R. C. (1999). Recovery rates in generalized anxiety disorder following psychological therapy: an analysis of clinically significant change in the STAI-T across outcome studies since 1990. *Psychological Medicine, 29*, 1425-1434.

Foa, E. B., & Kozak, M. J. (1996). Psycological treatment for obsessive-compulsive disorder. In M. R. Mavissakalian & F. F. Prien (Eds.), *Long-term Treatments of Anxiety Disorders* (pp. 285-309). Washington, DC: American Psychiatric Press, Inc.

Franklin, M. E., Abramowitz, J. S., Kozak, M J., Levitt, J. T., & Foa, E. B. (2000). Effectivenss of exposure and ritual prevention for obsessive-compulsive disorder: Randomized compared with nonrandomized samples. *Journal of Consulting and Clinical Psychology, 68 (4)*, 594-602.

Friedman, S., Hatch, M., & Paradis, C. M. (1993). Obsessive compulsive disorder in two black ethnic groups: Incidence in an urban dermatology clinic. *Journal of Anxiety Disorders, 7*, 343-348.

Frost, R. O., & Steketee, G. (1997). Perfectionism in obsessive-compulsive disorder patients. *Behaviour Research & Therapy, 35*, 291-296.

Gallup Organization, Inc. (1990). *A Gallup Study of Obsessive-Compulsive Sufferers.* Princeton, New Jersey.

Goodman, W. K., Price, L. H., Rasmussen, S. A., Mazure, C., Delgado, P., Heninger, G. R., & Charney, D. S. (1989). The Yale-Brown Obsessive Compulsive Scale: II. Validity. *Archives of General Psychiatry 1989, 46*, 1006-1011.

Gorman, J. M., Goetz, R. R., Fyer, M., King, D. L., Fyer, A. J., Liebowitz, M. R., & Klein, D. F. (1988). The mitral valve prolapse-panic disorder connection. *Psychosomatic Medicine, 50*, 114-122.

Gould, R. A., Otto, M. W., & Pollack, M. H. (1995). A meta-analysis of treatment outcome for panic disorder. *Clinical Psychology Review, 15*, 819-844.

Gould, R. A., Otto, M. W., Pollack, M. H., & Yap, L. (1997). Cognitive behavioral and pharmacological treatment of generalized anxiety disorder: A preliminary meta-analysis. *Behavior Therapy, 28*, 285-305.

Greist, J. H., Jefferson, J. W., Kobak, K. A., Katzelnick, D. J., & Serlin, R. C. (1995). Efficacy and tolerability of serotonin transport inhibitors in obsessive-compulsive disorder: A meta-analysis. *Archives of General Psychiatry, 52*, 53-60.

Hollander, E., Kwon, J. H., Stein, D. J., Broatch, J., Rowland, C. T., & Himelein, C. A. (1996). Obsessive-compulsive and spectrum disorders: Overview and quality of life issues. *Journal of Clinical Psychiatry, 57 (8, suppl.)*, 3-6.

Hudson, J. I., & Pope, H. G. (1987). Depression and eating disorders. In O. G. Cameron (Ed.), *Presentations of Depression: Depressive Symptoms in Medical and other Psychiatric Disorders*. Oxford, England: Joohn Wiley & Sons.

Jacobs, R. J., Davidson, J. R., Gupta, S., & Meyerhoff, A. S. (1997). The effects of clonazepam on quality of life and work productivity in panic disorder. *American Journal of Managed Care, 3*, 1187-96.

Jacobson, N. S., & Truax, P. (1991). Clinical significance: a statistical approach to defining meaningful change in psychotherapy research. *Journal of Consulting and Clinical Psychology, 59*, 12-19.

Jenike, M. A., Baer, L., & Carey, R. J. (1986). Coexistent obsessive-compulsive disorder and schizotypal personality disorder: A poor prognostic indicator. *Archives of General Psychiatry, 43 (3)*, 296.

Kamphius, J. H., & Telch, M. J. (1998). Assessment of strategies to manage or avoid perceived threats among panic disorder patients: The Texas Safety maneuver Scale (TSMS). *Clinical Psychology and Psychotherapy, 5*, 177-186.

Kane, F.J. Jr, Harper, R. G., & Wittels, E. (1988). Angina as a symptom of psychiatric illness. *Southern Medical Journal, 81*, 1412-1416.

Karajgi, B., Rifkin, A., Doddi, S. & Kolli, R. (1990). The prevalence of anxiety disorders in patients with chronic obstructive pulmonary disease. *American Journal of Psychiatry, 147*, 200-201

Kasvikis, Y. G., Tsakiris, F. Marks, I. M., & Basoglu, M. (1986). Past history of anorexia nervosa in women with obsessive-compulsive disorder. *International Journal of Eating Disorders, 5 (6)*, 1069-1075.

Katon, W., Von Korff, M., & Lin, E. (1990). Distressed high utilizers of medical care: DSM-III-R diagnoses and treatment needs. *General Hospital Psychiatry, 12*, 355-362.

Keijsers, G. P. J., Hoogduin, C. A. L., & Schaap, C. P. D. R. (1994). Predictors of treatment outcome in the behavioural treatment of obsessive-compulsive disorder. *British Journal of Psychiatry, 165 (6)*, 781-786.

Kennedy, B. L., & Schwab, J. J. (1997). Untilization of medical specialists by anxiety disorder patients. *Psychosomatics, 38 (2)*, 109-112.

Kessler, R. C., McGonagle, K.A., Zhao, S., Nelson, C. B., Hughs, M., Eshelman, S., Wittchen, H. U., & Kendler K. S. (1994). Lifetime and 12-month prevalence of DSM-III-R psychiatric disorders in the United States. *Archives of General Psychiatry, 51,* 8-19.

Klein, D. F. (1984). Psychopharmacologic treatment of panic disorder. *Psychosomatics, 25,* 32-6.

Koran, L. M., Thienemann, M. L., & Davenport, R. (1996). Quality of life for patients with obsessive-compulsive disorder. *American Journal of Psychiatry, 153 (6),* 783-788.

Kozak, M. J., Liebowitz, M. R., & Foa, E. B. (2000). Cognitive behavior therapy and pharmacotherapy for obsessive-compulsive disorder: The NIMH-sponsored collaborative study. In W. K. Goodman, M. V. Rudorfer, & J. D. Maser (Eds.), *Obsessive-Compulsive Disorder: Contemporary Issues in Treatment* (pp. 501-530). Mahwah, New Jersey: Lawrence Erlbaum Associates.

Leckman, J. F., Peterson, B. S., Pauls, D. L., Cohen, D. J. (1997). Tic disorders. *Psychiatric Clinics of North America, 20,* 839-861.

Leon, A. C., Olfson, M., & Portera, L. (1997). Service utilization and expenditures for the treatment of panic disorder. *General Hospital Psychiatry, 19,* 82-88.

Lydiard, R. B., Fossey, M. D., Marsh, W., & Ballenger, J. C. (1993). Prevalence of psychiatric disorders in patients with irritable bowel syndrome. *Psychosomatics, 34,* 229-234.

Mancuso D. M., Townsend, M. H., & Mercante, D. E. (1994). Long-term follow up of generalized anxiety disorder. *Comprehensive Psychiatry, 34 (6),* 441-446.

Margraf, J., Barlow, D. H., Clark, D. M., & Telch, M. J. (1993). Psychological treatment of panic: Work in progress on outcome, active ingredients, and follow-up. *Behaviour Research & Therapy, 31,* 1-8.

Margraf, J., & Schneider, S. (1995). *Cost-effectiveness of cognitive-behavioral treatment: a prospective study.* Paper presented at the World Congress of Behavioural and Cognitive Therapies, Copenhagern, Denmark.

Markowitz, J. S., Weissman, M. M., Ouellette, R., Lish, J. D., & et al. (1989). Quality of life in panic disorder. *Archives of General Psychiatry, 46,* 984-992.

Massion, A. O., Warshaw, M. G., & Keller, M. B. (1993). Quality of life and psychiatric morbidity in panic disorder and generalized anxiety disorder. *American Journal of Psychiatry, 150,* 600-607.

McDougle, C. J., Epperson, C. N., Pelton, G. H., Wasylink, S., & Price, L. H. (2000). A double-blind, placebo-controlled study of risperidone addition in seratonin reuptake inhibitor-refractory obsessive-compulsive disorder. *Archives of General Psychiatry, 57,* 794-801.

Moras, K., & Barlow, D. (1992). Definitions of secondary depression: Effects on comorbidity and outcome in anxiety disorders. *Pyschopharmacology Bulletin, 28 (1),* 27-33.

Mundo, E., Bianchi, L., & Bellodi, L. (1997). Efficacy of fluvoxamine, paroxetine, and citalopram in the treatment of obsessive-compulsive disorder: A single-blind study. *Journal of Clinical Psychopharmacology,. Vol 17 (4)*, 267-271.

Narrow, W.E., Regier, D. A., Rae, D. S., Manderscheid, R. W., & Locke, B. Z. (1993). Use of services by persons with mental and addictive disorders. *Archives of General Psychiatry, 50*, 95-107.

O'Sullivan, G., Noshirvani, H., Marks, I., Monteiro, W., & Lelliott, P. (1991). Six-year follow-up after exposure and CMI therapy for obsessive compulsive disorder. *Journal of Clinical Psychiatry, 52 (4)*, 150-155.

Orloff, L. M., Battle, M. A., Baer, L., & Ivanjack, L. (1994). Long-term follow up of 85 patients with obsessive-compulsive disorder. *American Journal of Psychiatry, 15*, 441-442.

Ormel, J., Koeter, M. W. J., van den Brink, W., & van de Willige, G. (1991). Recognition, management, and course of anxiety and depression in general practice. *Archives of General Psychiatry, 48*, 700-706.

Otto, M.W., Pollack, M.H., & Maki, K.M. (2000). Empirically supported treatments for panic disorder: Costs, benefits, and stepped care. *Journal of Consulting & Clinical Psychology, 68*, 556-563.

Pollack, M. H., Otto, M. W., Rosenbaum, J. F., & Sachs, G. S. (1992). Personality disorders in patients with panic disorder: association with childhood anxiety disorders, early trauma, comorbidity, and chronicity. *Comprehensive Psychiatry, 33*, 78-83.

Power K. G., Simpson, R. J., Swanson, V., Wallace, L. A., Feistner, A. T. C., & Sharp, D. (1990). A controlled comparison of cognitive-behaviour therapy, diazepam, and placebo, alone and in combination, for the treatment of generalised anxiety disorder. *Journal of Anxiety Disorders, 4*, 267-292.

Rapoport, J. (1988). The neurobiology of obsessive-compulsive disorder. *Journal of the American Medical Association, 260*, 2889.

Rapoport, J. (1989). The biology of obsessions and compulsions. *Scientific American, March issue.*

Rasmussen, S. A. (1985). Obsessive-compulsive disorder in dermatologic practice. *Journal of the American Academy of Dermatology, 13*, 965-967.

Rasmussen, S. A., & Eisen, J. L. (1990). Epidemiology of obsessive compulsive disorder. *Journal of Clinical Psychiatry, 51 (2, Suppl.)*, 10-13.

Rasmussen, S. A., & Eisen, J. L. (1992). The epidemiology and differential diagnosis of obsessive complsice disorder. *Journal of Clinical Psychiatry, 53*, 4-10.

Rasmussen, S. A., & Tsuang, M. T. (1986). Clinical characteristics and family history in DSM-II obsessive-compulsive disorder. *Journal of Clinical Psychiatry, 51 (2, suppl.)*, 10-13.

Ravizza, L., Barzega, G., Bellino, S., Bogetto, F., & Maina, G. (1996). Drug treatment of obsessive-compulsive disorder (OCD): Long-term trial with CMIand selective seratonin reuptake inhibitors (SSRIs). *Psychopharmacology Bulletin, 32 (1)*, 167-173.

Ravizza, L., Maina, G., Bogetto, F., Albert, U., Barzega, G., & Bellino, S. (1998). Long term treatment of obsessive-compulsive disorder. *Cns Drugs, 10 (4)*, 247-255.

Ravizza, R., Barzega, G., Bellino, S., Bogetto, F., & Maina, G. (1995). Predictors of drug treatment response in obsessive-compulsive disorder. *Journal of Clinical Psychiatry, 56*, 368-373.

Robins, L. N., Helzer, J. E., Weissman, M. M., & Orvaschel, H. (1984). Lifetime prevalence of specific psychiatric disorders in three sites. *Archives of General Psychiatry, 41*, 949-958.

Rogers, M. P., White, K., Warshaw, M. G., Yonkers, K. A., Rodriguez-Villa, F., Chang, G. & Keller, M. B. (1994). Prevalence of medical illness in patients with anxiety disorders. *International Journal of Psychiatry in Medicine, 24*, 83-96.

Roy-Byrne, P. P. (1996). Generalized anxiety and mixed anxiety-depression: Association with disability and health care utilization. *Journal of Clinical Psychiatry, 57 (Suppl 7)*, 86-91.

Sanderson, W. C., Beck, A. T., & McGinn, L. K. (1994). Cognitive therapy for generalized anxiety disorder: Significance of comorbid personality disorders. *Journal of Cognitive Psychotherapy, 8 (1)*, 13-18.

Sanderson, W. C., Di Nardo, P. A., Rapee, R. M., & Barlow, D. H. (1990). Syndrome comorbidity in patients diagnosed with a DSM–III–R anxiety disorder. *Journal of Abnormal Psychology, 99*, 308-312.

Schmidt, N. B., & Telch, M. J. (1997). Nonpsychiatric medical comorbidity, health perceptions, and treatment outcome in patients with panic disorder. *Health Psychology, 16*, 114-122.

Schmidt, N. B., & Woolaway-Bickel, K. (2000). The effects of treatment compliance on outcome in cognitive-behavioral therapy for panic disorder: quality versus quantity. *Journal of Consulting and Clinical Psychology, 68*, 13-8.

Steketee, G. (1993). Social support and treatment outcome of obsessive compulsive disorder at 9-month follow-up. *Behavioural Psychotherapy, 21 (2)*, 81-95.

Steketee, G., & Shapiro, L. J. (1995). Predicting behavioral treatment outcome for agoraphobia and obsessive compulsive disorder. *Clinical Psychology Review, 15(4)*, 317-346.

Steketee, G., Grayson, J. B., & Foa, E. B. (1987). A comparison of characteristics of obsessive-compulsive disorder and other anxiety disorders. *Journal of Anxiety Disorders, 1 (4)*, 325-335.

Steketee, G., Henninger, N. J., & Pollard, C. A. (2000). Predicting treatment outcomes for obsessive-compulsive disorder: Effects of comorbidity. In W. K. Goodman, M. V. Rudorfer, & J. D. Maser (Eds.), *Obsessive-Compulsive Disorder: Contemporary Issues in Treatment* (pp. 257-274). Mahwah, New Jersey: Lawrence Erlbaum Associates.

Stuart, G. L., Treat, T. A., & Wade, W. A. (2000). Effectiveness of an Empirically Based Treatment for Panic Disorder Delivered in a Service Clinic Setting: 1-Year Follow-Up. *Journal of Consulting and Clinical Psychology, 68*, 506-512.

Telch, M. J., Lucas, J. A., Schmidt, N. B., Hanna, H. H., Jaimez, T. L., & Lucas, R. (1993). Group cognitive-behavioral treatment of panic disorder. *Behaviour Research and Therapy, 31*, 279-287.

Telch, M. J., Schmidt, N. B., Jaimez, L., Jacquin, K., & Harrington, P. (1995). The impact of cognitive-behavioral therapy on quality of life in panic disorder patients. *Journal of Consulting and Clinical Psychology, 63*, 823-830.

Turner, S. M., Beider, D.C., Spauling, S. A., & Brown, J. M. (1995). The practice of behavior therapy: a national survey of cost and methods. AABT: *The Behavior Therapist, 18*, 1-4.

Wade, W. A., Treat, T. A., & Stuart, G. L. (1998). Transporting an empirically supported treatment for panic disorder to a service clinic setting: A benchmarking strategy. *Journal of Consulting and Clinical Psychology, 66*, 231-239.

Warshaw, M. G., Massion, A. O., Shea, M. T., Allsworth, J., & Keller, M. B. (1997). Predictors of remission in patients with panic with and without agoraphobia: prospective 5-year follow-up data. *Journal of Nervous and Mental Disease, 185*, 517-9.

Weissman, M. M., Markowitz, J. S., Ouellette, R., Greenwald, S., & Kahn, J. P. (1990). Panic disorder and cardiovascular/cerebrovascular problems: Results from a community survey. *American Journal of Psychiatry, 147*, 1504-1508.

Wittchen, H. U., Carter, R. M., Pfister, H., Montgomery, S. A., & Kessler, R. C. (2000). Disabilities and quality of life in pure and comorbid generalized anxiety disorder and major depression in a national survey. *International Clinical Psychopharmacology, 15 (6)*, 319-328.

Wittchen, H. U., Zhao, S., Kessler, R. C., & Eaton, W. W. (1994). DSM-III-R generalized anxiety disorder in the National Comorbidity Survey. *Archives of General Psychiatry, 51*, 355-364.

Wulsin, L.R., Arnold, L. M., & Hillard, J. R. (1991). Axis I disorders in ER patients with atypical chest pain. *International Journal of Psychiatry in Medicine, 21*, 37-46.

Yonkers, K., Dyck, I. R., Warshaw, M., & Keller, M. (2000). Factors predicting the course of generalised anxiety disorder. *British Journal of Psychiatry, 176*, 544-549.

Zajecka, J. (1997). Importance of establishing the diagnosis of persistent anxiety. *Journal of Clinical Psychiatry, 58 (Suppl 3)*, 9-13.

Zandbergen, J., Bright, M., Pols, H., Fernandez, I., deLoof, C., & Griez, E. J. (1991). Higher lifetime prevalence of respiratory diseases in panic disorder? *American Journal of Psychiatry, 148*, 1583-1585.

Preventing Excess Disability in Dementia Care

Debra W. Fredericks
Jane E. Fisher
Jeffrey A. Buchanan
Valerie Luevano
University of Nevada, Reno

Nationally, an increase in the elderly population is placing a great strain on the U.S. economy. Population trends indicate that the costs for government sponsored services, such as Medicare, under the current system will be staggering by the year 2030 as those aged 65 and older will increase from approximately 12% to 25% of the total U.S. population (US Census). In the elderly, chronic physical conditions are more disabling, require more care and are more costly to treat than for younger age groups. Over 34% of those aged 65-74 and 45% of those aged over 75 are disabled due to chronic health conditions (National Academy on an Aging Society, 2000). Annual per capita U.S. health care costs in 1997 were $1,286 for those under 65, $5,360 for those 65–85, and $9,000 for those over 85 (Butler, Lewis, & Sunderland, 1998). The largest segment with highest medical care utilization, those over the age of 85, is the fastest growing portion: between 1995 and 2030 it is expected that this group will double and quadruple by 2050 (Butler, et al., 1998). Adding to this burden, the incidence of Alzheimer's Disease (AD) is greatest after the age of 85. By the year 2030, it is estimated that in the US alone, persons with AD will double to approximately 9 million. Currently, AD accounts for $80 to $100 billion in total treatment costs yearly and is expected to increase to over $200 billion over the next few decades (Butler, et al., 1998). It is the third most expensive disease to treat in the US, preceded only by cancer and cardiac disease (National Alzheimer's Association). Already strained, both Federal and State resources will have difficulty meeting the demand of our aging population.

Given these staggering statistics, strategies to reduce the cost of AD care have become an important concern of legislators and care providers. In this chapter, we will present an overview of dementia, its symptoms, diagnosis, and a comprehensive description of the economic impact of AD. We propose that preventing excess disabilities in both patients and informal caregivers will be key to medical cost offset and describe an integrated model of care that may provide a strategy for care providers to prevent excess disability.

Overview of Dementia

"Dementia" is an umbrella term describing symptoms of cognitive impairment. "Cognition" refers to a variety of behaviors, including memory, thinking and problem solving. Healthy cognitive aging does not result in the types of cognitive symptoms of memory loss and confusion seen in diseases of the brain. There are numerous causes of cognitive impairment in the elderly, some of which are reversible, such as depression or vitamin B12 deficiency. Of the irreversible causes, AD is the most common, accounting for approximately 75%. AD is a terminal, slowly progressive, neurodegenerative disease of the brain. There is high inter-individual variation in symptom trajectory and length of the disease. Patients live, on average, for 2-20 years and most die of adventitious infections, such as pneumonia.

Symptoms of Alzheimer's Disease. Symptoms of AD include: (a) memory loss, (b) aphasia, (c) agnosia, (d) apraxia, and (e) impaired executive functioning. Memory loss is mild in the early phases and generally restricted to recent events and some word-finding difficulty during conversation. As the disease progresses, remote memory becomes impaired along with significant difficulty in recalling events that occurred even moments earlier. Aphasia (i.e., problems with speaking and under-standing language) is also an early sign of AD. Anomia (i.e., naming impairment) is the most common aphasic symptom. Agnosia, or problems recognizing objects, appears in a few different forms. Temporal agnosia affects the recognition of time and length of time. Visual agnosia affects the ability to recognize familiar objects by sight, whereas, tactile agnosia is the inability to recognize familiar objects by touch. The inability to recognize significance of sounds is called acoustic agnosia. Symptoms of apraxia include problems using objects appropriately, forgetting the sequence of tasks (i.e., amnesic apraxia), and forgetting the function of objects (i.e., sensory apraxia). Executive Functioning refers to logical thinking and problem solving skills.

Symptom Trajectory. Early in the disease, symptoms are very subtle: mild memory problems and minor word-finding problems often are attributed to normal aging. Early impairments are difficult to recognize by casual observation such as during short primary care check-up visits (Boise, Camicioli, Morgan, Rose, & Congleton, 1999). Additionally, the types of dissociations between different discrete language impairments probably allow the patient to appear unimpaired during conversation until well into the disease process (Fredericks & Fisher, unpublished). Conse-quently, only those closest to the patient may notice early symptoms and often wait years before visiting the appropriate specialist (Gori, et al., 1998). Thus, by the time a diagnosis is received, significant others often have already experienced years of uncertainty and stress, impacting their own health and psychological well-being.

Even during the earliest phases, the combination of impaired memory and impaired executive functioning can place individuals at risk for a number of health and safety concerns, thus requiring 24 hour supervision. Thus, high utilization of personal and financial resources can begin early in the disease and continues to increase over the course of the disease. Additionally, the emotional impact on families cannot be underestimated; however, despite this, families are responsible for providing the supervision and care required. The economic and health impact on informal care providers will be addressed in greater detail later in this chapter. First, we will turn to a brief overview of the diagnostic procedure and its necessitating costs.

Diagnosis. The National Institute of Neurologic Communicative Disorders and Stroke – Alzheimer's Disease Related Disorders Association (NINCDS-ADRDA) task force has established diagnostic criteria (McKhann, et al., 1984). Accurate clinical diagnoses in specialized clinics have reached high levels: between 80% to 90% (Butler, et al., 1998) with approximately 11% of dementia due to irreversible causes (Boise, et al., 1999). Accurate diagnosis, however, can be time consuming for the medical provider. It involves interviews with significant others, a thorough neurological exam, memory testing, laboratory studies, and brain imaging at a minimum (Kukull, et al., 1990).

Excess Disability

Excess disability can be defined as an impairment of function disproportionate to that directly attributable to the disease (Dawson, Wells, & Kline, 1993). For AD, this model can be expanded to include a social or physical environment that provides either insufficient support or excessive support. Simply stated, if there is not an optimal balance between opportunities to engage in spared skills along with compensation for impaired skills, excess disability can occur.

Our Westernized medical culture, however, prescribes that health care providers view the treatment of disease in a very limited way. It is an acute care based system that separates "mental" and physical events in such a way as to often dismiss or de-legitimize psychosocial influences on disease trajectory. Kitwood (1990) argues that focus should shift to the dementing process occuring within a "social-psychological" milieu that includes not only conditions of the brain and the patient's psychology but also the developmental and learning history that occurred over the lifespan. Thus, neurological impairment is viewed as an interactive process between physiological degeneration and psychosocial degeneration. Simply stated, variables contributing to degeneration are not limited to physiological changes. This perspective has implications for assumptions regarding treatment and may provide an explanation for the high degree of interindividual variability between AD patients.

A broader conceptualization of the dementing process, such as outlined by Kitwood (1990), has a number of implications for analyzing costs associated with the care of AD. Most notable is the assumption that disease trajectory is assumed to be affected by influences other than biomedical treatment. For example, once a particular constellation of symptoms, such as memory loss and anomia, are labeled "Alzheimer's Disease," social contingencies are such that the individual experiences vulnerability, disempowerment, loss of social skills, stigmatization, and radical depersonalization along an interactive continuum with neurodegenerative processes (Kitwood, 1990). The family also experiences these social contingencies.

Simply stated, treatments targeting the "social-psychological" milieu can be considered preventative care for more costly future conditions.

Medical Management. Most often, families do not pursue a diagnosis until well after the onset of behavioral and cognitive symptoms simply because these symptoms are attributed to stress or age (Gori, et al., 1998). Additionally, a number of obstacles to diagnosis by primary care physicians have been identified. These include a failure to recognize early symptoms, negative attitudes toward the utility of diagnosis, and limited time (Boise, et al., 1999). Primary practice physicians diagnose less than 50% of AD cases (Wind, Van Staveren, Jonker, & Eijk, 1994). As previously discussed, early symptoms are subtle, however, adherence to a particular health care ideology by primary physicians can also result in delays in accurate diagnosis. For instance, physicians may believe that since medical treatment options have no real benefit and since there is no cure, there is no reason to cause the patient and significant others undue anxiety or differentially diagnose from "dementia" (Boise, et al., 1999). Ideally, primary care physicians recognize that diagnosis is an important gateway to receiving support services; physicians must be able to look beyond "treatment" as cure and understand the impact that preventing excess disabilities can have. When a diagnosis is delayed, the opportunity to prevent excess disability is delayed, and greater costs will incur.

Effective medical management can significantly impact cost savings for the care of AD. As previously noted, AD is one of the costliest diseases to treat. A 1999 study (Gutterman, Markowitz, Lewis & Fillit) demonstrated that costs of a large managed care organization were 1.5 times greater for AD when adjusted for level of comorbidity for their 80,000 Medicare enrollees. Higher medical utilization costs have been shown to be directly related to disease progression and likely realized during the years prior to the severe phase of the disease (Souetre, Thwaites, & Yeardley, 1999). In support of this conclusion, a 2001 study by McCormick et al. found that during the last 3 years of life, AD enrollees did not incur higher costs than non-AD enrollees in a managed care organization. Populations accounting for the highest annual per capita health care expenses in 1997, also account for the highest probability of AD: $6,000 and $9,000 for aged 65-84 and 85 and above, respectively compared to less that $2,000 for under age 65 (Butler, et al., 1998). Considering that after diagnosis, an individual might live on average 7-10 years, delaying disease progression and preventing excess disability may provide substantial savings.

Slowing the progression of dementia. It has been estimated that annual savings of $996 to $24,348 in formal costs could be accrued if interventions to slow the progression of AD were implemented (Leon, Cheng, & Neumann, 1998). Currently, no medical interventions exist that provide cure or that can halt the progression of plaque and tangle formation. Current AD medications target acetylcholinestaerase, allowing increased levels of acetylcholine, a neurochemical active in areas of the brain thought to participate in higher mental functions. These medications offer a potential for economic benefit if they can help patients maintain higher function and slow progression. However, these medications are relatively new, therefore there are few long-term studies. Much of the published research is on tacrine, a medication rarely used currently. One study has estimated that individuals taking the drug tacrine from the time of diagnosis to the time of death were 2.3 times less likely to enter a nursing home and delayed nursing home placement by 440 days (Knopman, et al., 1997). Other studies have found that cost savings of $9,250 can be achieved over a patient's lifetime if the drug tacrine is started at the time of diagnosis (Henke & Burchmore, 1997).

In general, it is estimated that prevention of a 2 point decline in Folstein Mini Mental State Exam (MMSE) scores translates to a savings of $3,700 annually and a MMSE score improvement of 2 points translates to $7,100 savings annually per capita for in-home care of moderately and severely impaired patients (Ernst, Hay, Fenn, Tinklenberg, & Yesavage, 1997). Research indicates that treatment with donepezil in patients with mild to moderate AD can prevent a 2 point MMSE score decline compared to placebo, measured at one year (Winblad, et al., 2001). A study by Mohs et al. (2001) demonstrated that in moderate AD treated with donepezil, all subjects showed detectable disease progression, however after one year, measures demonstrated a 38% reduction in functional decline compared to placebo for both basic activities of daily living (ADL) and instrumental ADLs. Differences between decline in donepezil treated groups versus placebo groups have also been demonstrated for more severely impaired subjects (Feldman, et al., 2001) and on measures of caregiver burden (Fillit, Gutterman, & Brooks, 2000). Research on the effects of rivastigmine demonstrate similar results to those reported on donepezil; basically, all subjects declined but at a less rapid rate than those in the placebo group (Farlow, Anand, Messina, Hartman, & Veach, 2000). However, theories exist arguing that medications, such as rivastigmine, that also target butyrylcholinestarase may provide better effect for severe AD and, perhaps, influence neuritic plaque formation (Greig, et al., 2001).

Preventing Excess Disability in Caregivers. For in-home care, family members constitute over 70% of caregivers for individuals with physical and cognitive limitations (National Academy on an Aging Society, 2000). High medical care utilization can result for informal caregivers who are at risk for many disorders as a result of caring for a cognitively impaired family member. Research has consistently demonstrated that family caregivers are at risk for several negative consequences including severe depression, anxiety, and anger (Gaugler, et al., 2000), multiple health problems, addictive disorders, and increased rates of cancer, cardiac and infectious disease (Light, Niederehe, & Lebowitz, 1994). A recent study published in the Journal of the American Medical Association found that caregiving and its associated emotional strain is also an independent risk factor for premature death in spouses (Schulz & Beach, 1999). The negative consequences to the psychological and physical health of caregivers also place the care-receiver at risk for physical and emotional abuse, social isolation, depression, and institutionalization (Light, et al., 1994).

However, despite the formidable challenges families face in caring for their elderly family members, the majority of caregiving families go to extreme lengths in order to maintain their elderly relative in their home. Family caregivers of elderly adults consistently report that long term institutional care is sought only as a last resort (Gaugler, Zarit, & Pearlin, 1999), when the perceived stress of caregiving overwhelms their emotional, instrumental, and financial resources.

Economic Impact of Residential Care

Much of the high health care costs of AD are due to long term care costs. Federal/State Medicaid programs pay for 40% of these long term care costs. Although other special populations utilize long term care, the vast majority are elderly due to an increase in chronic conditions that necessitate assistance with ADLs. In 1990, over 40% of nursing home residents were cognitively impaired, requiring more intensive, 24 hour care than those who are not cognitively impaired. Compared to residential care, in-home care is decidedly more cost effective to public systems: in 1994 the cost of in-home care was $13 billion compared to $41 billion for residential care (Light, et al., 1994). Additionally, the positive off-set value of in-home care by family members is estimated to exceed $195 billion (National Academy on an Aging Society, 2000). Thus, resource allocations at the Federal and State levels have emphasized maintaining AD patients in their homes as long as possible.

Some studies have attempted to provide a combination of case management services as well as increases in reimbursement through Medicare or Medicaid for community-based services such as personal care, homemaker services, respite care, day care, or companion services. Nocks, Learner, Blackman, and Brown (1986) in a random clinical trial found that providing a combination of case management services and increasing reimbursement for community-based services resulted in significantly fewer nursing home admissions and a 38% reduction in nursing home use when compared to a control group. However, other studies providing a similar package of services found no differences in nursing home entry rates and no delay in the time to institutionalization (Miller, Newcomer, & Fox, 1999). In-home care and community based services may not, overall, be more cost effective than residential care when indirect costs of informal caregiving are accounted. Before examining this relation further, however, we will turn toward a discussion of the continuum of residential care available, as these options vary greatly with regard to services offered and costs.

Residential Care Options for Dementia

Residential care options generally fall under three categories: assisted living facilities, extended care facilities (nursing homes), and special care units for patients with dementia (which are often separate units within nursing homes). The following section will describe these types of residential care, the types of services they provide, what they cost in relation to in-home care, and what they cost in relation to each other.

Assisted Living Facilities. Assisted living facilities (ALFs) are defined as residences that combine housing, support services, and health care to meet the needs of those who need help with activities of daily living (Assisted Living Federation of America, 2001). ALFs usually provide a number of services including assistance with activities of daily living, 24-hour supervision, meal preparation, transportation, housekeeping, laundry, social activities, and an emergency call system. In reality, however, ALFs tend to vary widely in their intensity and level of services provided (General Accounting Office, 1997). Although some health related services might provide medications administration, services such as 24-hour skilled nursing care or rehabilitation are not available in ALFs.

ALFs offer an alternative to institutional care in that they provide a home-like atmosphere and have physical arrangements that are designed to meet the needs of frail, elderly individuals. ALFs were designed to maintain or enhance the capabilities of disabled elderly individuals such that they remain as independent as possible for as long as possible. The types of services provided usually are flexible and can change according to the changing needs of the individual resident.

ALFs have been growing in number since the early 1980s in response to several factors. First, as previously discussed, the elderly population continues to grow, particularly those who need assistance with activities of daily living. Second, there are an increasing number of elderly individuals who live alone, perhaps due to rising divorce rates and a more mobile society. Third, women traditionally serve as caregivers for dementia patients. However, the number of women in the workforce has steadily increased over the past 100 years, thereby reducing the pool of available in-home caregivers. Fourth, the net worth of older Americans has increased, making assisted living more affordable for more elderly individuals. Finally, the emergence of managed care and the need for reducing health care costs have made assisted living an attractive alternative to nursing home placement for state policy makers because of its lower cost. This is illustrated by the fact that Medicaid, the largest third party payer of health care services for dementia patients, is now covering (or plans to cover) assisted living services in 35 states for low-income, frail older persons (Mollica, 1998).

It is estimated that, in the U.S., about 1 million individuals live in assisted living facilities (Assisted Living Federation of America, 2001). Of these, approximately 50% of residents have some kind of cognitive impairment (General Accounting Office, 1997). Residents in ALFs tend to have levels of cognitive impairment, levels of dependency, and numbers of behavioral disturbances that are greater than those patients living at home, but less than those living in nursing homes (Kopetz, et al., 2000). Therefore, dementia patients with moderate care needs seem to be best suited for ALFs.

Extended Care Facilities (Nursing Homes). Nursing homes differ from ALFs in that they provide medical services such as skilled nursing care and rehabilitation services in addition to the services provided by ALFs. Therefore, individuals with medical conditions that require constant medical monitoring are most appropriate for nursing homes. It is estimated that roughly half of all nursing home residents have some form of diagnosed cognitive impairment, which translates into about 750,000 individuals (Krauss & Altman, 1998).

In general, nursing home residents have more severe cognitive impairments, more behavioral disturbances, and are more dependent than residents in ALFs (Kopetz, et al., 2000). However, Leon and Moyer (1999) found that anywhere from 23-65% of nursing home residents had levels of disability that could be adequately accommodated in ALFs. The implications of these finding in terms of costs will be discussed in more detail below.

Special Care Units. Special care units (SCUs) are a form of residential care found within an estimated 16% of nursing homes (Leon, 1994). SCUs are designed to cater to the specialized needs of patients with dementia and have been increasing in numbers for the last two decades. SCUs are defined by several features including minimal usage of physical and chemical restraints, modified physical environment (i.e., low stimulation), availability of appropriate physical and mental activities, specially trained staff, and preservation of residents' dignity (Phillips, Potter, & Simon, 1998). However, it is generally agreed upon that considerable variability among SCUs exists in terms of environmental design, philosophy of care, staff training, and criteria for admission.

There has been a considerable amount of controversy regarding SCUs. Although SCUs are purported to provide specialized care for patients with dementia, there is mixed evidence as to the efficacy of SCUs in terms of improving functioning (see Sloane, Lindeman, Phillips, Moritz, & Koch, 1995 for a review). One of the largest studies designed to determine the efficacy of SCUs found no statistical differences between residents in SCUs and nursing homes in terms of the rate of functional decline experienced by residents (Phillips, et al., 1997). However, other smaller scale studies have found SCUs to be beneficial on measures of patient distress, frequency of disruptive behaviors, and lower use of physical and chemical restraints (e.g., Sand, Yeaworth, & McCabe, 1992; Volicer, et al., 1994). Whether SCUs provide additional benefits for dementia patients above and beyond traditional nursing care is an important question because if SCUs are found to provide no additional benefits, then the extra costs associated with care in SCUs would be unwarranted.

Costs of Residential Care

Assisted Living Facilities. Regarding ALFs, the average monthly cost has been estimated to be $72 a day, or $2,200 a month (Citro, 1998). Other studies estimate monthly costs to be slightly higher, around $2,767 (Leon & Moyer, 1999). Therefore, the annual cost of ALFs may range from $26,400 to $33,204.

ALFs are generally private pay by residents. Medicaid waiver programs or subsidies in the form of additional payments for Social Security Income are available in some states (e.g., Oregon). Although Medicaid reimbursement is growing, it is still not widely available and has not had a major impact on the industry (National Center for Assisted Living, 1998). This is expected to change over the coming years because of the growing evidence that care in ALFs are more cost effective than nursing home care, which is already covered under Medicaid.

Nursing homes. Nursing homes cost about $3,800 per month on average (Citro, 1998). Yearly estimates are generally between $35,000 and $52,000, with an average somewhere around $45,000 (Ernst & Hay, 1994; Maas, Specht, Weiler, Buckwalter, & Turner, 1998; Rice, et al., 1993; Welch, Walsh, & Larson, 1992).

Nursing home payment is covered both by private and public sources. According to the Heath Care Financing Administration (HCFA), total nursing home expenditures in 1999 were $90.0 billion. Medicaid covered 47% ($42.4 billion) of this total, while out-of-pocket payment covered 26.6% ($23.9 billion). Public sources overall covered about 60.1% ($54.1 billion) of nursing home costs. Therefore, Medicaid and out-of-pocket payment are the two largest sources of nursing home payment.

Special Care Units. There is currently less information about the cost of SCUs within nursing homes. However, Maas and associates (1998) estimated the monthly cost of SCUs to be about $5,600, which translates into $67,200 per year. Because SCUs are found within nursing homes, financing of SCU care is similar to that of nursing home care as described above.

Cost comparisons among residential care options. Some studies have directly compared the costs of care associated with different forms of residential care. For instance, Leon and Moyer (1999) found that ALFs cost an average of $761 less than nursing homes. In addition, ALFs costs have been found to be 21-30% less than nursing homes (Leon, et al., 1998). As a rule of thumb, ALFs cost about two-thirds of what nursing homes cost (ALFA, 2001). When SCUs are compared with traditional nursing home care, Maas and colleagues (1998) estimated that SCUs cost $16 more per day, or roughly $480 more a month.

As can be seen from the discussions above, the literature concerning costs of residential care have been fairly consistent - ALFs are the least expensive of residential care options, followed by nursing home placement, with SCUs being the most expensive. The burden of cost, however, is much different, with ALFs being mostly paid for out-of-pocket and nursing homes and SCUs being paid for nearly equally among private and public sources.

Offsetting Costs Associated with Dementia Care

As can be seen above, residential care, and nursing home care in particular, are quite expensive for both families of dementia patients and for government funded programs, particularly Medicaid which covers roughly 78% of public spending for nursing homes (Health Care Financing Administration Office of the Actuary, 1999). In addition, nursing home care in 1999 cost the Medicaid program a total of $42.4 billion, which accounted for nearly 25% of total Medicaid spending that year (HCFA, 1999). In 1999, roughly 73% of Medicaid expenditures on long-term care (including both institutional and in-home) went toward institutional care (HCFA,

1999). This indicates that Medicaid money for long-term care currently is spent primarily on institutional care. Furthermore, expenditures for nursing home placement covered by Medicaid are expected to increase 60%; to $69 billion by the year 2008 (HCFA, 1998). Therefore, it is apparent that finding ways to slow the rising cost of institutional care, particularly nursing home care, will be a high priority for policy makers at the federal and state level.

It seems clear that the greatest potential impact for cost offset in the area of dementia care is in reducing utilization of nursing home care. The literature points to at least three ways that cost offset can be achieved in dementia care: developing comprehensive programs for family caregivers that delay institutionalization, delaying institutionalization by slowing the progression of the disease, and substituting nursing home placement with less expensive ALF placement when appropriate.

Programs designed to delay institutionalization. Keeping dementia patients at home for as long as possible is likely the primary way in which costs can be offset. Some studies have indicated that home care is half as costly as nursing home care (Hu, Huang, & Cartwright, 1986). A few studies have developed successful programs for delaying institutionalization. For example, in two studies, Mittelman and colleagues (1993; 1996) provided an intervention directed at reducing family caregiver stress in an effort to delay institutionalization. Their program required attendance at individual and family counseling sessions followed by additional supportive services. After one year, the intervention group had less than half as many nursing home placements as the control group (Mittelman, et al., 1993). In the second study, intervention group participants delayed institutionalization 329 days longer than those in the control group. (Mittelman, Ferris, Schulman, Steinberg, & Levin, 1996). In addition, caregivers in the intervention group were two-thirds less likely to place their spouse in a nursing home at any given point during the study.

Although Mittelman and associates did not calculate cost savings associated with their intervention, estimates of cost savings can be made. Other studies have estimated the mean monthly cost of nursing home care to be about $3650 (Maas, et al., 1998). Therefore, the program described by Mittelman and associates could potentially produce annual savings of $40,150 per individual. Still other studies have estimated that a one-month delay in institutionalization could save $1863 (Leon, et al., 1998). Based upon these estimates, Mittelman's program could potentially save $20,493 annually. Nationwide, this translates into a yearly savings of $1.23 billion.

The savings for families, however, would be substantially less given that caring for a patient with dementia at home is also costly. Yearly estimates of in-home care vary from roughly $18,000 (Stommel, Collins, & Given, 1994) to $34,500 (Max, Webber, & Fox, 1995) to $47,000 (Rice, et al., 1993). Estimates likely vary because they include different types of costs such as formal services costs (e.g., physicians visits, housekeeping services) or informal services (e.g., caregiving provided by friends or family). Generally, for in-home patients, informal services are the greatest

(Max, et al., 1995; Rice, et al., 1993). Some of these estimates may be underestimates because many do not include costs associate with increased utilization of medical services or lost paid work time by caregivers themselves. Therefore, it is clear that some of the cost savings produced by institutionalization will likely be at least partially offset by costs associated with caregiving (Neumann, 2000).

Other studies have examined home and community based services as a substitute for nursing home care. For example, one large-scale study implemented a Medicaid waiver system to cover home and community based services in three states: Colorado, Oregon, and Washington (Alecxih, Lutzky, Corea, & Coleman, 1996). The authors found that the number of people receiving Medicaid funded nursing facility care in these states grew at a slower rate than the rest of the nation. Furthermore, the number of people in nursing homes as a proportion of the population aged 75 and over decreased faster than the rest of the nation. Overall, the states saved between 9% and 23% of the amount that they would have spent on long-term care.

Substituting nursing home placement with assisted living care. As has been mentioned, Medicaid covers a large portion of nursing home costs in the United States, but currently covers relatively little of the costs associated with assisted living. Therefore, one way to cut costs associated with dementia care is to find alternative institutional placements for individuals needing care that cannot be provided in the home.

Assisted living may serve as a less expensive alternative to institutional care, particularly for mild to moderately impaired dementia patients. Studies have found ALFs to be from 21% to 30% less than nursing homes, (Leon, et al., 1998). Other studies have estimated that from 23% to 65% of mild to moderately impaired nursing home residents could be adequately cared for in ALFs (Leon & Moyer, 1999). By replacing nursing home care with ALF care for these individuals, an estimated $1.0 to $2.7 billion a year could be saved (Leon & Moyer, 1999).

Given these findings, two recommendations can be made. First, Medicaid coverage needs to expand to assisted living in more states. Fortunately, this is occurring in more and more states, although Medicaid currently covers only a small portion of assisted living costs nationwide. Second, other authors have called for the formation of a well-defined continuum of care for dementia (Leon & Moyer, 1999). Nursing homes and ALFs provide different services designed to serve dementia patients with different needs. ALFs tend to serve patients with mild to moderate dementias that have intermediate care needs, while nursing homes tend to serve individuals who have greater needs and cognitive impairments (Kopetz, et al., 2000). However, many nursing home patients could be sufficiently served in ALFs (Leon & Moyer, 1999). In fact, 82% of individuals over the age of 45 would prefer not to be placed in an institutional (e.g., nursing home) setting when they can no longer live at home (American Association of Retired Persons, 2000). Therefore, it appears as if each industry could develop its own niche on the continuum of care and consumers may prefer this.

Much more work will need to be done to create standardized criteria for determining where a particular patient will best be served and when clients need to be transferred from ALFs to nursing homes. Clearly this is a very complicated issue that could create tension between the two industries. However, with the growing costs associated with nursing home care and the growing numbers of dementia patients expected in the coming years, a continuum of care appears essential to provide the optimal level of care at lowest possible cost.

In summary, given population predictions and our current system of reimbursement for care, cost containment will continue to depend upon families absorbing the majority of caregiving costs, both formal and informal. Keeping AD patients at home for as long as possible will help the government to offset costs. However, delaying institutionalization inherently creates secondary costs to our medical system related to increased caregiver burden and its associated health risks. One approach toward preventing excess disability for AD patients and their informal caregivers is to provide an integrated treatment approach in outpatient medical care settings. Interventions targeting stress effects of informal caregiving may potentially affect both the quality of care and a family's ability to continue to care for their elderly relative in the home.

Integrated Care

The Nevada Caregiver Support Center is an integrated healthcare program that focuses on the prevention of excess disability in both persons with dementia and their caregivers. The Center is funded through a state grant program designed to foster independent living in older adults. Services are provided by an interprofessional team comprised of clinical psychologists, physicians, nurses, and social workers. A goal of the Center is to increase the ability of families to continue caregiving at home, thereby delaying residential treatment. The Center also provides support services to older persons with cognitive disorders in order to enhance the maintenance of their skills and promote a high quality of life. The integration of behavioral and medical healthcare is particularly important for dementia patients and their families given the high incidence of stress related problems experienced by family caregivers and the myriad of behavioral and psychological problems that emerge for persons with a degenerative dementia. Given that family caregivers are most likely to first report problems to a medical professional, the Center's integrated care model, wherein behavioral and medical healthcare specialists work side by side, allows the staff to provide patients and caregiving families with behavioral healthcare support in a timely manner. Integrated healthcare services for persons with dementia and their families serve several important preventative functions: At the point of diagnosis, behavioral healthcare providers have the unique opportunity to initiate primary prevention programs by providing patients and families with the educational and emotional support services they need in order to prepare for the inevitable changes in their future life circumstances. The behavioral healthcare specialists can also help families begin to develop the skill set necessary for preventing the development of problems (or worsening of extant problems) as the dementing illness advances.

The prevention programs within the Center are structured within a stepped care model targeting primary, secondary, and tertiary prevention functions wherein cost-effectiveness is achieved by identifying the least intensive interventions that can provide the maximum benefit. Simply stated, cost-effectiveness is achieved by identifying the least intensive and intrusive intervention that can provide the maximum benefit. The stepped care model has been found to be a cost-effective means of providing health-care services within organizations that provide care for a population on a pre-determined budget (Freeman, 1999). A needs assessment is conducted at first contact in order to determine the appropriated level of support for patients and their family caregivers. Respite services are offered in order to increase families' ability to take advantage of the services. Programs that are designed to prevent excess disability in patients and families include the following.

Primary prevention programs. Caregiver education programs provide instruction in empirically supported interventions for high prevalence problems (e.g., communication based problems, home safety design, problem solving skills deficits). Instruction in caregiving skills is ideally initiated early in the disease process in order to prevent the common consequences of these problems from emerging as the disease progresses (e.g., depression in the caregiver and patient, agitation and aggressive behavior in the patient, injuries to the patient and caregiver associated with ineffective hands on care, excessive levels of stress due to inadequate access to community resources, etc.). Persons with cognitive disorders are invited to enroll in a wellness program that is based on a behavioral activation model (Lewinsohn & Gotlib, 1995) that promotes the continued use of skills through environmental and social support. The wellness program provides opportunities for socialization (e.g., through a social club or community volunteer projects), physical activity (e.g., Tai Chi), and cognitive stimulation (e.g., through an arts program). Patients and their families are offered support services at the time of diagnosis and are eligible for these and other services over the course of the disease as needed.

Secondary prevention programs. Families caring for persons with cognitive disorders commonly delay seeking assistance until after a problem becomes severe. A challenge emerges in providing educational and case management support to families and patients in crisis when the family member is too emotionally distressed to benefit from didactic skills training or to participate in the problem solving necessary to navigate the medical and social services needed by persons with cognitive disorders. Recognizing this common scenario, focused support groups are offered to families in order to improve their ability to cope with problems such as depression, frustration, and anger. The Center needs assessment is designed to identify caregiver's specific difficulties. Based on the results of the assessment, distressed caregivers are invited to participate in an educational support group targeting their specific difficulty (e.g., depression, anger control, coping with stress, bereavement). The focused support groups are time-limited and structured and use guided mastery to promote the development of behavioral, cognitive, and emotional self-regulation skills. Skills are taught through direct instruction, in-session practice, and between session assignments. A goal of each of the interventions is for the targeted skills to generalize to future problems.

Tertiary prevention programs. Families experiencing high levels of distress are offered intensive, individualized support in the form of family and/or individual counseling. Individualized services are provided either at the Center or in the home depending on the caregiver's ability to travel. Criteria for referral to these services include but are not limited to: (a) evidence of risk of the caregiver or care receiver harming self or others, (b) substance abuse, and/or (c) severe depression. The individualized treatments are based on empirically supported interventions for assisting caregivers (e.g., Gallagher-Thompson & Steffen, 1994; Mittelman, et al., 1996; Dick, Gallagher-Thompson, & Thompson, 1996). Based on surveys of caregiver needs published over the past several years (e.g., Gaugler, et al., 2000; Ory, Hoffman, Yee, Tennstedt, & Schulz, 1999) it was anticipated that the most frequently needed services would be for the treatment of depression, severe anxiety, and anger management problems. Manualized protocols targeting these problems are available to the staff.

References

Alecxih, L. M., Lutzky, S., Corea, J., & Coleman, B. (1996). *Estimated cost savings from the use of home and community-based alternatives to nursing facility care in three states.* Washington, DC: AARP/Public Policy Institute.

American Association of Retired Persons. (2001). The AARP Research Center. http://researh.aarp.org.

Assisted Living Federation of America. (2001). *What is assisted living?*

Bayer, A., & Harper, L. (2000). *Fixing to stay: A national survey on housing and home modification issues.* Washington, DC: AARP.

Boise, L., Camicioli, R., Morgan, D. L., Rose, J. H., & Congleton, L. (1999). Diagnosing dementia: perspectives of primary care physicians. *The Gerontologist, 39* (4), 457-464.

Butler, R. N., Lewis, M. I., & Sunderland, T. (1998). *Aging and mental health: Positive psychosocial and biomedical approaches.* Boston: Allyn and Bacon.

Citro, J. (1998). *Assisted living in the United States.* Washington, DC: AARP/Public Policy Institute.

Dawson, P., Wells, D. L., & Kline, K. (1993). *Enhancing the abilities of persons with Alzheimer's and related dementias: A nursing perspective.* New York: Springer Publishing Company.

Dick, L. P., Gallagher-Thompson, D., & Thompson, L. W. (1996). Cognitive-behavioral therapy. In R. T. Woods (Ed.) *Handbook of the clinical psychology of ageing* (pp. 509-544). New York, NY: John Wiley & Sons.

Ernst, R. L., & Hay, J. W. (1994). The US economic and social costs of Alzheimer's disease revisited. *American Journal of Public Health, 84,* 1261-1264.

Ernst, R. L., Hay, J. W., Fenn, C., Tinklenberg, J., & Yesavage, J. A. (1997). Cognitive function and the costs of Alzheimer disease. *Archives of Neurology, 54*, 687-693.

Farlow, M., Anand, R., Messina, J., Hartman, R., & Veach, J. (2000). A 52-week study of the efficacy of rivastigmine in patients with mild to moderately severe Alzheimer's disease. *European Neurology, 44*, 236-241.

Feldman, H., Gauthier, S., Hecker, J., Vellas, B., Subbiah, P., Whalen, E., & the Donepezil MSAD Study Investigators Group. (2001). A 24-week, randomized, double-blind study of donepezil in moderate to severe Alzheimer's disease. *Neurology, 57*(4), 613-620.

Fillit, H. M., Gutterman, E. M., & Brooks, R. L. (2000). Impact of donepezil on caregiving burden for patients with Alzheimer's disease. International Psychogeriatrics, *12*(3), 389-401.

Fredericks, D. W. & Fisher, J. E. (unpublished). *Listener repair of referential problems during conversation with Alzheimer's disease speakers.* Dissertation, University of Nevada, Reno, 2001.

Freeman, R. K. (1999). Information management in behavioral healthcare. In: W. O'Donohue & J.E. Fisher (Eds.), *Management and administration skills for the mental health professional.* New York: Academic Press.

Gallagher-Thompson, D., & Steffen, A. M. (1994). Comparative effects of cognitive-behavioral and bridf psychodynamic psychotherapies for depressed family caregivers. *Journal of Consulting and Clinical Psychology, 62* (3), 543-549.

Gaugler, J. E., Edwards, A. B. Femia, E. E., Zarit, S. H., Stephens, M. P., Townsend, A., & Greene, R. (2000). Predictors of instutionalization of cognitively impaired elders: Family help and the timing of placement. *Journal of Gerontology: Psychological Sciences, 55*(4), P247-P255.

Gaugler, J. E., Zarit, S. H., & Pearlin, L. I. (1999). Caregiving and institutionalization: perceptions of family conflict and socioemotional support. *International Journal of Aging and Human Development, 49* (1), 1-25.

Greig, N. H., Utsuki, T., Yu, Q., Holloway, H. W., Perry, T., Lee, B., Ingram, D. K., & Lahiri, D. K. (2001). *Current Medical Research and Opinion, 17*(3), 150-165.

Gori, M. C., DelNero, P., Argentino, C., Girardi, P., Giubilei, F., Buttinelli, C., Buonfrate, G., & Tatarelli, R. (1998). Medical costs preceding diagnosis of probable Alzheimer Disease. *Archives of Gerontology and Geriatrics, supple 6*, 247-254.

Gutterman, E. M., Markowitz, J. S., Lewis, B., & Fillit, H. (1999). Cost of Alzheimer's Disease and related demenia in managed-Medicare. *Journal of the American Geriatrics Society, 47*, 1065-1071.

Health Care Financing Administration Office of the Actuary. (1999). *National health expenditures.* Washington, DC: National Health Statistics Group.

Health Care Financing Administration Office of the Actuary. (1998). *National health expenditures.* Washington, DC: National Health Statistics Group.

Henke, C. J., & Burchmore, M. J. (1997). The economic impact of tacrine in the treatment of Alzheimer's disease. *Clinical Therapy, 19*, 330-345.

Hu, T., Huang, L., & Cartwright, W. S. (1986). Evaluation of the costs of caring for the senile demented elderly: A pilot study. *The Gerontologist, 26,* 158-163.

Kitwood, T. (1990). The dialectics of dementia: With particular reference to Alzheimer's Disease. *Ageing and Society, 10,* 177-198.

Knopman, D., Schneider, L., Davis, K., Talwalker, S., Smith, F., Hoover, T., & Gray, S. (1997). Long-tem tacrine (Cognex) treatment: Effects on nursing home placement and mortality. *Neurology, 47,* 166-177.

Kopetz, S., Steele, C. D., Brandt, J., Baker, A., Kronberg, M., Galik, E., Steinberg, M., Warren, A., & Lyketsos, C. G. (2000). Characteristics and outcomes of dementia residents in an assisted living facility. *International Journal of Geriatric Psychiatry, 15,* 586-593.

Krauss, N., & Altman, B. (1998). *Characteristics of nursing home residents, 1996.* Agency for Health Care Policy and Research MEPS Research Findings No. 5 [AHCPR Pub. No. 99-00006]. Rockville, MD: U.S. Government Printing Office.

Kukull, W. A., Larson, E. B., Reifler, B. V., Lampe, T. H., Yerby, M. S., & Hughes, J. P. (1990). The validity of three clinical diagnostic criteria for Alzheimer's disease. *Neurology, 40,* 1364-1369.

Leon, J. (1994). The 1990/1991 national survey of special care units in nursing homes. *Alzheimer's Disease and Associated Disorder, 8,* S72-S86.

Leon, J., & Moyer, D. (1999). Potential cost savings in residential care for Alzheimer's disease patients. *The Gerontologist, 39,* 440-449.

Leon, J., Cheng, C. K., & Neumann, P. J. (1998). Alzheimer's disease care: Cost and potential savings. *Health Affairs, 17,* 206-216.

Lewinsohn, P. M., & Gotlib, I. H. (1995). Behavioral theory and treatment of depression. In E.E. Becker & W.R. Leber (Eds.), *Handbook of depression* (pp. 352-375). New York: Guilford Press.

Light, E., Niederehe, G., & Lebowitz, B. D. (Eds). (1994). Stress effects on family caregivers of Alzheimer's patients. N.Y.: Springer.

Maas, M. L., Specht, J. P., Weiler, K., Buckwalter, K. C., & Turner, B. (1998). Special care units for people with Alzheimer's disease: Only for the privileged few? *Journal of Gerontological Nursing, 24,* 28-37.

Max, W., Webber, P., & Fox, P. (1995). Alzheimer's disease: The unpaid burden of caring. *Journal of Aging and Health, 7,* 179-199.

McCormick, W. C., Hardy, J., Kukull, W. A., Bowen, J. D., Teri, L., Zitzer, S., & Larson, E. B. (2001). Healthcare utilization and costs in managed care patients with Alzheimer's Disease during the last few years of life. *Journal of the American Geriatrics Society, 49,* 1156-1160.

McKhann, G., Drachman, D., Folstein, M., Katzman, R., Price, D., & Stadlan, E. M. (1984). Clinical diagnosis of Alzheimer's Disease: Report of the NINCDS-ADRDA work group under the auspieces of Department of Health and Human Services task force on Alzheimer's disease. *Neurology, 34,* 939-944.

Miller, R., Newcomer, R., & Fox, P. (1999). Effects of the Medicare Alzheimer's disease demonstration on nursing home entry. *Health Services Research, 34,* 691-714.

Mittelman, M. S., Ferris, S. H., Schulman, E., Steinberg, G., & Levin, B. (1996). A family intervention to delay nursing home placement of patients with Alzheimer's disease: A randomized control trial. *Journal of the American Medical Association, 276*, 1725-1731.

Mittelman, M. S., Ferris, S. H., Steinberg, G., Shulman, E., Mackell, J. A., Ambinder, A., & Cohen, J. (1993). An intervention that delays institutionalization of Alzheimer's disease patients: Treatment of spouse-caregivers. *The Gerontologist, 33*, 730-740.

Mollica, R. (1998). *State assisted living policy: 1998.* National Academy for State Health Policy.

Mohs, R. C., Doody, R. S., Morris, J. C., Ieni, J. R., Rogers, S. L., Perdomo, C. A., & Pratt, R. D. (2001). A 1-year, placebo-controlled preservation of function survival study of donepezil in AD patients. *Neurology, 57*(3), 481-488.

National Academy on an Aging Society. (2000). *Chronic conditions: a challenge for the 21st century.* Washington, DC: Author.

National Center for Assisted Living. (1998). *The assisted living sourcebook.* American Health Care Association.

Neumann, P. J. (2000). Estimating the long term cost savings from the treatment of Alzheimer's disease: A modeling approach. *Pharmacoeconomics, 17*, 109.

Nocks, B. C., Learner, M., Blackman, D., & Brown, T. E. (1986). The effects of a community-based long term care project on nursing home utilization. *The Gerontologist, 26*, 150-17.

Ory, M. G., Hoffman, R. R., Yee, J. L., Tennstedt, S., & Schulz, R. (1999). Prevalence and impact of caregiving: A detailed comparison between dementia and nondementia caregivers. *The Gerontologist, 39*(2), 177-186.

Phillips, C. D., Sloane, P. D., Hawes, C., Koch, G., Han, J., Spry, K., Dunteman, G., & Williams, R. L. (1997). Effects of residence in Alzheimer disease special care units on functional outcomes. *Journal of the American Medical Association, 278*, 1340-1344.

Phillips, V. L., Potter, S. J., & Simon, S. L. (1998). Special care units for Alzheimer's disease patients: Their role in the nursing home market. *Journal of Health and Human Service Administration, 20*, 300-310.

Rice, D. P., Fox, P. J., Max, W., Webber, P. A., Lindeman, D. A., Hauck, W. W., & Segura, E. (1993). The economic burden of Alzheimer's disease care. *Health Affairs, 13*, 164-176.

Sand, B. J., Yeaworth, R. C., & McCabe, B. W. (1992). Alzheimer's disease special care units in long-term care facilities. *Journal of Gerontological Nursing, 18*, 28-34.

Schulz, R., & Beach, S. R. (1999). Caregiving as a risk factor for mortality: the Caregiver Health Effects Study. *Journal of the American Medical Association, 282*(23), 2215-2219.

Sloane, P. D., Lindeman, D. A., Phillips, C., Moritz, D. J., & Koch, G. (1995). Evaluating Alzheimer's special care units: Reviewing the evidence and identifying potential sources of bias. *The Gerontologist, 35*, 103-111.

Souetre, E., Thwaites, R. M. A., & Yeardley, H. L. (1999). Economic impact of Alzheimer's disease in the United Kingdom. *British Journal of Psychiatry, 174*, 51-55.

Stommel, M., Collins, C. E., & Given, B. A. (1994). The costs of family contributions to the care of persons with dementia. *The Gerontologist, 34*, 199-205.

U.S. Congress General Accounting Office. (1997). *Long-term care – Consumers protection and quality of care issues in assisted living.* [GAO Pub. No. HEHS-97-93]. Washington, DC: U.S. Government Printing Office.

Volicer, L., Collard, A., Hurley, A., Bishop, C., Kern, D., & Karon, S. (1994). Impact of special care unit for patients with advanced Alzheimer's disease on patient's discomfort and costs. *Journal of the American Geriatrics Society, 42*, 597-603.

Welch, H. G., Walsh, J. S., & Larson, E. B. (1992). The cost of institutional care in Alzheimer's disease: Nursing home and hospital use in a prospective cohort. *Journal of the American Geriatrics Society, 40*, 221-224.

Winblad, B., Engedal, K., Soininen, H., Verhey, F., Waldemar, G., Wimo, A., Wetterholm, A. L., Zhang, R., Haglund, A., Subbiah, P., & the Donepezil Nordic Study Group. (2001). A 1-year, randomized, placebo-controlled study of donepezil in patients with mild to moderate AD. *Neurology, 57*(3), 489-495.

Wind, A. Van Staveren, G., Jonker, C., & Van Eijk, J. T. M. (1994). The validity of the judgement of general practitioners on dementia. *International Journal of Geriatric Psychiatry, 9*, 543-549.